# LEADING THE
# PASSOVER
# JOURNEY

# LEADING THE PASSOVER JOURNEY

## The Seder's Meaning Revealed, the Haggadah's Story Retold

RABBI NATHAN LAUFER

JEWISH LIGHTS Publishing
Woodstock, Vermont

*Leading the Passover Journey:*
*The Seder's Meaning Revealed, the Haggadah's Story Retold*

2005 First Printing
© 2005 by Nathan Laufer

**Library of Congress Cataloging-in-Publication Data**
Laufer, Nathan, 1957–
Leading the Passover journey : the Seder's meaning revealed, the Haggadah's story retold / Nathan Laufer.
p. cm.
Includes index and bibliographical references.
ISBN 1-58023-211-6 (hardcover)
1. Seder. 2. Haggadah. 3. Passover—Customs and practices. I. Title.
BM695.P35L355 2005
296.4'5371—dc22

2004024964

Manufactured in the United States of America

Published by Jewish Lights Publishing
A Division of LongHill Partners, Inc.
Sunset Farm Offices, Route 4, P.O. Box 237
Woodstock, VT 05091
Tel (802) 457-4000     Fax (802) 457-4004
www.jewishlights.com

To my parents,
for showing me the way

# Contents

# Acknowledgments

I have wonderfully fond memories of growing up, celebrating Passover with my family. The elegantly set table in our small apartment, the arrival of my grandmother, aunt, uncle, and cousins bearing sweets and gifts, the aromatic scents and poignant songs of the Seder meal, and the drama of hearing my people's founding story, often told to accompanying song, are all as real to me today as they were then.

Each year, as our family read the Haggadah, the story of our people's liberation from Egypt 3,250 years ago, we inevitably segued into my family's personal stories of survival and liberation from the Nazi concentration camps during World War II. Often, the talk came around to the cup of Elijah sitting on the table.

The cup had a tale: As my father's family was preparing to be sent off to the camps, my grandfather, a charming gentleman who had excellent relationships with the local townspeople, convinced his non-Jewish neighbors to allow them to bury their silver in their backyards. My grandfather, may his memory be for a blessing, was sent to and perished in Auschwitz. After the war was over, my father, his mother, and his sister returned to their hometown to unearth their possessions. Alas, they found that the buried silver had been ransacked by the local population and was gone—all except for the cup of Elijah that my grandfather had used at his Passover Seders. My grandmother gave that cup to my father, and he has since bequeathed that cup—that cup of survival, hope, and redemption—to me.

In a way, the story of that cup is my personal Jewish story. The intense Jewish passion of my grandfather—actually of both my grandfathers, who each perished in the Holocaust—was saved in the hearts and souls of my parents, who transmitted it lovingly to me. Stoked by my teachers, that passion moved me to devote my life to my people and to share the richness of our people's heritage. Strange as it may sound, my own Jewish journey, like the redemption from Egypt, which was foreseen by Abraham hundreds of years before it occurred, felt like it had a sense of inevitability to it. I experienced my love for Judaism and embrace of my people as if it had to be—as if it could not be otherwise.

This commentary on the Haggadah, the culmination of nearly twenty years of teaching and work, has written itself. Almost every insight that occurred to me over the years seemed to come out of the blue, as if my deceased grandfathers shared with me in inaudible whispers the wisdom that they were unable to personally transmit during their truncated lifetimes.

Aside from my parents, my heroes of Jewish survival, to whom this book is dedicated, there are several key people to whom I owe a profound debt of gratitude. First, to my teachers and colleagues with whom I have had the privilege of studying, in particular Rabbi Joseph B. Soloveitchik, Professor Nechama Leibowitz, Rabbi David Hartman, Rabbi Yitz Greenberg, Rabbi Saul Berman, and Rabbi David Silber; if I have been able to discover lost horizons and articulate previously unexpressed ideas, it is only because I stand on the shoulders of these spiritual titans. Any errors that I have made are, of course, solely my own.

I owe a singular debt of gratitude to my professional mentor, Rabbi Herbert A. Friedman, and to my patrons, Leslie and Abigail Wexner, for giving me the opportunity over the past two decades to realize my life's mission of serving the Jewish People. My thinking has ripened and matured thanks to the collegiality of the faculty and the thirst for knowledge of the thirteen hundred students of the Wexner Heritage Foundation program, who have allowed me to teach them and, even more frequently, to learn from them. I would especially like to thank one of my students, Mr. Michael Halbert of Toronto, Canada, for his valuable comments upon reading the manuscript. I was privileged to complete this manuscript while on sabbatical in Jerusalem. I am deeply appreciative of the opportunity given to me by my long-time friend and colleague Rabbi Donniel Hartman and The Shalom Hartman Institute to complete my research and writing of this manuscript on their beautiful Jerusalem campus. I would also like to thank my colleague Dr. Daniel Polisar, president of the Shalem Center in Jerusalem, for his many helpful suggestions upon reviewing this manuscript.

I am grateful to my publisher, Stuart M. Matlins of Jewish Lights, for the confidence that he expressed in this project, and I feel a special sense of kinship with my editor, Ms. Elisheva Urbas, for her brilliant insights and ongoing editorial support. I am deeply appreciative of the tireless efforts which were invested by the staff at Jewish Lights, particularly Amanda Dupuis, Emily Wichland, and Tim Holtz.

Words of thanks are insufficient to express my gratitude to my wife, Sharon, and my children, Becky, Michael, Leslie, and Matti, for their steady encouragement and the many joys that they have brought to my life. Nevertheless, I want to express my special thanks to Sharon, for formatting this entire manuscript: *Yishar Kochaych!* I am immensely grateful to my friends, who have stood by me through thick and thin and whom I have experienced time and time again as God's angels. May God bless them according to their many, many kindnesses.

Finally and most importantly, I offer my humble thanks to the Creator of the world, who has given me and my loved ones infinite gifts and whose Strength and Love fills the world. I pray that my life and words fulfill God's purpose in my creation.

Rabbi Nathan Laufer
Jerusalem, Israel

# Introduction

## Rediscovering the Meaning of the Seder

Over the past eighteen years I have traveled and taught extensively around North America. Wherever I go I find an almost unquenchable thirst to learn more about Judaism. People of all ages—young, middle-aged, and senior adults—are desperately seeking a deeper understanding of themselves as Jews and of the Jewish tradition. While life in North America is full of economic opportunity and material abundance, the rich spiritual heritage of the Jewish people has been harder to come by.

One of the most welcoming gateways to understanding Judaism and feeling part of the Jewish People is through the Passover Haggadah. Nine out of every ten Jews attend some sort of Passover Seder, the festival meal at which the Haggadah is read. The story of the Exodus, which reverberates with the themes of political liberation and religious freedom, aligns well with our cultural values as North Americans. People want to learn more about their own community's founding story but often come away from the Passover experience feeling unsatiated and unfulfilled. I have found that this is true for Jews from all walks of life.

For those Jews or non-Jews who have not had ample opportunity to study Judaism at all or in any great depth, the language and sheer length of the Haggadah can be alienating and simply daunting. Often such Jews find themselves at Passover Seders where just about the only substantive Jewish content of the evening is the blessing over the wine and the symbolic eating of a piece of dry matzah. The participants mostly forego the reading of the Haggadah and transform the Passover Seder into the Jewish ethnic equivalent of an American Thanksgiving dinner among family and friends.

For other Jews who have had a bit more Jewish education—perhaps gone to Hebrew school, taken a couple of adult education courses, and the like—or who feel a greater commitment to doing Passover somewhat traditionally, more of the Haggadah text may be covered and discussed. Participants usually share some fragmentary knowledge about this or that piece of the Passover Seder that they have come across haphazardly here and there over the years. Related issues of contemporary freedom and human rights issues may be discussed by association. Some songs like the "Dayenu" (usually only the first two lines) may be sung by those around the table. After about forty-five minutes or an hour, people usually tire of trying so hard to find meaning and joy and skip to the meal, which expands to take up the rest of the evening.

Then there are the Jews who have had a rigorous and extensive Jewish education growing up. Day school graduates, Jewish camp enthusiasts, often Orthodox or raised in a traditional Conservative Jewish home, these individuals read the entire Haggadah front to back. Often they cite a plethora of Jewish commentaries on this or that paragraph, can access a dozen or more traditional melodies to enliven the proceedings, and generally engage in much of what the Seder has to offer. Nevertheless, when one listens carefully to their telling of the Exodus story, one still frequently hears a very disjointed tale, one that does not hang together, one that does not sound at all coherent. While deeply and irrevocably committed to the practice of Jewish ritual they sometimes—often?—go through the motions without fully grasping the deeper spiritual meaning of the transformative experience in which they are engaged. They too come away from the Seder feeling vaguely dissatisfied or ill at ease.

Here, as in so much of Jewish educational experience, what is lacking is an understanding of how the pieces of Judaism fit together to form a powerful and compelling whole. For it is not merely a truism that the whole is greater than its individual parts; in Judaism, failing to grasp the whole, the big picture, means that one often misses the main point, the end goal of the Jewish ritual experience. One literally misses the grandeur and mystery of the forest because one is distracted by this or that individual tree.

I have found that this is especially true in teaching the Haggadah. Even when people have a lot to say about this or that item of the Seder, they are often unable to connect those pieces into a single, meaningful, cohesive story. The need to do so, to understand how the Haggadah conveys a coherent narrative with a beginning, middle, and end, is a deeply human impulse. This is what this book endeavors to do: to connect the dots so that one grasps the complete and beautiful saga of our people's redemption by the conclusion of the evening.

## What Is Necessary to "Lead" the Seder

This view of the Haggadah's big picture is valuable to everyone at a Seder, but especially so for those who may lead a Seder. Anyone who has ever had to lead a Passover Seder is intimidated by the prospect. This is especially true in post-modern America, where so many families go away to hotels, resorts, and cruises to celebrate Passover. While freeing the family from the onerous preparations for the holiday, these contemporary exoduses from one's home often sap the spiritual vitality out of the Passover experience. Instead of being able to experience a parent or grandparent lead family and friends through their own personally meaningful interpretation of the Haggadah, the night of the Seder is transformed into a mass, impersonal performance by some distant rabbi or cantor who occupies center stage. How is one to learn to lead a meaningful Seder under such circumstances?

In addition to this, for the novice as well as for the veteran, leading the Seder is felt to be an awesome responsibility. This is as it should be: leadership of any group of people engaged in an important activity is a serious matter and requires certain prerequisites. First, leadership requires a thorough knowledge of the area you are leading. Leaders are expected to have command of the terrain in which they are leading their followers. Facile knowledge on the leader's part will quickly be detected by the members of the group, and trust in the leader will be undermined. Second, leaders must be able to communicate the "story" of the group in cogent and compelling terms and explain how the individual details fit into the larger story. If the details of the story don't fit together or are familiar to the point of boredom, then the members will quickly become distracted and "tune out" the message and the messenger. Third, to be knowledgeable leaders and effective communicators, leaders must prepare themselves in advance of the actual event that they will lead. No one would think of taking center stage to lead an important discussion without thoroughly preparing an outline of the agenda, with clear talking points highlighting the key items. Finally, the litmus test of successful leadership is inspiring those around you to aspire to leadership themselves based on the example you have set. Emulation is the highest form of flattery, and succession is the ultimate standard of leadership success.

What is required of leaders generally is certainly required of the leader of the Passover Seder. In fact, the importance of achieving these leadership prerequisites is contained in two long-standing pre-Passover traditions. The first tradition is that you begin studying the *halakhot* (literally: "pathways") of Passover thirty days before the holiday. The logic behind this tradition is that by becoming acquainted with the ins and outs of the Passover journey, you become more knowledgeable and feel more comfortable once Passover begins. The second tradition is the custom to read much of the *Maggid* section of the Haggadah, the fifth item in the Seder, on the Shabbat afternoon prior to Passover, the Shabbat that the tradition calls "The Great Shabbat," *Shabbat HaGadol.* Reading through the Haggadah narrative awakens latent knowledge and previously unexplored questions, offers you an opportunity to practice communicating the Passover story, and prepares you to undertake the soon to be embarked upon Passover journey with confidence.

Following the spirit of these traditions, if you, whether leader or participant, begin to read through this book thirty days prior to Passover, focusing on those parts that seem to be particularly germane on the Shabbat prior to Passover and using this volume as a resource guide throughout the actual Seder, you will find yourself much better prepared to undertake and lead the pilgrimage, the spiritual journey, that the Seder represents. You will understand the Haggadah's narrative and feel empowered to chart the course of redemption told by the Seder. You will be able to communicate the flow of the Seder to others in a coherent and compelling way, with the participants coming away knowing both the message of the whole and the meaning of the parts of the Seder. Finally, you may even inspire the other participants to lead a future Seder themselves one day.

# A Word (or Two) about God

My publisher and I have struggled together with the question of how to translate God's name Y-H-W-H in the English text. The word is pronounced in the Hebrew as *Ah-Doe-Nay*, which means "My Lord" or "My Master." *Ah-Doe-Nay* is another name used to denote God in the Bible (e.g., Deuteronomy 3:24). Even though it is self-evident from the letters that "*Ah-Doe-Nay*" is not really the pronunciation of Y-H-W-H, Jews have, from time immemorial, used this pronunciation in order to avoid violating the third of the Ten Commandments—not to utter the Divine name Y-H-W-H inappropriately, that is, in vain. To emphasize this pronunciation of Y-H-W-H, publishers have inserted the vowels for the word *Ah-Doe-Nay* under the Hebrew word Y-H-W-H, and have generally used the masculine and somewhat archaic word *Lord* as its standard translation.

The Bible itself is self-conscious about using God's name appropriately. In the twenty-fourth chapter of the Book of Leviticus, the Bible tells the story of the person who blasphemed God's name. In telling this tale of subversion, the Bible refuses to say that the blasphemer cursed Y-H-W-H or even that he cursed *Ah-Doe-Nay*. Instead, the Bible says that the blasphemer cursed *Ha-Shem*, "The Name," thus avoiding printing in the biblical text what the accused was condemned of violating in practice. Based on this text (and a close reading of Exodus 3:15, cited below), pious Jews, most notably among the Orthodox community, avoid pronouncing and writing God's Y-H-W-H name as *Ah-Doe-Nay* except in the context of performing one of the 613 commandments—for example, in reciting a blessing or reading from a Torah Scroll in the context of prayer. In all other contexts they refer to Y-H-W-H as *Ha-Shem*. Non-Orthodox Jews as well as non-Jews, perhaps unaware of its biblical roots, are unfamiliar and vaguely uncomfortable with the use of the term *Ha-Shem* as referring to God.

In all of my educational work, and in this book with the help of the superb editorial staff at Jewish Lights, I have striven to be genuinely pluralistic and maximally inclusive. I have sought to embrace all my potential readers and been concerned not to consciously alienate any denomination within my broad audience. Accordingly, I have chosen to eschew the use of the words *Ah-Doe-Nay*, Lord, or *Ha-Shem* as translations for Y-H-W-H. I have also avoided the impersonal translation "Eternal" or the untranslated and unpronounceable Y-H-W-H to denote God's name. Rather, I have chosen to use the term "EverPresent God" as the translation for Y-H-W-H.

The choice of EverPresent God emerges organically from within the biblical story of the Exodus. In the third chapter of the Book of Exodus, while standing in God's glowing presence at the Burning Bush, Moses raises the question of how to refer to God when he brings the news of the coming redemption to his enslaved people in Egypt:

> Moses said to God, "When I come to the Israelites and say to them 'The God of your fathers has sent me to you,' and they ask me, 'What is God's name?' what shall I say to them?" And God said to Moses, *"Ehyeh-Asher-Ehyeh."* God continued, "Thus shall you say to the Israelites, '*Ehyeh* sent me to you.'" And God said further to Moses, "Thus shall you speak to the Israelites: Y-H-W-H, the God of your fathers, the God of Abraham, the God of Isaac, and the God of Jacob, has sent me to you: This shall be My name forever, This My appellation for all eternity.
>
> Exodus 3:13–15

The meaning of the term *Ehyeh* is "I will be." The best-known of classical biblical exegetes, the eleventh-century French commentator Rabbi Shlomo Yitzchaki (referred to by the acronym Rashi) translates *Ehyeh* as "I will be with them (in this suffering)" and *Ehyeh asher Ehyeh* as "I will be with them in this suffering just as I will be with them in future oppressions." While *Ehyeh* assures the Jewish People of God's presence in the future, Y-H-W-H (Y-H-W-H, the God of your Fathers ...), a combination of the Hebrew words *Ha-yah, Ho-Weh, Ye-hee-yeh,* asserts God's Presence in the past, present, and future—which is how God wants to be known and recalled "for all eternity." In this spirit, we have translated Y-H-W-H as EverPresent God.

A parallel term for describing God's Presence, *HaMakom,* the "OmniPresent," used to denote God's Presence in the entire universe (i.e., space) rather than for all eternity (i.e., time), is used by the Haggadah to refer to God in *Maggid,* the verbal retelling of the Exodus story (see p. 43). My teacher, Rabbi Joseph B. Soloveitchik, once pointed out to my rabbinical school class that the term *HaMakom* is used specifically to express the attribute of God's empathetic Presence with human beings in their suffering. Thus, for instance, it is the way that God is referred to in the formula of solace that visitors recite to comfort those grieving in a house of mourning: *HaMakom yenachem etchem...,* "the OmniPresent should console you...." Rabbi Soloveitchik continued, "There is no greater expression of empathy that a person can give another human being than to assure them that God is Present in their struggles and suffering."

Similarly, the translation of God's name Y-H-W-H as EverPresent God is meant to convey the sense of God's personal, caring presence. This name for God assured the Jewish People of God's caring presence in Egypt, and reassures us, who identify with their experience of slavery and redemption from Egypt, on the night of the Passover Seder.

# 1

# Preparing for Passover:
## Why We Rid Ourselves
of *Chametz*

Every Jewish holiday entails some degree of preparation, but most anyone who has prepared for a traditional celebration of Passover would agree that Passover is in a class by itself. Jewish tradition tells us that we begin studying the laws and customs of Passover thirty days before the holiday. A month's time is also about how long it takes to turn one's house upside down in order to get rid of every bit and morsel of *chametz*, "leavened food." While in a free society and abundant economy there is no problem buying matzot for Passover, ridding your home, office, automobiles, and possessions of any leavened product seems as onerous and burdensome now as it was millennia ago. Many of us have asked ourselves, while slaving away cleaning for Passover, what the Jewish tradition could possibly have had in mind (aside from reexperiencing our ancestors' slavery!) in outlawing *chametz* throughout Passover. After all, while we eat *maror* (bitter herbs) at the Seder to symbolize the bitterness of our experience in Egypt, we do not shun other vegetables either at the Seder or during the remainder of Passover. Yet, both the Torah and the rabbinic interpretations of the Torah, when commanding us to eat matzah, are unequivocal in absolutely outlawing any trace of *chametz*.

In fact, the Jewish tradition is far more stringent in its restrictions on Passover regarding *chametz* than it is in the dietary discipline the rest of the year regarding nonkosher meat. For instance, during the rest of the year, if a small amount of a nonkosher substance accidentally falls and disappears into a pot of kosher food, then the pot of food is still deemed kosher so long as the ratio of kosher to nonkosher is 60:1; the nonkosher substance is, in effect, neutralized. However, if a tiny amount of *chametz* flies into your kitchen on Passover and lands in your ten-gallon vat of kosher-for-Passover chicken soup, then even if the *chametz* is only 1/1000 of the amount of Passover chicken soup, it renders the contents of the vat, and the vat itself, impermissible for use during the holiday.

In addition, according to Jewish tradition, not only may *chametz* not be eaten on Passover, it may not be owned, possessed, or provide any benefit. The tradition even instructs us, in the blessing and formula for removing *chametz* that follows, to search exhaustively for, renounce legal ownership of, and destroy/burn any *chametz* in our possession prior to Passover. The only other item with which our tradition deals as severely as *chametz* is idolatry, which has a similar set of laws all year round. In some way, *chametz* on Passover must be similar to idolatry throughout the year, but how and why is that?

The Haggadah, in the recitation of the passage *Ha lakhma anya* ("This is the bread of affliction/poverty"; see pp. 40–42), provides a clue. The word *anya* is derived from the word *ani,* which denotes a poor person. Matzah, made only from flour and water hastily mixed and baked, is poor man's bread. What then is rich man's bread? *Chametz,* which has yeast and other enriching ingredients (e.g., eggs, baking soda, fruit juice) and which, in addition, has the luxury of time to allow for the fermentation of the dough. Our Israelite ancestors were consigned to eating dry, flat matzot made only from flour and water, baked and eaten hastily because of the relentless pace of their slave labor. The matzot reflected their very existence: a dry, flat monotony of endless labor under pressure of time from dawn to dusk, every day of every week of every year.

In contrast, who ate rich man's bread, bread made with the

finest ingredients, prepared slowly, given the time to rise and savored when eaten? The Egyptians, of course. It is well known that fermented bread was invented by the Egyptians and was used as a form of currency in the Egyptian economy. Fundamentally, then, by eating matzot on Passover, we are identifying with and reliving the experience of our Israelite ancestors. By shunning *chametz*, we are rejecting the lifestyle and values of their Egyptian taskmasters. As we will see when we begin the Passover Seder, *Kadesh* or *Kiddush*, the blessing over wine, will take us back in time to the period of the Exodus. There we will assume the very identities and personae of our ancient, enslaved Israelite ancestors. Therefore, it is only fitting and proper that we eat what our ancestors ate, and avoid the food that our cruel taskmasters enjoyed.

But the dichotomy between *chametz* and matzah goes deeper than that, much deeper. For how could the Egyptians afford to eat rich man's bread? And why could the Israelites only afford to eat poor man's bread? Answer: The Egyptians earned their wealth the good, old-fashioned way—by impoverishing and enslaving our grandfathers and grandmothers. Our people's enslavement and economic exploitation stripped the Jewish nation of their wealth and provided for the unjust enrichment of the Egyptian populace.

Slavery is, after all, an institution that is motivated and sustained by two factors: economic greed and an unquenchable desire for absolute control. Slavery provides nearly free labor to the slave owner. Imagine how much wealth you could accumulate if you merely had to provide your workers with the most minimal subsistence and did not otherwise have to pay your employees for their services or the goods that they produced. Slavery also equates human beings with chattel, objects that can be manipulated and disposed of at will. In a slave society, greed and abusive control trump human dignity and worth. Since the Jewish tradition posits that every human being is created in the image of God, to systematically violate human dignity and diminish human value through enslaving others are tantamount to denying God and worshiping idolatry—not in a metaphoric sense but in reality:

greed and power are no less idols than golden statues and natu-ralistic fetishes. The products of that idolatrous enslavement are spiritually contaminated and constitute unjust enrichment. On Passover, *chametz*, rich man's bread, is the embodiment of that spiritual contamination and unjust enrichment and is therefore taboo. On Passover, *chametz* becomes morally repugnant in the Jewish tradition because it symbolizes what is called in American tort law the product of "unclean hands." Therefore, even an infin-itesimal amount of *chametz* on Passover renders everything it comes in contact with impermissible for consumption during the duration of the festival.

This equation of *chametz* with unjust enrichment also explains an unusual tradition regarding *chametz* owned by a Jew that remains in the Jew's legal possession over the Passover holiday. This *chametz*, if intentionally kept by a Jewish person in his or her possession contrary to Jewish tradition, is referred to as *chametz she-avar alav HaPesach*. If not sold or otherwise properly disposed of, such *chametz* may not be used even after the holiday of Passover. For a Jew to benefit from *chametz* that was not properly disposed of before Passover would constitute a similar unjust enrichment (albeit this time benefiting a Jew) to that derived by the ancient Egyptian slave owners. Therefore, such *chametz* remains taboo in perpetuity.

On Passover, instead of eating rich man's bread, *chametz*, we eat poor man's bread, matzah. (This accounts for the prevalent custom in traditional Ashkenazic circles on Passover to even avoid eating enriched matzah, *matzah ashirah*, such as egg matzot, which are enriched with eggs and fruit juice, unless one has no choice because of health concerns.) Although the "bread" we eat on Passover is poor, we have earned it through our own work and the sweat of our own brow (literally!). As the Psalmist says: "Happy is everyone who fears the Lord; who walks in God's ways. For when you eat the labor of your hands, happy will you be and it will be good for you" (Psalm 128:1–2).

# Searching for *Chametz*/בְּדִיקַת חָמֵץ

One of the distinctive trademarks of Jewish tradition is that it gives expression to its values through the performance of concrete actions. On the night and morning before Passover, the tradition is to search for, renounce ownership of ("nullification"), and burn or otherwise permanently dispose of any *chametz* that is in our possession. Prior to beginning the search for *chametz*, we praise God for differentiating us from our ancient Egyptian enslavers by commanding us to remove all leavened products:

> *Blessed are You, EverPresent God, our God, Sovereign of the universe, who has sanctified us through Your commandments, commanding us to remove all* chametz.

בָּרוּךְ אַתָּה יְיָ אֱלֹהֵינוּ מֶלֶךְ הָעוֹלָם, אֲשֶׁר קִדְּשָׁנוּ בְּמִצְוֹתָיו, וְצִוָּנוּ עַל בִּעוּר חָמֵץ.

After completing the search for the *chametz*, we proclaim:

> *All* chametz *in my possession that I have not seen or removed or of which I am unaware is hereby nullified and ownerless as the dust of the earth.*

כָּל חֲמִירָא וַחֲמִיעָא דְּאִכָּא בִרְשׁוּתִי, דְּלָא חֲמִתֵּהּ וּדְלָא בְעַרְתֵּהּ וּדְלָא יְדַעְנָא לֵהּ, לִבָּטֵל וְלֶהֱוֵי הֶפְקֵר כְּעַפְרָא דְאַרְעָא.

# Destroying One's *Chametz*/בִּעוּר חָמֵץ

In the morning, after we have eaten our last meal of *chametz*, we take whatever *chametz* we gathered in the previous night and burn

it or otherwise dispose of it. By doing so we symbolically disassoci-
ate ourselves from any trace of Egyptian values. We then declare:

> All chametz *in my possession, whether I have seen it or
> not, whether I have removed it or not, is hereby nullified
> and ownerless as the dust of the earth.*

כָּל חֲמִירָא וַחֲמִיעָא דְּאִכָּא בִרְשׁוּתִי, דַּחֲזִתֵּהּ וּדְלָא
חֲזִתֵּהּ, דַּחֲמִתֵּהּ וּדְלָא חֲמִתֵּהּ, דְּבַעַרְתֵּהּ וּדְלָא
בַעַרְתֵּהּ, לִבָּטֵל וְלֶהֱוֵי הֶפְקֵר כְּעַפְרָא דְאַרְעָא.

# 2

# Understanding the Order of the Seder

As a young person, I had the good fortune to receive a fine Jewish education. I was taught by my teachers that the biblical and rabbinic texts that I studied were very carefully crafted. The more I studied, the more I became convinced that my teachers were right. Yet somehow the Haggadah seemed an exception to the rule. Rather than being carefully crafted in some sort of conscious order (in a *seder,* "order"), the Haggadah seemed to lack an organizing principle. The elements of the Seder appeared to be fragmented and, if not irrelevant, then at times "quaintly antiquated."

Several examples from the early part of the Haggadah will make the point.

The Seder begins with *Kadesh,* or *Kiddush,* the blessing over wine, which inaugurates the festival meal. Since every Shabbat and festival meal begins with a *Kiddush,* its recitation is nothing out of the ordinary. What is extraordinary is that this *Kiddush* is the first of four cups of wine over which the participants in the Seder recite a blessing during the course of the meal. What connection is there, if any, between the four cups, and why are they positioned as they are in the course of the meal? What function do these cups play in the saga of the Seder?

The second item in the Seder (in the "order" of the

Haggadah) is called *U-Rechatz,* washing the hands without saying a blessing. As a youngster I was told that the reason for washing the hands related to a rather arcane law about a wet vegetable having the potential to become *tamei,* spiritually contaminated. I was puzzled by this explanation, since this kind of spiritual contamination, *tum-ah,* has been a void legal category since the destruction of the Second Temple in Jerusalem in 70 C.E. Nor does Jewish tradition mandate the ritual washing of the hands prior to the eating of vegetables during the remainder of the year. As to why no blessing was said, I was usually told by my teachers that no blessing was recited so as to prompt the young to ask why no blessing was recited and to pique their interest. Talk about circular reasoning!

The explanation for the third item in the Seder, *Karpas,* eating a green vegetable dipped in salt water, sounded equally improbable. I was told that "we ate a green vegetable because Passover is a spring festival, and we dipped the vegetable in salt water to remind us of the tears of our Israelite ancestors."

First of all, all we need to do to know that spring is in the air is to take a deep breath and look outside the window at the budding of the trees. The Rabbis of the third century C.E., who put together the Haggadah, were not in the business of asserting the obvious. A meaningful ritual that reminded people to celebrate the upcoming spring festival might have been helpful to communicate to the participants a month or two weeks prior to the festival. For people already sitting at the Passover meal, however, such a reminder would be superfluous at best and an insult to people's intelligence at worst. And why mix spring, which is the season and symbol of our liberation, with tears, a symbol of our embittered enslavement? Talk about a mishmash of concepts!

Finally, there is the fourth item in the Passover Seder, *Yachatz,* the breaking of the middle matzah. The larger broken portion was wrapped up and hidden away, while the smaller broken portion was reinserted between the two remaining whole matzot. What this item had to do with the previous item, *Karpas,* was never made clear. The reason that was given for *Yachatz* by my teachers was "to arouse the curiosity of the young people and stoke their interest in the Seder." While this particular ruse often worked, it still left me wondering if the Seder was nothing more than a long-winded trick to keep the children awake while the adults fell asleep with confusion or apathy.

While most of my peers accepted these sometimes odd, disjointed explanations of the components of the Seder, I was troubled by them. I reasoned that if the Haggadah was in a particular *seder*, in a particular order, then the order of the pieces of the Haggadah should form a coherent whole rather than just a series of disjointed parts that had nothing, or little, to do with each other. Moreover, whatever that whole was, it needed to relate in some way to the underlying story of the Exodus, which the Haggadah, presumably, was telling. I wondered whether we had perhaps forgotten the original, holistic meaning of the Seder. Could the passage of time and nearly two thousand years of persecution and Diaspora wandering have caused us to forget what the rabbinic authors intended with the Haggadah? Could the organic connection between the Haggadah and the story of the Exodus have somehow evaporated?

When the Passover Haggadah and the story of the Exodus are read together, we can see that the meaning of the Seder is the chronological reenactment and retelling of the highlights of the Jewish People's journey from physical slavery to spiritual redemption as recorded in the Book of Exodus. To engage in the Passover Seder is to embark on a spiritual pilgrimage through time. It is to journey from the successful entry of the Jewish People into Egypt, through slavery and infanticide, to political freedom and spiritual redemption. Every item in the Seder mirrors the precise order of that journey as it appears in the second book of the Bible.

This *seder*, this order, not only mirrors the experience of the Jewish People in ancient Egypt, but closely approximates the experience of the Jewish People throughout their journeys in the Diaspora, including our people's most recent past. In nearly every Diaspora—Spain, Portugal, Poland, Germany, Russia, and so on—

the Jewish People were at first welcomed into their host countries with open arms. Often, the Jews brought a set of economic skills or international connections that the host country found useful to building up the local economy. Then as the Jewish population began to be overly successful, their very prosperity elicited a counterreaction from the ruling elites, who felt threatened by the obvious flourishing of the Jewish minority. This reaction would usually take the form of discriminatory laws to help "contain" the Jews. Often these laws would create physical boundaries between the Jews and the local population—ghetto walls, or restrictions on social and economic intercourse. As the Jews continued to be successful despite these efforts at containment, the local authorities would resort to violence or physical expulsion. This pattern of Jewish success and reactionary discrimination, which culminated in the twentieth century with the Holocaust, has its origins in the Jewish experience in ancient Egypt thirty-five hundred years ago. To reenact this experience is therefore to relive not only the Exodus from Egypt, but the recurrent cycle of Jewish history.

Metaphorically, the Seder also reflects our personal pilgrimages, the patterns of our individual life journeys. While our birth and arrival on this planet is often celebrated with great fanfare, as was the arrival of the Jewish people in Egypt, much of growing up and becoming an adult is about the struggle to achieve independence, material sustenance, and spiritual meaning—not so unlike the struggles of the Jewish People in Egypt and in their desert wanderings. Along the way, more often than not, we are likely to encounter setbacks and moments of crisis when the world seems dark and hopeless. The Jewish story reenacted every year in the Passover Seder is the reassurance that just as our people overcame our challenges in the distant past, so too, with God's help, will we as individuals overcome the obstacles that we face in the present and the future. The Seder therefore serves as a type of personal catharsis in which we recall the struggles of our past and exult in our experience of personal redemption.

## Three Ways of Telling the Story

The Rabbis in the Haggadah chose to tell the story of the Exodus using all three primary senses:

1. Visually, through the Seder plate
2. Kinesthetically, through the ritual actions of the Seder
3. Verbally, through *Maggid*, the narrative at the Seder's center

## The Seder Plate: The Visual Telling

The Haggadah begins by telling the story visually. Before we even sit down to the Passover Seder, the presence of the Passover Seder plate sitting in the center of the table begins to communicate the story visually. Although there is a myriad of different customs as to how one arranges the Seder plate,[1] none of them is arbitrary or arranged at random. Rather, each of them represents the author's understanding of the crucial elements of the Seder and their role in telling the story of the Exodus. What follows is my own arrangement based on my analysis of the Seder.

The plate is called a Seder plate not merely because it is the platter used at the Seder, but because, like the Seder itself, it has a purposeful order: in my understanding, the order of the Jewish People's pivotal moments in the Book of Exodus. The Seder plate itself is round, like a clock, reflecting the pilgrimage through time through which we journey during the Seder and the cyclical nature of Jewish history. The items are placed on the plate in chronological order (i.e., in a *seder*) going clockwise. The Seder plate is placed above the cloth or enclosure containing the three matzot.

The first item on the plate, placed at the one o'clock position on the "Seder clock," is the *karpas,* parsley, representing the initial fertility and growth of the Jewish People in Egypt (Exod. 1:7). The next item on the plate, placed at the three o'clock position of the Seder clock, is the *charoset,* symbolizing the mortar used in constructing Pharaoh's cities. This represents the next stage in the Jewish People's experience in Egypt—one of harsh labor and unrelenting toil (Exod. 1:13–14). At the five o'clock position is a bit of *maror*, symbolizing the bitter enslavement of the Jews (ibid.). It is customary to use either romaine lettuce or ground horseradish to represent the *maror*. At the seven o'clock position is a piece of solid horseradish called *chazeret*. The difference between *maror* and *chazeret* is that while the *maror* can be eaten, the *chazeret* cannot be swallowed. As *Yachatz* will symbolize in the Seder, the *chazeret* represents Pharaoh's decree of infanticide which the Jewish People were unable to "assimilate" or "swallow" (Exod. 1:22). This stands in contrast to Pharaoh's previous attempts to stem the prodigious growth of the Jewish People, which, however difficult and bitter, the people were able to "swallow" and overcome (Exod. 1:12, 1:17, 1:21).

At the nine o'clock position is a roasted bone, called the *zeroa*. This bone represents the Passover sacrifice, which was roasted over the fire on the night of the Exodus (Exod. 12:8–9). The use of the word *zeroa* instead of the normally used *etzem* to describe the bones of the Passover sacrifice (see Num. 9:12) is also meant to invoke God's promise to the Jewish People to redeem them "...with an outstretched arm [*zeroa netuyah*]" (Exod. 6:6). As will be explained in the section on the third cup, God's outstretched arm alludes to the miracle of the splitting of the sea, in which Moses, stretching out his arm, in effect acted as God's extension (see Exod. 14:16, 14:21, 14:26). Thus the bone and name of *zeroa* symbolize the two pivotal events of the physical redemption of the Jewish People from Egypt: the night of the plague of the first-born on which God passed over the Israelite homes and the night on which God parted the Sea of Reeds.

At the eleven o'clock position is a roasted egg, called the *betzah*. This represents the roasted holiday sacrifice *(korban chagigah)*, which could only be brought to one place: the Temple in Jerusalem on the Pilgrimage Festivals. Because of its association with the *Beit HaMikdash,* the sacred Sanctuary, the *betzah* corresponds to *Nirtzah,* or acceptance in the kinesthetic Seder, and symbolizes the final stage of the redemption process, "spiritual redemption"—the complete acceptance of the people by God and of God by the people. This joyful, mutual acceptance occurred when the Divine Presence came to dwell among the people in the *Mikdash,* the Tabernacle, which the people built for God to conclude the Book of Exodus (Exod. 40:34–38).

In the center of the plate, my family's custom is to place a bowl of salt water. The salt water is used for the dipping of the *karpas,* to symbolize the sweat-drenched Israelites toward the beginning of the story, as well as to remind us of the splitting of the sea toward the end of the Seder's story. In a sense, the salt water represents the two "hands" of the Seder's clock: one "hand" is pointed toward two o'clock, between the *karpas* and *charoset,* denoting the first half of the Jewish People's experience in Egypt (the sweat of slavery); and the other "hand" is pointed toward ten o'clock, between the *zeroa* and *betzah,* reminding us of the latter portion of the Jewish People's experience (the waters of redemption). Like the double washing of the hands and the symbolic meaning of the matzah, the salt water takes on a different significance depending on where in the spiritual journey through time we find ourselves.

## The Seder: The Kinesthetic, Ritual Telling

After seeing the visual story of the Seder in the plate, we sit down at the table for the Seder proper. Each item of the Seder contains some kinesthetic ritual action (e.g., the drinking of the first cup of wine for *Kadesh;* the washing of the hands for *U-Rechatz;* the dipping and eating of parsley for *Karpas*). Even *Maggid,* which, as we will see, is the "verbal Seder," still contains kinesthetic elements to mark its key moments. This emphasis on symbolic ritual actions is central to the educational philosophy of the Rabbis who wrote the Haggadah. Like William James and Thomas Dewey's pragmatic/experiential educational theory, the Rabbis believed that we learn best by doing and experiencing, not merely by seeing and hearing. Anyone who has ever observed infant behavior or undergone physical rehabilitation knows that the body teaches the mind even before the mind teaches the body. The Seder therefore tells us the story of the Exodus through a series of kinesthetic actions that together coalesce into a single transformative educational experience.

## *Maggid:* The Verbal Seder

The section of *Maggid,* which will commence with the recitation of the Four Questions, will begin the verbal retelling of the Exodus story. In *Maggid,* the fifth item in the Seder, we will use primarily words, rather than food, drink, or actions, to review and imaginatively retell the part of the story that we have already "told" visually and kinesthetically through the first four items on the Seder plate *(karpas, charoset, maror,* and *chazeret)* and the first four items of the Seder *(Kadesh, U-Rechatz, Karpas,* and *Yachatz).* We will then proceed further in *Maggid,* continuing to both verbally and ritually tell the rest of the Exodus story.

Why did the Rabbis add a verbal telling to the visual and kinesthetic tellings? Because the Rabbis understood that in order to have the Exodus story speak to all the people of their generation and future generations, they had to speak to all their primary senses.[2] For those who learn best by seeing (visual learners), the Rabbis fashioned the Seder plate, which visually tells the Exodus story. For those who learn best by doing (kinesthetic learners), the Rabbis designed the kinesthetic, ritual actions of the Seder. Finally, for those who absorb information best by hearing (audial learners), they authored *Maggid*—the verbal Seder. I call *Maggid* the verbal *Seder* because, like the Seder plate and the Seder proper, *Maggid* too has a purposeful order and structure. Like the plate and the Seder, which follows the order of the verses in the Book of Exodus, *Maggid* will follow the order of a single verse in the Book of Exodus, the verse upon which the entire Haggadah is based:

"And you should tell your child on that day, saying: 'Because of this [*or:* This is because of what], the EverPresent God did for me when I left Egypt.'"

Exodus 13:8

וְהִגַּדְתָּ לְבִנְךָ בַּיּוֹם הַהוּא לֵאמֹר: בַּעֲבוּר זֶה עָשָׂה
יְיָ לִי, בְּצֵאתִי מִמִּצְרָיִם.

How the lengthy and complex section of *Maggid* follows the order of this verse will be fully explored when we arrive at that way station in our spiritual journey. For now, having set up and eyed the Seder plate, it is time to commence our Seder, the kinesthetic "telling" of the Exodus story.

## The Seder

1. *Kadesh*/קַדֵּשׁ
2. *U-Rechatz*/וּרְחַץ
3. *Karpas*/כַּרְפַּס
4. *Yachatz*/יַחַץ
5. *Maggid*/מַגִּיד
6. *Rochtzah*/רָחְצָה
7. *Motzi*/מוֹצִיא
8. *Matzah*/מַצָּה
9. *Maror*/מָרוֹר
10. *Korekh*/כּוֹרֵךְ
11. *Shulchan Orekh*/שֻׁלְחָן עוֹרֵךְ
12. *Tzafun*/צָפוּן
13. *Barekh*/בָּרֵךְ
14. *Hallel*/הַלֵּל
15. *Nirtzah*/נִרְצָה

## Why the Seder Is Sung

It is customary to begin the evening by singing through the fifteen items of the Seder. This is because the Seder is not merely a table of contents for the evening's program; no one that I know sings the table of contents of a book. Rather, there is something about the order, the *seder*, of the evening that is intrinsically important. The singsong employed to recite the Seder helps all those around the table to give expression to and remember all the items of the Seder in their correct order. As in any song, the melody pulls together the words into a unified whole with a beginning, a middle, and an end. As we will see, this is because the Seder is just that—a unified, ordered, whole story with a beginning, middle, and end.

## What's in a Number? Seven Instances of the Number Fifteen

There are fifteen steps to the Seder. The Jews were liberated from Egypt and we celebrate Passover on the fifteenth day of the Hebrew month of Nisan. There are fifteen steps (*Ma'alot Tovot*) for which we praise God when all the participants at the Seder join together to sing "Dayenu" (pp. 101–108). In the Torah scroll, the "Song at the Sea" (sung by the Jewish People after God rescued them from the pursuing Egyptian legions—Exodus 15) is written as a poem in three vertical columns. The center column, which appears to be an ascending ladder, has fifteen steps. There were fifteen steps on the southern side of the Temple Mount that led up to the sacred Temple in Jerusalem, and there are fifteen psalms (Psalms 120–134) that begin with the words *Shir HaMa'alot*, "A Song of the Steps."[3] Finally, there are fifteen words in the Priestly Blessing.

      Are all these "fifteens" mere coincidence? Highly unlikely. For there is yet another "fifteen" that may explain all the previous fifteens: God's name, *Yah*, equals fifteen in *gematria*, a system of numerology equating Hebrew letters with their corresponding numbers (e.g., *aleph* = one, *bet* = two, *gimel* = three). All of the previous fifteens share one thing in common—they are all fifteens that lead to a direct experience of the Divine Presence. Whether singing the fifteen *Shir HaMa'alot* psalms while ascending the fifteen stairs to the Temple in Jerusalem where God's Presence was manifest, experiencing God's love emanating from the recitation of the fifteen words of the Priestly Blessing, seeing God's strong hand smite the first-born of Egypt on the fifteenth day of the Hebrew month of Nisan, or witnessing God's awesome power at the Sea of Reeds poetically "laddered" in the fifteen lines of the Torah scroll, the Jews, in all these instances, experienced the immediacy of the Divine Presence in their lives. (In fact, as we explicate the Seder, we will find that all of these fifteens are associated with the experiencing of the Divine Presence in a particular place: the sacred Temple in Jerusalem. We will return to this point at *Nirtzah,* the very end of the Haggadah.) For the Jewish People, the unmitigated contact with the Divine was the ultimate meaning of redemption. Everything else—miracles, freedom, even commandments—were only means to achieving that direct contact with the Divine. Achieving that union with the Divine Presence was no easy matter. It took many steps of preparation—fifteen, to be precise.[4]

Another metaphor for understanding these fifteens generally, and the fifteen steps of the Seder in particular, is as a "spiritual pilgrimage." In the times of the Temple, Passover was the first of the three "Pilgrimage Festivals" in which the Israelites journeyed from all over the Land of Israel to the Temple Mount. There, they would experience the singing of the fifteen psalms by the Levites on the fifteen steps of the Temple; they would receive the Priestly Blessing by the splendidly robed priests on those same stairs, and then would ascend those steps, bringing their offerings and gifts before God in God's very house. The fifteen steps, psalms, and words of blessing were meant to prepare the pilgrims before they encountered the awesome sight of the Divine Presence dwelling in the Temple's cloud of aromatic incense.

The Seder is a virtual pilgrimage experience. It is a fifteen-step voyage through time and space in which the "pilgrim" imagines himself/herself living in Egypt, being enslaved and persecuted, and being liberated and redeemed by a loving God. We prepare to embark on the pilgrimage in the first fifteen days of the month of Nisan, journey through the people's experience from slavery to freedom in the fifteen steps of the Seder, praise God for each step in the "Dayenu," and burst out in fifteen steps of song on the safe shores of the Sea of Reeds. Ultimately, like the more literal pilgrimages in Temple times, our spiritual pilgrimage arrives at the same destination: we encounter the loving presence of God hovering in our homes, God's miniature abode, which acts as a contemporary substitute for the Temple, God's permanent home, accepting our offerings and gifts of thanksgiving.

For now it is time to turn to the beginning of the Seder, the first two items in the list of fifteen: *Kadesh* and *U-Rechatz,* to understand their particular role in the Seder.

# Traveling Back to Sacred Time and Sacred Space

How can we transform ourselves from being American Jews living in the twenty-first century of the Common Era, to being ancient Israelites, living in Egypt 1,250 to 1,500 years before the Common Era? How do we help our imaginations take flight and prepare not only our minds and our souls but our very bodies for the tumultuous journey upon which we are about to embark? The genius of the Rabbis who authored the Haggadah is that they knew these transitions of time and place needed to be structured into the evening. That is why they begin the Seder with *Kadesh,* to empower our minds to return to our people's first sacred time, and *U-Rechatz,* to prepare our bodies for entering sacred space.

## *Kadesh*/קַדֵּשׁ: Preparing Our Minds to Travel through Time

If we were telling a story about ourselves, we would begin by telling when and where the story took place. Similarly, to tell the story of the Exodus and to learn something of spiritual significance from that story, we first have to set its historical context. We have to locate it both chronologically and geographically. This is what the

Torah does to open its telling of the Exodus story in the first six verses of the Book of Exodus. It reiterates the time, place, and major characters of the story that follows, even though that information was already conveyed to us in chapters 46–50 of the Book of Genesis.

The Book of Exodus begins:

> And these are the names of the children of Israel who came to Egypt with Jacob, each man came with his household: Reuven, Shimon, Levi, and Yehudah; Issachar, Zevulun, and Binyamin; Dan, Naftali, Gad, and Asher. All the descendants who came from Jacob totaled seventy souls including Joseph who was already in Egypt. Then Joseph and all his brothers and all those of that generation died.
>
> Exodus 1:1–6

The Seder, which symbolically retells the story of the Exodus, likewise begins by setting the historical context of our people's journey. The first purpose of *Kadesh* is to take us back to the time of the Exodus. How do we know this? From the text of *Kiddush* itself:

> *Blessed are You, EverPresent God, our God, Sovereign of the universe, who creates the fruit of the vine.*
>
> *Blessed are You, EverPresent God, our God, Sovereign of the universe, who has chosen us and exalted us from all nations and has sanctified us with Your commandments. And You, EverPresent God, our God, has lovingly bestowed upon us, appointed times for happiness, holidays and times for joy, this Feast of Matzot, our time of freedom, called sacred, recalling the Exodus from Egypt. For it was us that You chose and us that You sanctified from among all the peoples. In Your gracious*

*love, You granted us Your appointed times for happiness and joy. Blessed are You, EverPresent God, who sanctifies Israel and the appointed times.*
*Blessed are You, EverPresent God, our God, Sovereign of the universe, who has granted us life and sustenance and permitted us to reach this time.*

סַבְרִי מָרָנָן וְרַבָּנָן וְרַבּוֹתַי:

בָּרוּךְ אַתָּה יְיָ, אֱלֹהֵינוּ מֶלֶךְ הָעוֹלָם, בּוֹרֵא פְּרִי הַגָּפֶן.

בָּרוּךְ אַתָּה יְיָ, אֱלֹהֵינוּ מֶלֶךְ הָעוֹלָם, אֲשֶׁר בָּחַר בָּנוּ מִכָּל-עָם, וְרוֹמְמָנוּ מִכָּל-לָשׁוֹן, וְקִדְּשָׁנוּ בְּמִצְוֹתָיו. וַתִּתֶּן-לָנוּ יְיָ אֱלֹהֵינוּ בְּאַהֲבָה מוֹעֲדִים לְשִׂמְחָה, חַגִּים וּזְמַנִּים לְשָׂשׂוֹן, אֶת-יוֹם חַג הַמַּצּוֹת הַזֶּה, זְמַן חֵרוּתֵנוּ, מִקְרָא קֹדֶשׁ, זֵכֶר לִיצִיאַת מִצְרָיִם. כִּי בָנוּ בָחַרְתָּ וְאוֹתָנוּ קִדַּשְׁתָּ מִכָּל-הָעַמִּים וּמוֹעֲדֵי קָדְשֶׁךָ בְּשִׂמְחָה וּבְשָׂשׂוֹן הִנְחַלְתָּנוּ: בָּרוּךְ אַתָּה יְיָ, מְקַדֵּשׁ יִשְׂרָאֵל וְהַזְּמַנִּים.

בָּרוּךְ אַתָּה יְיָ, אֱלֹהֵינוּ מֶלֶךְ הָעוֹלָם, שֶׁהֶחֱיָנוּ וְקִיְּמָנוּ וְהִגִּיעָנוּ לַזְּמַן הַזֶּה.

As with every blessing, the theme for *Kiddush* is contained in the closing summary, the *chatimah*. The first theme of *Kiddush* is *zeman*, "time": "times for happiness, holidays and times for joy … our time for freedom … who sanctifies Israel and the appointed times … who has granted us life and sustenance and permitted us to reach this time." Which time? The time of the Exodus from

Egypt, *zecher litziat Mitzrayim*. *Kadesh* is a time machine that transports our minds (*zecher litziat Mitzrayim*, reminding us of the Exodus
from Egypt) back to the sacred events surrounding the Exodus.[1]

This also explains why we recite *Kiddush* over wine and drink
a total of four cups of wine during the course of the Seder. Each
cup of wine, recited with its own blessing, helps focus our minds,
shifts our consciousness to a different time, to a different point in
the Exodus story. The first cup takes us back to the beginning of
the story, to the first day our ancestors arrived in Egypt (Exod. 1).
Since we are undertaking a long, 3,500-year journey, the *Kiddush*
blessings that we recite are the lengthiest of the four cups. The second cup will take us forward 210 years to the final night that the
Jewish People were in Egypt (Exod. 12); the third cup will transport us seven days later to the shore of the Sea of Reeds (Exod.
14–15); and the fourth cup will leave us six weeks after that, at the
foot of Mount Sinai, where the Jewish People witnessed the Divine
Presence revealing the Ten Commandments and coming to symbolically dwell among the Jewish People (Exod. 19–20, 40).

This progressive journey through time is what the Rabbis
meant when they linked the drinking of the four cups to the four
promises of redemption that God made to Moses in Exodus 6:6–8:

> "Therefore say to the Jewish People, I am the EverPresent
> God, and I will take you out from under the suffering of
> Egypt and I will rescue you from their enslavement, and I
> will redeem you with an outstretched arm and with great
> judgments. And I will take you to be My people and I will
> be your God, and you will know that I am the EverPresent
> God, your God, who takes you out from under all the suf-
> ferings of Egypt."

The first cup, which chronicles the history of the Jewish
People from the time they descend to Egypt through their enslavement and God's bringing of the ten plagues, corresponds to the
first promise of redemption: taking them out from under the suf-

fering of Egypt. As God began to stand up for the Jewish people, the psychological suffering of the Jewish People occasioned by their sense of abandonment and hopelessness began to ease. Once the Jewish People saw that they had a real champion for their cause, their spirits, which had been crushed by the weight of suffering, began to be lifted. The first cup therefore corresponds to the period in which they were taken out from their suffering.

The second cup, which corresponds to the Jewish People's last meal in Egypt, corresponds to the second promise of redemption: rescuing the people from slave labor. As they ate their meal of freedom on the last night of their sojourn in Egypt, their slavery was relegated to a memory. Never again would they be enslaved to their Egyptian taskmasters.

The third cup transports us in our time machines to the confrontation at the Sea of Reeds. It corresponds to the promise of being "redeemed with an outstretched arm and with great judgments." Why does this refer to the miracles at the sea? Because the miracles were done before the eyes of the Jewish People with Moses acting as God's extension, as God's "extended arm." In fact, twice in the story of the splitting of the sea, God tells Moses to stretch out his arm to perform the miracles, and twice more the Torah tells us that Moses extended his arm to perform God's miracles.

Finally, the fourth cup, which corresponds to the fourth promise of redemption ("And I will take you to be My people and I will be your God, and you will know that I am the EverPresent God, your God, who takes you out from under all the sufferings of Egypt") will transport us to the Jewish People standing at the foot of Mount Sinai, where God took them to be God's people (Exod. 19:4–6) and revealed God's identity in the first commandment, as "the EverPresent God, your God, who took you out from the land of Egypt from the house of bondage" (Exod. 20:2).

The wine of the four cups loosens up our consciousness and helps us suspend our critical faculties. Drinking a substantial but not inebriating amount of alcohol allows our imagination to hover in the period of 1250 B.C.E., much as God's presence hovered above the Israelite houses as God struck down the Egyptian first-born. It helps us smooth over the bumpy roads of time travel and journey almost seamlessly from one pivotal moment in historical time to the next. The wine enables us to really believe that we are slaves of Pharaoh about to be liberated from Egyptian bondage and redeemed by God's loving presence.

This is why four pieces of matzah or four servings of the Passover sacrifice would not do the trick. Neither matzah nor sacrificial meat nor bitter herbs has the effect of loosening up our sense of reality the way wine does. On the other extreme, drinking a beverage with higher alcoholic content would undermine our ability to discern reality with any degree of definition and would make the entire Seder one big illusory blur.

The second purpose of *Kadesh* is to identify who the "us" is that is returning to Egypt. "Us" is *Yisrael,* the ancient Israelites who came down to Egypt at the beginning of the Book of Exodus; the children of Israel descended from Abraham, Isaac, and Jacob, whom God chose in Genesis to be a blessing to all the nations of the world (Gen. 12); the Israelites whom God predicted to Abraham in the "Covenant of the pieces" would be strangers and enslaved for 400 years before God redeemed them with great power and abundant wealth (Gen. 15). *Kadesh* tells us that for the night of Passover we are not North American Jews living in material comfort and freedom in the early twenty-first century. Instead, we are ancient Israelites living in Egypt in the thirteenth century B.C.E. who are about to embark on an extraordinary metamorphosis that will alter our identity not only on this night, but for all time to come.

## *U-Rechatz*/וּרְחַץ: Preparing Our Bodies to Enter Sacred Space

Of all the items in the Seder, only the second one begins with the Hebrew letter *vav,* meaning "and." Whenever someone writes "this and that," the writer intends to forge a connection between those items—in this case, between *Kadesh* and *U-Rechatz*. The connection becomes even more pronounced by the absence of any grammatical conjunctions between the remaining items in the Seder.

While *Kadesh* is meant to prepare our minds and alter our consciousness to enter sacred time, *U-Rechatz* is meant to prepare our bodies, to sanctify our physicality before we enter sacred space. *Kadesh* and *U-Rechatz* are a complementary pair that enables us to enter sacred time and tread on sacred space.

What is it that makes time and space sacred? The encounter with the Divine Presence. When we meet God in our lives, the moment of that meeting and the place of that meeting become sacred, "holy," or, to use a more prosaic expression, "special." To experience that encounter, our physical selves must be symbolically purified and thereby sanctified. For example, before the Revelation of the Torah by the Divine Presence on Mount Sinai, Moses instructed the Israelites to wash their bodies and their garments in preparation for their meeting the Divine (according to the plausible explanation of Exod. 19:10 by the rabbinic Sages). Later on, after the Sanctuary was built, the priests were instructed to wash their hands and feet with a pitcher and washbasin before entering the sacred precincts of the "Tent of Meeting" and doing the priestly service in the presence of the Divine (Exod. 30:17–21). Human beings have to sanctify their bodies and become holy to merit being in the presence of the Holy One.

Having journeyed back in time to approximately 1250 B.C.E. and assumed the identity of our Israelite forebears, we must now prepare our bodies to enter the sacred precincts of ancient Egypt. What makes ancient Egypt (of all places!) sacred? The same phenomenon that made Mount Sinai and the Tent of Meeting sacred: the Divine Presence, which became manifest there. As the Haggadah makes explicit during the *Maggid* section in the comment on *VeAvarti,* "I will pass," God did not redeem the Jewish People by proxy; God did not use messengers, angels, or any other intermediaries to do God's work (see pp. 92–93). Rather God personally, with God's own identifiable Presence, swooped down to smite the Egyptians and redeem the Israelites. In *Maggid* (see pp. 92–94), the Haggadah will tell us that the Divine Presence was revealed in Egypt, *Uvemora gadol: zeh gilui Shekhinah,* "'Great awe' alludes to the divine Revelation [in Egypt]." Since we are reliving that experience of divine Revelation, we have to symbolically wash our bodies and prepare to witness the Divine, as did the Israelites at Mount Sinai and as did the priests at the entrance to the biblical Sanctuary.

It is interesting to note the similarities between our washing of the hands for *U-Rechatz,* the figurative entrance to the Passover Seder, and the priests laving of their hands and feet at the physical entrance to the biblical Tabernacle. Like the priests who acted as the representatives of the Jewish People in ministering before God in the Tabernacle, many Jews have the custom of designating the leader of the Seder to ritually wash his/her hands as their representative for *U-Rechatz.* The leader also often has the custom of wearing a *kittel,* a plain white robe, at the Seder, which is reminiscent of the white linen garments that the priests wore before ministering in the biblical Tabernacle. The donning of a clean white robe reminds us, as well, of the washing of the clothes with which the Israelites were instructed to prepare themselves before the Revelation at Mount Sinai. Some have a custom of washing the hands using a pitcher and basin that is brought to the table rather than utilizing a standard washing cup at the sink. The pitcher and basin reenact the pitcher and basin used by the priests at the entrance to the Tent of Meeting in the biblical Sanctuary.

Since it is the body that is being symbolically prepared for encountering the Divine, there is no "mindfulness" required—that is, there is no blessing. Unlike *Kiddush,* in which we are altering our consciousness and being reminded of the period of the Exodus through the recitation of the blessing, in *U-Rechatz* it is our bodies and not our minds that are being prepared and transformed.

The lack of a blessing not only makes the distinction of mind *(Kadesh)* and body *(U-Rechatz)* clear by contrast, but also brings to the fore a central point: the redemption from Egypt was first and foremost a physical rather than a spiritual redemption. It was our individual bodies, as well as the collective body politic of the ancient Israelites, that were liberated from the rigors of slavery, rather than our individual and collective souls. Theoretically, God could have "saved our souls," much as the Christians understand Jesus to have done later on in history, while leaving the bodies of the Jews enslaved in Egypt. Having an item in the Seder that emphasizes the physical (i.e., washing the hands) while absenting the spiritual (not reciting a blessing) drives home the point that for the Jews the liberation of the soul is not complete without the liberation of the body.

Together, *Kadesh* and *U-Rechatz* serve as the introduction to the Seder. They symbolically communicate who we are (ancient Israelites), where we are (ancient Egypt), when we are living (1500–1250 B.C.E.), and whom we are about to encounter (none other than the Divine Presence). With that spiritual and historical context, both mind and body are prepared to enter the sacred precincts of the Exodus experience.

# From the Triumph of Life to the Kingdom of Death

*Karpas* and *Yachatz* tell the story of the early years of the Jewish people in Egypt. These two items in the Seder dramatically portray how the successful growth of the Jewish people in the first part of their life in Egypt eventually led to the imposition of a regime of harsh labor, oppressive slavery, and the draconian decree of infanticide. Fortunately, rather than leave us on such a dreadful note, the author of the Seder concludes *Yachatz* by pointing us, however obliquely, toward the birth of Moses, our people's human redeemer, who is born and hidden away until the time of redemption.

## *Karpas*/כַּרְפַּס: The Teeming Beginning of the Jewish People in Egypt

The Book of Exodus tells us how the Jewish People in the beginning of their stay in Egypt took root in the land and achieved extraordinary fecundity; how they grew from a single family of seventy souls into a teeming, muscular nation within a nation:

> All the persons who descended from Jacob, including Joseph who was in Egypt, amounted to [only] seventy

29

souls.... Yet the Jewish People became fertile and multiplied and increased and became very, very powerful, and the earth was filled with them.

Exodus 1:5–7

In fact, this growth represented an actualization of God's blessing to humanity in the Garden of Eden: "Be fruitful and multiply and fill the earth" (Gen. 1:28). Thus, the beginning of the Jewish People's experience in Egypt was indeed a blessed and bountiful one.

The Seder tells us the identical tale of extraordinary, bountiful growth using symbolic tools. We take in our hands the *karpas,* a vegetable, preferably green, symbolizing vitality and fertility, which grows abundantly (as the ancient Israelites did) in the ground (of Egypt); we dip the vegetable in salt water and bless God, who creates the fruit of the ground:

> *Blessed are You, EverPresent God, our God, Sovereign of the universe, who creates the fruit of the earth.*

בָּרוּךְ אַתָּה יְיָ, אֱלֹהֵינוּ מֶלֶךְ הָעוֹלָם, בּוֹרֵא פְּרִי הָאֲדָמָה.

How do we know that the vegetable is supposed to signify this prolific growth of the Jewish people? In the *Maggid* section, the fifth item of the Seder, while commenting on the phenomenal growth of the Jewish People in Egypt, the Haggadah cites the verse "I made you as numerous as the plants of the field" (Ezek. 16:7) to draw the analogy between God's abundant vegetation on the ground and the proliferation of the Jewish People in the land of Egypt (see p. 85). In *Nirtzah,* the conclusion of the Seder, when we beseech God to establish us once again as an innumerable people, we refer to ourselves as *nitei khannah,* "planted seedlings." We therefore take as the *karpas* a "plant of the field," that is, a vegetable, which grows in abundance, to represent the abundant growth of the Jewish people in Egypt.

It is interesting to note that the prevalent custom in North America is to use parsley as the vegetable for *karpas*. When one looks carefully at parsley, one notices that each stem has multiple green flowers growing (often six or seven flowers per stem). This reminds us of the rabbinic commentary that accounts for the exponential growth of the Jewish People from the paltry 70 souls who entered Egypt to the teeming 600,000 males between the ages of twenty and sixty who exited Egypt, by suggesting that the Israelite women gave birth to six children, sextuplets, at a time.

Having established that the green vegetable symbolizes the enormous fertility and growth of the Israelites in Egypt, why do we then take this symbol of fertility and dip it in salt water? Let us return to the narrative of the Book of Exodus to discern the answer:

> A new king arose over Egypt.... He said to his people: "Behold the people of the children of Israel are more numerous and stronger than we. Come let us deal cunningly with them, lest they become more numerous than us, and in the event of war they will join with our enemies and uproot us from the land" [translation according to Rashi]. So they appointed conscription officers over the Israelites to crush their spirits with harsh labor. And they built up supply cities for Pharaoh, the cities of Pithom and Ra'amses. But the more the Egyptians made the Israelites suffer, the more they grew and spread out. The Egyptians dreaded the Israelites. The Egyptians worked the Israelites oppressively [*bepharech*], and they embittered their lives with hard work in mortar and bricks and all sorts of work in the field. All the works that they had them do were oppressive [*bepharech*].
>
> Exodus 1:8–14

If we visualize the scene that the Bible is painting, we see the Israelites drenched in sweat, laboring in heavy construction and field work under the hot Egyptian sun. What is the cause of the Israelites' predicament? Their very growth and empowerment. Pharaoh's plan is to work them to the bone, drain the vitality and virility from their bodies, and thereby stem their prodigious growth. The Torah makes clear, however, that at this stage of the story at least, Pharaoh's plan boomerangs. The harder the Jews are worked, the more they grow. The mysterious life force that pulses within them grows stronger with their oppression.

Therefore, at the Seder we take a stem of parsley, the symbol of the Jewish People's growth and vitality, drench it in salt water as the Israelites were drenched in the sweat of slavery, and following the dictum "we are what we eat," ingest it, becoming, as it were, one of those virile, sweat-soaked Israelites ourselves.

The custom of dipping the vegetable in salt water is the dominant one among Ashkenazic Jews, whose ancestry hails from Germany and most of the European continent. The custom of Sephardic Jews, whose ancestry stems from Spain and North Africa, is to dip the vegetable in *charoset* (Maimonides, *The Book of Seasons*, "Laws of Leavened and Unleavened Bread," 8:2). The *charoset* resembles the brown mortar with which the Israelites worked. Those of us who saw the movie *The Ten Commandments* can still remember Moses, played by Charlton Heston, caked in mud and mortar, being brought in chains before Pharaoh in his opulent palace. For Sephardic Jews, dipping the vegetable in *charoset* rather than in salt water is the way we recall that harsh experience of slave labor.

There is another reason for the Sephardic custom of dipping the *karpas* in *charoset*. One of the elements that go into making *charoset* is red wine. Why red wine? The Haggadah's commentary in *Maggid* on the word *varav*, "as numerous," describing the prodigious growth of the Jewish People, offers us the clue:

"Varav," *as it says (Ezek. 16:7, 16:6): "I made you as numerous as the plants in the field; you grew and developed and became beautiful of figure, your breasts firm and your hair growing. And I passed over you and saw you wallowing in your blood [of childbirth] and I said to you, 'Through your blood will you live,' and I said to you, 'Through your blood will you live.'"*

According to the Jerusalem Talmud (*Pesachim* 10:3), a lesser known but significant Talmudic compilation of rabbinic law and lore from the fifth century C.E., the red color of the wine in the *charoset* is *zecher ladam,* a reminder of the blood of childbirth graphically described in Ezekiel, which enabled the Jewish people to survive and thrive despite their oppressive slavery. Thus the Sephardim conflate three images in this one ritual: the people's prolific growth, the blood of childbirth, and the mortar of slavery. It might well be that the Ashkenazic community shied away from this practice of dipping their vegetable in *charoset* and switched to salt water because of the long history of blood libels under which Ashkenazic Jews suffered in Christian Europe. Nevertheless, there is textual support for the Ashkenazic custom, because immediately prior to and after the verses from Ezekiel cited in *Maggid,* there is a reference to water and salt (Ezek. 16:4, 16:9).

In either the Ashkenazic or Sephardic custom the symbolism is the same: the symbol of growth, rootedness, and fertility (the green vegetable) is dipped in the symbol of our new oppressed state of slave labor (salt water/*charoset*). Despite being drenched in salt water/sweat or caked in *charoset*/mud, the Israelites continued to proliferate. It is almost as if the brackish salt water and the muddy, reddish *charoset* served to irrigate and fertilize the roots of the Jewish People.

The very word *karpas* has traditionally been explained as deriving from two words: *samekh, parech. Samekh,* which in Jewish numerology *(gematria)* equals sixty, is short for the number 600,000—the number of males who left Egypt. *Parech* is the word that the Torah uses, twice, to designate the extreme harshness and oppressive nature of the labor. The word *karpas* thus encapsulates the exponential growth of the Israelites (from 70 to 600,000) as well as the oppressive slavery that this growth triggered.

The *karpas* symbolizes not only the early stages of the Israelites' immigration to Egypt but almost every major migration in Jewish history. More often than not, Jews have been initially welcomed in their new places of exile, whether it was in Spain, Poland, Germany, and so on. In those hospitable Diaspora surroundings, the Jewish people took root and became powerful, numerous, and successful. Nevertheless over time, the Jewish people's very success led to discomfort and resentment among the native population. This in turn led to a process of discrimination and intensified persecution to "contain" them, sometimes resulting in the Jews being ghettoized and becoming permanent second-class citizens, sometimes resulting in inquisition and expulsion, and sometimes leading to attempted genocide.

## *Yachatz/* יַחַץ: The Kingdom of Death and the Birth of the Redeemer

The next item in the Seder is the breaking in half of the middle matzah. Why do we break the matzah in half? Let us return to the story in the Book of Exodus.

Having deduced that slave labor would not succeed in breaking the backs of the Jewish People, Pharaoh in the Bible resorts to an even more nefarious scheme:

> The king of Egypt spoke to the Hebrew midwives, whose names were Shifrah and Puah. He said to them: "When you deliver Hebrew women and you see on the birth stool that the infant is a boy, then kill him, but if it is a girl then let

her live." The midwives feared God and did not do as the Egyptian king told them—they allowed the infant boys to live. The king of Egypt summoned the midwives and said to them: "Why did you do this! Why did you allow the infant boys to live?" "The Hebrew women are not like the Egyptian women," replied the midwives to Pharaoh. "They deliver by themselves. By the time the midwives arrive, they have already given birth!" God was good to the midwives, and the people increased and became very numerous.... Pharaoh then gave orders to all his people: "Every boy who is born shall be thrown into the Nile, but every girl shall be allowed to live."

Exodus 1:15–22

At each step along the way, Pharaoh attempts to drain the life force of the Jewish People without success. Even the attempt to clandestinely smother the Israelite boys fails to stem the growth of the people; the Torah tells us that they continue to multiply. But when Pharaoh issues a public decree to all the Egyptian people that every boy is to be drowned, the Torah does not say that the Jews continue to multiply despite the decree. Apparently, Pharaoh's order of infanticide succeeds in breaking the backs and spirit of the Jewish People. To symbolize this notorious decree, which broke our people's spirit, we break the matzah in half.

Traditionally, matzah covers are made with separate sections for each of the three matzot: *Kohein* (Priests), *Levi* (Levites), and *Yisrael* (Israelites). These three sections represent the three divisions of the Israelite people who experienced the Exodus. Together, the three matzot represent the collective Jewish People at the time of the Exodus—"Corporate Israel." Breaking one of the matzot therefore symbolizes the breaking of the Jewish People.

The matzah that we break is the middle matzah, the matzah identified with the Levites. The smaller of the two broken pieces is put back between the two whole matzot; the larger of the two broken pieces, what will later be called the *afikoman,* is wrapped up in a cloth and hidden away until the latter part of the Seder. The retrieval and eating of the *afikoman* in the listing of the Seder is called *Tzafun*, which means "the hidden one."

Why do we perform this strange ritual? We must briefly return to the story in Exodus to locate the answer:

> And a man of the house of Levi went and married the daughter of Levi. The woman became pregnant and gave birth to a son. She saw how good he was and hid him [*Vatitzpeneihu*] for three months. And when she could no longer hide him [*Hatzfino*], she took for him a papyrus box and coated it with red clay and pitch and placed the child inside, placing the box among the uncut papyrus near the bank of the Nile. His sister stood at a distance to know what would happen to him.
>
> Exodus 2:1–4

What an amazing coincidence! A Levite man marries a daughter of Levi and they have a son. The son (who will later be named Moses) is wrapped in secrecy and hidden away. In fact he will remain hidden from the Jewish people for most of his life—growing up in Pharaoh's house, then fleeing to and living in the country of Midian. There he remains "out of sight" until many years later, when he is called upon by God to return and lead the Jewish People out of Egypt. At that time he reappears and redeems the people from bondage. In the interim, Moses's two siblings, Aaron and Miriam, who themselves will play important but smaller supporting roles in the later biblical story of the Exodus, remain with the rest of the Jewish People in Egypt.

The Torah, in describing the hiding of the child, twice uses variations of the root word *z-f-n* to denote the child's hiddenness. This is the only place in the Five Books of Moses that this root word is used to denote hiding (elsewhere in the Torah, the root word *ch-b-a* is used to denote hiding). Can it really be a coincidence that the Haggadah uses the same root word *z-f-n* to label the hidden matzah? Is it just serendipitous that the matzah, like Moses, is wrapped up and hidden away until it reappears much later in the Seder when it is time to leave Egypt and lead the redemption? Is it just an accident that the smaller piece of broken matzah, like Aaron and Miriam, remains sandwiched in between the other matzot, which symbolize the collective Jewish People, separated from the larger matzah with which they were originally one whole piece (family)? Clearly the hidden one, the larger one, the one who symbolizes redemption, is none other than Moses, the hero of the story of the Exodus. His siblings, Aaron and Miriam, the smaller ones in importance, remain with Jewish People to keep the people together until Moses returns. They are the glue that keeps the people together despite the absence of their sibling redeemer.

There is further congruence between the story of Moses and the ritual of hiding the wrapped matzah at the Seder. Recall that when Moses is placed on the Nile, his young sister watches intently from a distance to see what would happen to her baby brother. She then negotiates with the daughter of Pharaoh to retrieve the baby to the care of the child's biological mother who first hid him. Similarly at the Seder, the children watch intently as the parent hides the matzah in order to locate and retrieve the wrapped matzah. Like Miriam, the children then negotiate with the adults in order to return the matzah to the parent who hid the matzah in the first place. Moreover, in both the biblical story and our contemporary homes, there is an exchange of financial compensation.

But why then is Moses hidden? Not only is Moses hidden symbolically in a napkin, but he is hidden as well in the text of the Haggadah. Moses's name appears only once in the Ashkenazic version of the Haggadah. Even that one appearance is in a parenthetical proof-text on the number of plagues at the sea, which is easy to miss and where Moses is placed in a clearly subservient role to God: "And they [the Jewish people] believed in God and in Moses, God's servant." In Maimonides's authoritative Sephardic Haggadah text, even this one minor reference to Moses is omitted.

The reason for Moses's hiddenness in the Haggadah is that

the Haggadah is absolutely intent on telling the story of the Exodus from Egypt as a tale of the unmitigated love relationship between God and the Jewish People. The authors of the Haggadah did not want to hinge that relationship based on the presence—or absence—of a human leader, not even one as great as Moses. No one could come between God and His People.

In the text of the *Maggid,* the Haggadah brilliantly and clandestinely makes this point. In commenting on the words "the EverPresent God brought us out of Egypt," the Haggadah cites the Midrash (rabbinic exegesis) on Exodus 12:12, which says: "'I will pass through the land of Egypt on that night'—I and no angel [*Malach*]; 'I will slay all the first-born in the land of Egypt'—I and no fiery being [*Saraph*]; 'And upon all the Gods of Egypt I will execute judgments'—I and not the messenger [*Hashaliach*]; 'I, the EverPresent God,' it will be I and no other." The first letters of those named by the Midrash as being ones who would not take the Jewish people out of Egypt (mem-s[h]in-hei) together spell *Mosheh.* It is God and God alone whom the Haggadah wants to credit with the Exodus.

This was an especially important point to make, since the Jewish People who left Egypt confused Moses with God on at least two occasions in the Book of Exodus. In the first instance, when the people ran out of provisions in the desert thirty days after leaving Egypt, the nation accused Moses and Aaron of taking the Jewish People out of Egypt in order to starve them to death. In defending himself from the people's accusations, Moses twice parries their accusatory thrusts by telling the people to direct their complaints toward God rather than toward him and Aaron (Exod. 16:3, 16:7–8). Contrary to the people's assumption, Moses emphasizes that it was God who took them out of Egypt, not him or Aaron.

In the second instance, when Moses tarries on top of Mount Sinai receiving the Torah, the people demand of Aaron that he fashion them a "god" because "we don't know what happened to that man, Moses, who took us up out of the land of Egypt" (Exod. 32:1). The people's perception of Moses as the godlike figure who brought the people out of Egypt only forty days after they heard/saw God say to them, "I am the EverPresent God, your God, who took you out of the land of Egypt," shows how easy it was for even those who personally witnessed/experienced the Exodus in their flesh to confuse God and Moses.

Since we are imagining ourselves as those very Israelites who left Egypt, we are in danger of making the same error. Hence the Haggadah goes to great lengths to hide and intentionally diminish Moses's role in the saga of the Exodus by focusing the spotlight on God's role as the sole redeemer of the Jewish people from slavery.

Historical considerations at the time of the composition of the Haggadah may also have influenced the Haggadah's anonymous author to downplay Moses's role in the story of the Exodus. The Haggadah was put together around the time of the redaction of the Mishnah, about 200 C.E. This was only one or two generations after the disastrous defeat of Bar Kokhba in 135 C.E. The Jewish people were exiled and demoralized, believing that God had abandoned them and that without a strong Moses or Bar Kokhba-like figure, their future was hopeless. The point of the Haggadah was to restore the people's confidence in their relationship with a loving and redeeming God and diminish their dependence on the single, mythic, powerful leader. By emphasizing God's role in the story of the Exodus, the author of the Haggadah empowered the Jewish People to believe in their own redemptive potential, with or without a heroic figure of flesh and blood like Moses or Bar Kokhba.

Since Passover represents the passionate love relationship between God and God's people, we read in synagogue on the Shabbat of Passover the most passionate piece of biblical literature, the Song of Songs (some Jews have the custom of also reciting the Song of Songs in their homes after the conclusion of the Seder). In addition, on the first day of Passover we recite in our liturgy the prayer for *Tal,* the falling of the dew, which represents the *Shekhinah,* the palpable mist of the Divine Presence. On Passover,

more than any other time of the year, we can feel the loving closeness of the Divine Presence. We will return to this theme and rein-
force it at *Nirtzah,* the conclusion of the Seder. But we are getting
ahead of ourselves. For now we are left with a broken and enslaved
Israelite nation in Egyptian bondage and a human redeemer, too
young and too hidden to make an immediate difference.

## Concluding *Yachatz:* "This Is the Bread of Affliction" or Why We Eat Matzah on Passover

Since we have just broken the middle matzah, it is an appropriate
time to question why we eat matzah on Passover. Ask almost anyone and they will tell you it is because of the haste with which the
Jews left Egypt and the unleavened flour, which had no time to rise
and which the sun baked on their backs. In fact, toward the end of
the *Maggid* section, the Haggadah gives that very reason for eating
matzah:

> *This matzah—why do we eat it? Because the dough of
> our ancestors had not had a chance to ferment when the
> Sovereign of Sovereigns, the Holy One blessed be God,
> was revealed to them and redeemed them, as it is said
> (Exod. 12:39): "And they baked the dough which they
> took out of Egypt into unleavened cakes [matzot],
> because it had not fermented, for they were expelled from
> Egypt and could not delay, nor had they made any other
> provisions for themselves."*

In this understanding, matzah symbolizes what the Rabbis
later dubbed as *lechem decherutah,* "the bread of freedom," which
the famished but joyous Israelites ate when they left Egypt.

Nevertheless, at this point in the Haggadah, when we are still
in *Yachatz,* we encounter a very different understanding of the
meaning of matzah. The leader of the Seder picks up the (smaller)
broken piece of the middle matzah and says:

This is the bread of poverty that our ancestors ate in the land of Egypt. All who are hungry, let them enter and eat. All who are in need, let them enter and partake of the Passover. Now we are here, next year we will be in the Land of Israel; now we are enslaved, next year we will be free.

הָא לַחְמָא עַנְיָא דִּי אֲכָלוּ אַבְהָתָנָא בְּאַרְעָא דְמִצְרָיִם. כָּל דִּכְפִין יֵיתֵי וְיֵכוֹל, כָּל דִּצְרִיךְ יֵיתֵי וְיִפְסַח. הָשַׁתָּא הָכָא, לְשָׁנָה הַבָּאָה בְּאַרְעָא דְיִשְׂרָאֵל. הָשַׁתָּא עַבְדֵי, לְשָׁנָה הַבָּאָה בְּנֵי חוֹרִין.

Not the bread of freedom, but the bread of poverty! Not the bread eaten when our ancestors left Egypt, but the bread eaten by our ancestors while they were still in Egypt!

Well, which bread was it? Do we eat matzah because of the freedom we achieved as we exited Egypt, or do we eat matzah because of the poverty we endured as we were enslaved in Egypt? The answer, of course, is both—but not at the same time. At this point in the symbolic telling of our story, when Pharaoh has brutally enslaved us and has broken our backs and our spirits with the decree of infanticide, this broken piece of matzah symbolizes our poverty and affliction in the land of Egypt. But by the time we get to the portion of *Maggid* where we offer the "freedom" explanation of matzah, we will have reached the point in the story when the Jews are being freed. At that point in the narrative, the same physical substance, the same bread that now symbolizes pain and poverty, will symbolize freedom and the speed of redemption.

As the passage of *Ha Lakhma Anya* ("This is the bread of affliction/poverty") states, although our bread is poor, and we have only a broken piece of it in our hands, the beginning of our redemption is our willingness to share the little we do have with our sisters and brothers in need ("All who are hungry, let them enter and eat. All who are in need, let them enter and partake of the Passover"). Our attitude is the very opposite of the Egyptians—not greed, but sharing; not controlling others, but nurturing them. The Egyptians, through their actions of enslaving human beings, through their denial of our ancestors' "image of God," served the idol of their own insatiable greed and insecurity. We, through our actions of nurturing other less fortunate images of God, engage in true spiritual service and trust in God. Finally, despite our suffering and travail, we maintain hope: hope of reaching the destination of our dreams—the Promised Land—and hope of achieving the dignity of being a free people. "Now we are here, next year we will be in the Land of Israel; now we are enslaved, next year we will be free."

# The Narrative of Redemption

## Introduction to *Maggid*

### The Verbal Telling within the Seder

As noted in chapter 2, the Rabbis in the Haggadah chose to "tell" the story of the Exodus using all three primary senses: visually, through the Seder plate; kinesthetically, through the ritual actions of the Seder; and verbally, through the section of *Maggid*.

Till now the Haggadah had told the beginning of the story in two different symbolic ways: visually, through the presence of the *karpas, charoset, maror,* and *chazeret* on the Seder plate; and kinesthetically, through the ritual actions of *Kadesh, U-Rechatz, Karpas,* and *Yachatz* in the Seder. The section of *Maggid,* which commences with the Four Questions, begins the creative, verbal retelling of the Exodus story.

Why did the Rabbis interpolate *Maggid,* the verbal telling, immediately following *Yachatz* and preceding *Rochtzah* in the kinesthetic telling? Because in the Seder, *Maggid* marks the pivot point in the journey from slavery to freedom. *Maggid* contains the two redemptive elements of the Exodus story that are not found in the other fourteen elements of the Seder: God's remembering the covenantal promise to our founding father Abraham to redeem his descendants from slavery (this will provide one important explanation for why we were redeemed); and God's fulfillment of that promise through the miracles of the ten plagues (which will explain how we were redeemed). In the Book of Exodus, these two elements take up several chapters. The Exodus story could not be coherently "retold" in the Haggadah without an elaborate and creative verbal retelling of these two redemptive elements of the Exodus saga. In keeping with the Seder's chronological retelling of the Exodus story, the Rabbis placed the covenantal promise of redemption (Exod. 2:23–25) and the story of the ten plagues (Exod. 7–12) at the exact point in the Seder in which they chronologically appear in the Book of Exodus: after the decree of infanticide and the hiding of Moses (*Yachatz,* corresponding to Exod. 1:22–2:22) and before the commencement of the final meal in Egypt (*Rochtzah,* corresponding to Exod. 12). To further underline the importance of each of these two transformative moments in the Exodus story, the Rabbis, in *Maggid,* associated a kinesthetic action with their verbal retelling: raising our cup as a toast to God for recalling the covenantal promise, and dipping our finger ten times in our cup of wine for bringing the ten plagues upon the Egyptians. By verbally telling the story and performing these accompanying kinesthetic actions at this precise moment of the Seder, we reexperience the power of God's recalling the covenantal promise and miraculously bringing the plagues as it was originally experienced by the Israelites in the Book of Exodus.

## The Seder within the Telling

In the Bible, there are only three positive commandments regarding the celebration of Passover. The first, which we have already discussed, is the command to eat matzah. The second, the bringing of the Passover sacrifice, is not possible without the Temple in Jerusalem. The third positive command in the Torah is telling the story of the Exodus to the next generation.

The Torah instructs us to tell the story of the Exodus to future generations immediately following the Jewish People's exit from Egypt:

> "And you should tell your child on that day, saying: 'Because of this [*or:* This is because of what], the EverPresent God did for me when I left Egypt.'"
>
> Exodus 13:8

וְהִגַּדְתָּ לְבִנְךָ בַּיּוֹם הַהוּא לֵאמֹר· בַּעֲבוּר זֶה עָשָׂה יְיָ לִי, בְּצֵאתִי מִמִּצְרָיִם.

This verse, and especially the first word, *vehigadeta,* "and you should tell," is the basis for the entire book known as the Haggadah, "the telling." This verse also determines the structure of the section of the Haggadah called *Maggid,* "telling." Just as we were able to decipher the meaning of the first four items of the Seder by following the order of the verses in the first two chapters of Exodus, so too will we be able to decipher the meaning of the otherwise confusing section of *Maggid* by following the precise order of the words in this verse.[1]

Because this section seems complex and convoluted, it is usually the point in the Seder when the natives get restless and want to know when we are going to eat already. Apparently, in Temple times, this is exactly what they did—at this point in the Seder they ate the meal and then proceeded to *Maggid* rather than the other way around.[2] However, the Rabbis here, as elsewhere, employed a consistent principle of putting the spiritual act (of telling) before the physical act of eating. For instance, on Chanukah, the Rabbis insisted that the Chanukah candles be lit before one could eat dinner; similarly, on Purim, the Rabbis ordered that the Scroll of Esther be read before one could break the fast of Esther and eat the evening meal; daily, the Rabbis legislated that one should offer morning prayers every day of the year prior to eating breakfast. The Rabbis insisted on the primacy of the spiritual in order to ensure that the spiritual not be neglected once the physical cravings of the participants were satiated. Here too, the Rabbis changed the order of Passover night from what it was in Temple times so that the Seder participants would first fulfill the spiritual duty of telling the Passover story before reenacting the momentous final meal in Egypt.

## The Significance of "Order" in *Maggid*

Not only does the entire section of *Maggid* follow the order of the verse in Exodus 13:8, but the four questions that introduce *Maggid* also have an order. Later on we will see that the central subsection of *Maggid,* which we will label *Leimor: Ba'avur Zeh,* "saying, because of this," also has an implicit order. Why all this "order"? The author of the Haggadah uses the principle of order to convey a deeper spiritual message: amidst the seeming meaninglessness of hundreds of years of slavery and misery, there is a deeper divine order and meaning in history. Reality, despite often seeming cruelly absurd, haphazard, and arbitrary, actually has a deeper logic to it if we step back from the particular event that we are presently experiencing and reframe that event within a larger scope of time. By presenting us with *Maggid,* a text that seems on the surface to be disorganized but upon reflection turns out to be highly organized, the Haggadah's author has created a brilliant metaphor for the Jewish People's historical experience. The author is telling us that history, like the Haggadah, often seems to be meaningless and without purpose but is actually purposeful and meaningful. Our people's overall existence and continued survival are not a historical accident but a reflection of structured, divine intention.

## From Shame to Praise: The Theme of *Maggid*

Aside from the several ordering devices found in *Maggid,* there is also a recurring, organizing theme to this section. *Mishnah Pesachim* 10:4 tells us that the telling "begins in shame and concludes with praise." This motif of starting negatively but ending positively is interlaced throughout the *Maggid* section. It repeats itself, much as a musical fugue does, in successive entering voices that are arranged in the same, identifiable pattern to form a single harmonious whole.

This recurring theme of "shame to praise" is also apparently not a simple literary device but a euphemism for the Jewish—and perhaps the human—condition. In some mysterious and disturbing way, suffering appears as the precursor to redemption. Whether suffering acts as an educational corrective to alter behavior, as a form of karmic expiation for sins in this or past lives, or as the grounds for future rewards is not clear or agreed upon in Jewish tradition.[3]

Nevertheless, that Jewish suffering seems to precede Jewish redemption seems to be a given, not only in the text of *Maggid,* but in the historical experience of the Jewish people that *Maggid* is attempting to mirror. In fact, in the historical experience of the Jewish People, what characterizes a story as a Jewish story—and the Haggadah is the prototypical Jewish story—is precisely this motif of "beginning in shame and concluding with praise."

## The *Midrashic* Method of *Maggid*

Aside from the use of order and the recurring theme of "shame to praise," the Rabbis employ a distinctive methodology in *Maggid* called midrash, creative interpretation through commentary on the biblical text. The Rabbis reasoned that the Torah does not instruct us to simply read the story from the text as it does elsewhere on other occasions (e.g., Deut. 31:11). Rather, it instructs us to tell the story. The Rabbis understood from this that every generation has the obligation to creatively retell the story of the Exodus in such a way that it would be compelling to the next generation.

Moses himself modeled the midrashic method by creatively retelling the story of the Exodus in the Book of Deuteronomy to the next generation of Israelites who were about to enter the Promised Land. That generation had not personally experienced the Exodus as adults as had their parents. Moses retold the story to them as they were poised to conquer the Promised Land in such a way as to reassure and motivate them in their spiritual and military quest. Moses's retelling is used in *Maggid* to commence the response to the Four Questions: "We were slaves to Pharaoh in Egypt and the EverPresent God took us out with mighty force" (Deut. 6:21).

Moses went even further in Deuteronomy by providing a synopsis of the Exodus story for all future generations to retell each year when they brought their first fruits to the Temple (Deut. 26:5–10). This synopsis, which begins with the words "My father was a fugitive from Aram," forms the basis of rabbinic Midrash/commentary on the *Leimor* subsection of *Maggid,* as per the instructions in *Mishnah Pesachim* 10:4: *Vedoreish,* "one should do a creative exegesis."

Moses's disciple and successor, Joshua, whom the Torah tells us "was filled with the spirit that Moses instilled in him" (Deut. 34:9), followed his master's example by creatively retelling the Jewish People's story to the third generation of Israelites in yet a third version of the original Exodus story (Josh. 24:2ff). Joshua's retelling serves as the preamble to the entire *Leimor* subsection of *Maggid.*

All three of these retellings are included in the *Maggid* section. In fact, the entire *Maggid* section is a creative rabbinic exegesis, a midrash, on Exodus 13:8.

## Exodus 13:8—The Roadmap of *Maggid*

Before we begin to read the many layers of the rabbinic Midrash on this verse, let us examine the roadmap, the verse itself. By understanding the organizing principle of this verse and its midrash, we can make *Maggid* more accessible and meaningful.

וְהִגַּדְתָּ/*Vehigadeta.* "And you should tell": Every telling assumes a question. If we don't have a question that the telling answers, then the telling seems senseless and will not be retained in memory. Therefore the *Maggid* section will begin with the Four Questions. These questions will serve as a preamble to the telling that follows.

The first three paragraphs of the "telling" that will follow the Four Questions (We were slaves ... A tale is told ... Rabbi Elazar ben Azaryah said …) provide answers to both the spoken questions and the unspoken issues surrounding those questions. This section will inform us what to tell, why we tell it, who is supposed to do the telling, and how long we are supposed to tell.

לְבִנְךָ/**Levinkha.** "To your children": This word corresponds to the section of *Maggid* that begins with the words "Regarding four children" (wise, wicked, simple, unable to ask). This section will tell us to whom we tell the story and how to tailor the telling to fit the audience.

בַּיּוֹם הַהוּא/**Bayom Hahu.** "On that day": This phrase of the verse corresponds to the paragraph immediately following the four children, beginning with the words *Yakhol merosh Chodesh,* "Possibly from the first of the month." It will tell us which day and when in the day we tell.

לֵאמֹר: בַּעֲבוּר זֶה/**Leimor: ba'avur zeh.** "Saying: because of this": The purpose of this subsection will be to deepen our understanding of the saga of the Exodus by implicitly answering four of its own questions in the following order:

1. Why were we enslaved?
2. How were we enslaved?
3. Why were we redeemed?
4. How were we redeemed?

The author of the Haggadah will provide three alternative answers to these questions: the response of Rav, the response of the anonymous author of the Mishnah, and the response of Rabban Gamliel.

עָשָׂה יְיָ לִי/**Asah HaShem li.** "The EverPresent God did for me": These words correspond to the paragraphs immediately following Rabbi Gamliel's statement, which begins, "In every generation, each person must regard themselves as though he or she personally left Egypt," and continues with the paragraph

"Therefore we are obligated to praise...." This section will explain how it is possible for every Jew in history to say to their children in the first person that God redeemed him or her personally from Egypt. It will also explain why each Jew in every generation feels an obligation to offer praise to God for the Exodus.

בְּצֵאתִי מִמִּצְרָיִם/*Betzeiti miMitzrayim.* "When I left Egypt": These words correspond to the last paragraph of *Maggid,* which begins, "When the Israelites left Egypt." This section will verbally presage the spontaneous outburst of song and praise at the sea that we will experience in the *Hallel* section of the Seder.

Let us now go through the *Maggid* section piece by piece to explicate more fully how the Rabbis shaped the verbal story of the Exodus to correspond to the exact order of the biblical verse on which the entire Haggadah is based.

# *Maggid/*מַגִּיד

## *Vehigadeta*—"And You Should Tell"

> "And you should tell your child on that day, saying: 'Because of this [or: This is because of what], the EverPresent God did for me when I left Egypt." (Exod. 13:8)

וְהִגַּדְתָּ לְבִנְךָ בַּיּוֹם הַהוּא לֵאמֹר: בַּעֲבוּר זֶה עָשָׂה

יְיָ לִי, בְּצֵאתִי מִמִּצְרָיִם.

The Four Questions—there is not only a *seder* to the Seder, and a *seder* to *Maggid,* there is also a *seder* to the Four Questions. The central theme of the Four Questions is "Who are we?" Not coincidentally this is the same question with which we began the Seder. In *Kadesh,* we answered (with the imaginative help of the first cup of wine) that we are the ancient Israelites who experienced the Exodus from Egypt. But now we ask this question again verbally and in a more sophisticated and detailed manner:

*Why is this night different from all other nights?*

1. *On all other nights we eat chametz and matzah. Tonight, why do we eat only matzah?*
2. *On all other nights we eat any kind of herbs. Tonight, why do we eat the bitter herbs?*
3. *On all other nights we do not dip even once. Tonight, why do we dip twice?*
4. *On all other nights we eat sitting or reclining. Tonight, why do we all recline?*

מַה נִּשְׁתַּנָּה הַלַּיְלָה הַזֶּה מִכָּל הַלֵּילוֹת?

שֶׁבְּכָל הַלֵּילוֹת אָנוּ אוֹכְלִין חָמֵץ וּמַצָּה, הַלַּיְלָה הַזֶּה כֻּלּוֹ מַצָּה.

שֶׁבְּכָל הַלֵּילוֹת אָנוּ אוֹכְלִין שְׁאָר יְרָקוֹת, הַלַּיְלָה הַזֶּה מָרוֹר.

שֶׁבְּכָל הַלֵּילוֹת אֵין אָנוּ מַטְבִּילִין אֲפִילוּ פַּעַם אֶחָת, הַלַּיְלָה הַזֶּה שְׁתֵּי פְעָמִים.

שֶׁבְּכָל הַלֵּילוֹת אָנוּ אוֹכְלִין בֵּין יוֹשְׁבִין וּבֵין מְסֻבִּין, הַלַּיְלָה הַזֶּה כֻּלָּנוּ מְסֻבִּין.

Each of these four questions exposes some aspect of the underlying question "Who are we?":

Question 1: Are we poor people? We are eating poor man's bread exclusively during Passover. This is tangible evidence that we are impoverished.

Question 2: Are we subjugated slaves? The *maror* is reflective of the bitter psychological experience of feeling enslaved.

Question 3: Are we rich people? We are serving our food with dips—the poor cannot afford to serve hors d'oeuvres! This seems to provide tangible evidence of our affluence.

Question 4: Are we free noblemen? We are lounging about as if we don't have a care in the world. Unlike a slave who stands at the master's attention, we seem totally relaxed and psychologically at ease, as befits nobility.

The Four Questions are therefore really one question: Who are we? Are we impoverished slaves or wealthy nobility? From the innocent perspective of the questioner, the Seder, like our identities, seems to be something of a mishmash, the very opposite of an ordered event and of an integrated personality.

The question of identity is a crucial one, not only because we want to know who we are, but because the Jews of the Exodus also had to learn who they were. They were as puzzled about their identity as we are today. When they came down to Egypt, their identities were clear: they were the children of Israel, the family of Jacob, each one with their distinct name and household, "Reuven, Shimon, Levi, Judah ..." (Exod. 1:2). After the enslavement deepened and the decree of infanticide had been enacted, the people lost their identities—they lost their names. Moses's parents are not identified by name in chapter 2 of Exodus. Rather they are described as an anonymous man from the house of Levi who married a daughter of Levi. Moses's sister and Egyptian foster mother are not mentioned by name; neither, for that matter, is the Israelite whom Moses saves from the hands of the Egyptian overseer or the Israelites who are bickering with one another. Only Moses, who grows up in freedom and affluence, is given a name, and that name is bestowed upon him not by his enslaved Israelite parents, but by Pharaoh's daughter. The struggle of the entire slave generation that left Egypt was not merely to regain their political freedom but to regain their names—to reembody their own distinct identity and discover their national mission. Their challenge was to journey from being nameless, faceless "beasts of burden" in Egypt to being God's proud, holy, treasured people in their own country—the Land of Israel.

The Haggadah provides a clear answer as to who *we* are and, by extension (since we assume the identity of the ancient Israelites on Passover night), who the *Israelites* were:

*We were slaves to Pharaoh in Egypt, but the EverPresent God, our God, brought us out of there with a strong hand and an outstretched arm.*

עֲבָדִים הָיִינוּ לְפַרְעֹה בְּמִצְרָיִם. וַיּוֹצִיאֵנוּ יְיָ אֱלֹהֵינוּ מִשָּׁם, בְּיָד חֲזָקָה וּבִזְרוֹעַ נְטוּיָה.

We eat poor person's bread and bitter herbs because we were impoverished slaves; but we serve hors d'oeuvres and eat in a reclining position because God transformed us into free people with economic means. So on this night we are both poor slaves and affluent nobility—but not at the same time. Just as the matzot have two meanings—one at the beginning of the Seder (i.e., bread of poverty/suffering) and a very different one toward the end (i.e., bread of freedom and liberation), so too do we act in apparently opposite ways depending upon what period of our history we are reliving. First, we reexperience our story of being slaves (we begin with shame); then, and only then, do we undergo a metamorphosis and achieve freedom (we conclude with praise).

Having explained who we are, the Haggadah proceeds to answer the introductory question lying underneath the Four Questions: Why are we performing all of these strange rituals—or to use the Haggadah's language—why is this night different from all other nights? The reason we engage in these rituals is because were our ancestors not redeemed, we and all generations of Jews who assume the identity of our ancient Israelite forebears on this night would also not be redeemed.

*And if the Holy One, blessed be God, had not taken our ancestors out of Egypt, then we, our children, and our grandchildren would still be enslaved to Pharaoh in Egypt.*

וְאִלּוּ לֹא הוֹצִיא הַקָּדוֹשׁ בָּרוּךְ הוּא אֶת־אֲבוֹתֵינוּ
מִמִּצְרַיִם, הֲרֵי אָנוּ וּבָנֵינוּ וּבְנֵי בָנֵינוּ, מְשֻׁעְבָּדִים
הָיִינוּ לְפַרְעֹה בְּמִצְרַיִם.

Our story, and therefore our identities, would not be one of slavery to redemption, but one of perpetual, never-ending slavery. The only tale we would be able to tell our children would be one of unrelenting woe. Ours would be a sad lot indeed.

So far we have explained what we are supposed to tell and why we tell it. What remain to be defined is who is supposed to do the telling and for how long they are supposed to tell:

> And even if all of us were scholars, sages, elders learned in the Torah, it would still be a mitzvah to explain the story of the Exodus from Egypt, and whoever elaborates upon the story of the Exodus from Egypt is praised.

וַאֲפִילוּ כֻּלָּנוּ חֲכָמִים, כֻּלָּנוּ נְבוֹנִים, כֻּלָּנוּ זְקֵנִים,
כֻּלָּנוּ יוֹדְעִים אֶת־הַתּוֹרָה, מִצְוָה עָלֵינוּ לְסַפֵּר
בִּיצִיאַת מִצְרַיִם. וְכָל הַמַּרְבֶּה לְסַפֵּר בִּיצִיאַת
מִצְרַיִם, הֲרֵי זֶה מְשֻׁבָּח.

We stated at the outset that the recurring theme throughout *Maggid* is "beginning in shame and concluding with praise." In this very first paragraph, the author of the Haggadah uses that formula. The paragraph began in shame: "We were slaves to Pharaoh in Egypt," a statement of our disgraceful status. The paragraph now concludes with the words "whoever elaborates upon the story of the Exodus from Egypt is praised [*meshubach*]." The paragraph literally concludes with the word for "praise." This pattern of beginning in shame and ending in praise will recur, again and again, throughout the section called *Maggid*.

Everyone, no matter how much knowledge and understanding we possess, is to tell the story. How much are we to tell? The two paragraphs that follow in the Haggadah teach us that the more one tells the better. Why? Because in retelling the story we immerse ourselves in reliving and reexperiencing it. We lose our current selves in the story and become the characters of the story—we actually become our ancient Israelite forebears who journey from slavery to redemption. We lose track of time and enter what a modern psychologist, Mihaly Cziksentmihaly, calls the state of "flow," "The Zone."

*It happened that Rabbis Eliezer, Joshua, Elazar ben Azaryah, Akiva, and Tarfon were reclining at the Seder table in Bnei Brak. They spent the whole night discussing the Exodus until their students came and said to them: "Rabbis, it is time for the recitation of the* Shema."

*Rabbi Elazar ben Azaryah said: "I am like a seventy-year-old man and I have not succeeded in understanding why the Exodus from Egypt should be mentioned at night, until Ben Zoma explained it by quoting: 'In order that you may remember the day you left Egypt all the days of your life.' The Torah adds the word 'all' to the phrase 'the days of your life' to indicate that the nights are meant as well. The sages declare that 'the days of your life' means the present world and 'all' includes the messianic era."*

מַעֲשֶׂה בְּרַבִּי אֱלִיעֶזֶר, וְרַבִּי יְהוֹשֻׁעַ, וְרַבִּי אֶלְעָזָר
בֶּן־עֲזַרְיָה, וְרַבִּי עֲקִיבָא, וְרַבִּי טַרְפוֹן, שֶׁהָיוּ מְסֻבִּין
בִּבְנֵי־בְרַק, וְהָיוּ מְסַפְּרִים בִּיצִיאַת מִצְרַיִם כָּל־אוֹתוֹ

הַלַּיְלָה, עַד שֶׁבָּאוּ תַלְמִידֵיהֶם וְאָמְרוּ לָהֶם:
רַבּוֹתֵינוּ, הִגִּיעַ זְמַן קְרִיאַת שְׁמַע שֶׁל שַׁחֲרִית.

אָמַר רַבִּי אֶלְעָזָר בֶּן־עֲזַרְיָה: הֲרֵי אֲנִי כְּבֶן שִׁבְעִים
שָׁנָה, וְלֹא זָכִיתִי שֶׁתֵּאָמֵר יְצִיאַת מִצְרַיִם בַּלֵּילוֹת,
עַד שֶׁדְּרָשָׁהּ בֶּן זוֹמָא, שֶׁנֶּאֱמַר: לְמַעַן תִּזְכֹּר אֶת
יוֹם צֵאתְךָ מֵאֶרֶץ מִצְרַיִם, כֹּל יְמֵי חַיֶּיךָ. יְמֵי
חַיֶּיךָ, הַיָּמִים. כֹּל יְמֵי חַיֶּיךָ, הַלֵּילוֹת. וַחֲכָמִים
אוֹמְרִים: יְמֵי חַיֶּיךָ, הָעוֹלָם הַזֶּה. כֹּל יְמֵי חַיֶּיךָ,
לְהָבִיא לִימוֹת הַמָּשִׁיחַ.

As the experience of Rabbi Elazar ben Azaryah indicates, by retelling the story of the Exodus we gain deeper insight and understanding as to what the Exodus is about and how pervasive it ought to be all year long in our Jewish memory and self-understanding.

## *Levinkha*—"To Your Child": The Four Children

> *"And you should tell your child on that day, saying:*
> *'Because of this [or: This is because of what], the EverPresent*
> *God did for me when I left Egypt.'"* *(Exod. 13:8)*

וְהִגַּדְתָּ לְבִנְךָ בַּיּוֹם הַהוּא לֵאמֹר: בַּעֲבוּר זֶה עָשָׂה
יְיָ לִי, בְּצֵאתִי מִמִּצְרָיִם.

To whom are we supposed to tell the tale of the Exodus? From the episode of the five Rabbis we know that it is told to whomever shares the Passover meal. Nevertheless, the primary mitzvah, the essential directive, is to tell the tale to the next generation. The reason is simple: redemption in Judaism is a multigeneration, covenantal process. Even the generation of Jews who were redeemed from Egypt did not fully experience the redemption that they were promised. They perished in the desert instead of marching triumphantly into the Promised Land. Their children were the ones who were privileged to enter and inherit the land dripping with milk and honey. Furthermore, even after entering the land, it took many more generations of children and hundreds of years to consolidate power, establish the capital in Jerusalem, and witness God's Presence descend into the Temple.

Since redemption is not something that happens in one generation and then is over and done with, the story of redemption and the ideal of future redemption must be shared with each succeeding generation. Every generation plays an important role in the redemptive process. If we want to frame reality as a story of redemption and wish to remain intellectually honest, then we must bring the next generation into the story, and they in turn must bring the following generation, etc.

There is a further matter that is highlighted by the presence and participation of the children: the crucial role of family and community in the story of the Exodus. When the Jewish People descended to Egypt, they arrived with their families intact: "These are the names of the children of Israel who came to Egypt, each man and his family came" (Exod. 1:1). But after their enslavement, families are rarely mentioned again until the cusp of their liberation (Exod. 12). Why? Because slavery undermined the institution of the family. In slave families, it was the master who had conjugal rights to the slave's wife and authority over the slave's children. Being a husband or a wife and being a father or mother were and are privileges, rights that Egyptian slaves did not possess.

The midrash in *Shemot Rabbah* 28, a rabbinic commentary on the Book of Exodus, uses this very understanding of the precarious state of the Jewish family in Egypt to explain Moses's actions in slaying the Egyptian overseer who was beating a Jewish slave:

And it came to pass in those days, when Moses was grown, that he went out to his brothers, and looked on their burdens; and he saw an Egyptian beating a Hebrew, one of his brothers. And he looked this way and that way, and when he saw that there was no man, he slew the Egyptian and hid him in the sand.

Exodus 2:11–12

According to the midrash, the Egyptian overseer had assigned the Jewish slave the night shift at work to enable the overseer to bed the slave's wife while he was gone. When the Jewish slave found out what had occurred in his absence and apparently made his feelings known, the Egyptian overseer began to beat the slave with lethal force. Moses, incensed by the patent injustice of the situation, and seeing that there was no one else to stand up for the Jewish slave, intervened and used commensurate force to slay the Egyptian. The sanctity of the marital relationship was clearly not one that the Egyptians respected.

Nor were women slaves the only ones treated, or rather mistreated, as chattel in Egypt. Male slaves too were considered fair game for their Egyptian masters and mistresses. Recall the story of Joseph, whose mistress tried to seduce him and then, when Joseph refused her insistent invitations, ended up being thrown into the dungeons of Egypt (Gen. 39:7–20). Such was the world of slavery in Egypt: a society in which nothing was sacred—not one's spouse, not one's marital vows, and not one's life.[4]

As the Jewish People began the process of being liberated from Egypt through the Passover lamb sacrifice, the family unit was reconstituted in the biblical text and in the Seder meal, which reenacts that liberation. The Jewish family, no less than the individual Jew, regained its dignity and was redeemed by the Exodus from Egypt. Hence the importance of including the family in the central mitzvah or commandment of "telling" the Exodus story. Communicating the story of redemption in a family setting to the next generation is in itself an act of redemption. The medium is the message.

*Blessed be the Omnipresent; blessed be God. Blessed be
God, who has given the Torah to God's people Israel;
blessed be God. The Torah speaks of four children: a wise
one, a wicked one, a simple one, and one who is not able
to ask a question.*

בָּרוּךְ הַמָּקוֹם. בָּרוּךְ הוּא. בָּרוּךְ שֶׁנָּתַן תּוֹרָה לְעַמּוֹ
יִשְׂרָאֵל. בָּרוּךְ הוּא. כְּנֶגֶד אַרְבָּעָה בָנִים דִּבְּרָה
תוֹרָה. אֶחָד חָכָם, וְאֶחָד רָשָׁע, וְאֶחָד תָּם, וְאֶחָד
שֶׁאֵינוֹ יוֹדֵעַ לִשְׁאוֹל.

How do we tell the story of redemption in the most effective
way? Not with a single script. Within the biblical text itself, the text
poses hypothetical children asking various sorts of questions about
the Exodus and its observance. Likewise, the Torah provides different answers or teachings for the parents to tell their children.
Following the Bible's lead, *Mishnah Pesachim* 10:4 tells us: "The parent teaches according to the knowledge level of the child."
Different children of whatever age have different attitudes, varying
levels of knowledge, and multiple learning styles, which have to be
taken into account in the process of communication. We already
saw how the Rabbis told the story visually, kinesthetically, and verbally to accommodate the different learning styles of the Seder's
participants. Now within the verbal telling the Rabbis teach us how
to shape our message depending on the fundamental attitudes
and knowledge levels of our listeners.

But it is not only to "children" that this section of *Maggid* speaks.
The diversity of the children in the Haggadah reflects the diversity
that we experience among our various friends and members of our
extended families and communities in the twenty-first century. I, like
most of you who will be reading these pages, have had people sit at
my Passover Seders who were full of enthusiastic, detailed questions

about the proceedings and their deeper meanings; people who have come with open contempt for the Jewish tradition and barely veiled hostility to the evening's ritual; newcomers to Judaism and people outside the Jewish faith who have asked simple, straightforward questions, just trying to orient themselves to what was happening; and some, often the most thoughtful among the participants, who have quietly, albeit intensively, observed the evening's events without initiating questions of their own accord. The diversity of attitudes toward the Passover Seder seems to act as a kind of Rorschach test reflecting the multiplicity of attitudes toward organized religion generally, and toward Judaism in particular.

The Haggadah models a process of inclusion for all those present regardless of the knowledge and attitudes that they bring to the table. Everyone is encouraged to be part of the conversation whether they agree or disagree with the written text; whether they are articulate or inarticulate in expressing their thoughts and feelings; whether they appear to be sophisticated or simplistic in their approach to the Seder, Jewish tradition, or their Jewish identities. The Passover Seder represents the opportunity for the "whole house of Israel" (see Exod. 40:38) to share the experience of retelling and re-imagining our sacred past, our existential present, and our redemptive future.

> *The wise child asks: "What is the meaning of the testimonies, statutes, and laws that the EverPresent God, our God, has commanded us?" Explain to this child the traditions of the Pesach until "no dessert may be eaten after the Passover sacrifice."*

חָכָם מַה הוּא אוֹמֵר? מָה הָעֵדֹת וְהַחֻקִּים
וְהַמִּשְׁפָּטִים אֲשֶׁר צִוָּה יְיָ אֱלֹהֵינוּ אֶתְכֶם? וְאַף
אַתָּה אֱמָר־לוֹ כְּהִלְכוֹת הַפֶּסַח: אֵין מַפְטִירִין אַחַר
הַפֶּסַח אֲפִיקוֹמָן.

Two factors make the wise child "wise":

Attitude—The child is loyal to the child's people and tradition. The loyalty is implicit in the child's question.

Knowledge—The child has already assimilated the basic story of the Exodus. This child is now interested in the detailed, action implications of that story. We respond accordingly.

> The wicked child asks: "What does this service mean to you?" By the words "to you" this child implies that this service is only for you—not for him- or herself. By excluding him- or herself from the community, the child denies the essential principle of Judaism. So tell this child bluntly: "This is done on account of what the EverPresent God did for me when I came out of Egypt." For me, not for him or her; had this child been there, he or she would not have been redeemed.

רָשָׁע מַה הוּא אוֹמֵר? מָה הָעֲבֹדָה הַזֹּאת לָכֶם?
לָכֶם וְלֹא לוֹ. וּלְפִי שֶׁהוֹצִיא אֶת־עַצְמוֹ מִן הַכְּלָל,
כָּפַר בְּעִקָּר. וְאַף אַתָּה הַקְהֵה אֶת־שִׁנָּיו, וֶאֱמָר־לוֹ:
בַּעֲבוּר זֶה עָשָׂה יְיָ לִי, בְּצֵאתִי מִמִּצְרָיִם. לִי
וְלֹא־לוֹ. אִלּוּ הָיָה שָׁם, לֹא הָיָה נִגְאָל.

What makes the wicked child wicked is also twofold:

- The child's rebellious attitude to the Jewish People—Unlike many translations that assume that the wicked child denies God's providence, the real challenge is that this child views him- or herself outside of the Jewish community.

- The child is being scornful of the actions being used to reexperience the Exodus story. The child not only views him- or herself outside the current Jewish community, but also outside the historical Jewish community. This child lives as an outsider. Nevertheless, by challenging the previous generation, he or she has also engaged that generation. This defiance presents us with an opportunity, albeit an emotionally charged one, to challenge the child's point of view. We respond in kind: an emotionally charged answer that points out the painful consequences of removing him- or herself from the community.

> *The simple child asks: "What is this all about?" Tell the child, "With a strong hand the EverPresent God brought us out of Egypt from the house of slavery."*

תָּם מַה הוּא אוֹמֵר? מַה זֹּאת? וְאָמַרְתָּ אֵלָיו: בְּחֹזֶק
יָד הוֹצִיאָנוּ יְיָ מִמִּצְרַיִם מִבֵּית עֲבָדִים.

This simple child is innocent and curious, both in attitude and knowledge. We do not overwhelm this child with facts. In response to the simple question, "What is this?" we tell a clear, simple story.

> *As for the child who is unable to ask a question, you must open up the subject to this child, as it is written: "You shall tell your child on that day: 'This is on account of what the EverPresent God did for me when I came out of Egypt.'"*

וְשֶׁאֵינוֹ יוֹדֵעַ לִשְׁאוֹל, אַתְּ פְּתַח לוֹ. שֶׁנֶּאֱמַר: וְהִגַּדְתָּ
לְבִנְךָ בַּיוֹם הַהוּא לֵאמֹר: בַּעֲבוּר זֶה עָשָׂה יְיָ לִי,
בְּצֵאתִי מִמִּצְרָיִם.

The child "who does not know how to ask" lacks the knowledge and perhaps even the curiosity to formulate a question. So we provide the knowledge to prompt the child to begin to think and question. It is not coincidental that it is the youngest child who is usually asked to recite the Four Questions. Since the child cannot yet formulate his/her own questions, we script the questions for him/her. Interestingly the proof-text for responding to this child is Exodus 13:8, the very verse that provides the *seder* for the entire section of *Maggid*. Lest we think that this so-called inarticulate child is merely an afterthought, the Haggadah seems to be telling us that it was this very child that the Torah had in mind when it instructed us to tell the story of the Exodus to the next generation.

### *Bayom Hahu*—"On That Day": *Yakhol Merosh Chodesh*—"Possibly from the First of the Month"

> *"And you should tell your child on that day, saying: 'Because of this [or: This is because of what], the EverPresent God did for me when I left Egypt.' " (Exod. 13:8)*

וְהִגַּדְתָּ לְבִנְךָ בַּיּוֹם הַהוּא לֵאמֹר: בַּעֲבוּר זֶה עָשָׂה

יְיָ לִי, בְּצֵאתִי מִמִּצְרָיִם.

The paragraph that follows tells us what day in the month (the fifteenth day of Nisan) and when in the day (at nightfall) we are obligated to tell this story, as well as what conditions must be present for this telling to be effective (the visual props of matzah and *maror* must be present; see my commentary on Rabban Gamliel, pp. 109–113, for why this is so).

> One might think that the Haggadah should be recited on
> the first day of the month of Nisan, but the Torah says:
> "You shall tell your child on that day" [the first day of
> Passover]. One might think that the phrase "on that day"
> means that the story of the Exodus should be recited in the
> daytime; therefore, the Torah says: "This is on account of
> what the EverPresent God did for me" (Exod. 13:8). The
> word "this" refers to the time when this matzah and this
> maror are placed before you—on Passover night when
> you are obliged to eat them.

יָכוֹל מֵרֹאשׁ חֹדֶשׁ, תַּלְמוּד לוֹמַר בַּיּוֹם הַהוּא. אִי
בַּיּוֹם הַהוּא יָכוֹל מִבְּעוֹד יוֹם, תַּלְמוּד לוֹמַר בַּעֲבוּר
זֶה. בַּעֲבוּר זֶה לֹא אָמַרְתִּי, אֶלָּא בְּשָׁעָה שֶׁיֵּשׁ מַצָּה
וּמָרוֹר מֻנָּחִים לְפָנֶיךָ.

By citing Exodus 13:8, as it did for the inarticulate child in
*Levinkha,* the Haggadah is again cluing us, the reader, in that this
verse acts as the roadmap for the *Maggid* section. More than that,
the Haggadah is pointing out the importance of timing for the
telling of the story. Like the Jews in Egypt, who were told by Moses
to prepare for the coming redemption on the first day of Nisan
but did not actually exit Egypt until the fifteenth day of that
month, we too require fifteen days to prepare for the Revelation of
the Divine Presence. And just like the Jewish People witnessed
God's redemption while they were partaking of the Passover meal
with the matzah and *maror* before them, so too do we require the
same accoutrements to reenact and reexperience the night of
redemption.[5] The whole key to unlocking the Seder is knowing
where in the journey through time and space to locate ourselves in
order to understand what is about to unfold (see the commentary
on *Kadesh* and *U-Rechatz,* chap. 3).

## Leimor: Ba'avur Zeh—"Saying: Because of This"

> "And you should tell your child on that day saying:
> 'Because of this [or: This is because of what], the EverPresent
> God did for me when I left Egypt.'" (Exod. 13:8)

וְהִגַּדְתָּ לְבִנְךָ בַּיּוֹם הַהוּא לֵאמֹר: בַּעֲבוּר זֶה עָשָׂה
יְיָ לִי, בְּצֵאתִי מִמִּצְרָיִם.

Having thus far provided in *Maggid* a formula for what we tell and explained why we tell, who is obligated to tell, how much we tell, to whom we tell, how we vary our telling (depending on the audience), and when we tell, we are now interested in going deeper. The verse of Exodus 13:8 implies as much when it says: "And you should tell your child on that day, saying: Because of this, that the EverPresent God did for me when I left Egypt." Apparently, at this point in the narrative it is our duty to say/explain the "because," the cause for our enslavement and redemption. This is what the section of *Leimor* will attempt to do. The author of the Haggadah will offer three explanations of why the Jews were enslaved and redeemed. These explanations can be seen as complementary approaches, although they represent three distinct viewpoints of the rabbinic Sages.

### Rav's Explanation of Why We Were Enslaved and Redeemed: Our Idolatry and God's Covenant

Commenting on the *Mishnah* (*Pesachim* 10:4) that says the Exodus story is told by "beginning with shame and concluding with praise," the Talmud records a difference of opinion between two Rabbis as to what constitutes shame and praise (Tractate *Pesachim* 116a). Samuel, quoting Moses's retelling of the Exodus story in Deuteronomy, says that we begin with the shame of our people's slavery and conclude with the praise of God's bringing us to political freedom. We used

Samuel's formula at the commencement of *Maggid,* when we began the answer to the Four Questions: "We were slaves to Pharaoh in Egypt, but the EverPresent God, our God, brought us out of there with a strong hand and an outstretched arm." In contrast, Rav says that we commence with an entirely different shame: the fact that our ancestors worshiped idols; and we conclude with the corresponding praise of God bringing us closer to worshiping God. We use Rav's formula to begin the section of *Leimor* in explaining why our people were enslaved and redeemed.

The citing of Rav's opinion in addition to Samuel's opinion is indicative of the Haggadah's penchant to be respectful and inclusive of divergent opinions. Rather than take an "either/or" approach to truth, the Rabbis take a "both/and" approach, which allows for many interpretations to coexist side-by-side with each other. Thus, rather than present only one interpretation of the Exodus experience, the Haggadah, throughout *Maggid,* presents multiple perspectives of what occurred and what the deeper meanings of those events signify.

Rav, like Samuel, is answering the question of who we are. Samuel's answer was direct and to the point: we were slaves, and then God liberated us with power and might so that now we are free. Rav's answer is both more expansive and deeper. It is not that Rav denies Samuel's answer. But Rav wants to know why we were slaves—what caused the slavery of the Jewish People in Egypt. He is also interested in knowing why the Jews were redeemed and what we mean by redemption. Is the absence of slavery enough to constitute redemption? Or is redemption not merely freedom *from* slavery but actualization *to* our full human and spiritual potential? Without being able to answer the "why" questions, we will know neither how to avoid becoming enslaved again, nor what strategic goals to set for ourselves as we strive to achieve true and lasting "redemption" for ourselves and future generations.

The Haggadah supports this interpretation by quoting from chapter 24 of the Book of Joshua. There, Joshua, shortly before his death, like Moses his teacher before him, initiates a recovenanting ceremony with the new generation of Jews, whom he will soon leave behind (the children of the generation who conquered the Promised Land). Joshua prefaces that recovenanting ceremony by retelling the story of their ancestors. That retelling begins with the words *Va-yomer Yehoshua,* "and Joshua said." In effect, what Rav is saying is that if we want to know what Moses meant by the word "saying" in the verse "And you should tell your child on that day, saying …" what could be better than listening to what Joshua, Moses's prize student, said to his spiritual "children," the next generation of Israelites! After all, the Torah told us at the end of Deuteronomy (34:9) that Joshua "was filled with the spirit of wisdom because Moses had laid his hands upon him." Moses imbued Joshua with his own spirit. Joshua learned the importance of midrash, of retelling the Jewish People's story to the next generation, from Moses, his spiritual master. Who would know better than Moses's student what the real causes were for the enslavement and redemption from Egypt? Who would know better than Joshua what we are supposed to "say" to our children? So the Haggadah turns to what Joshua "said" to discern the underlying causes of our story:

At first our forefathers served idols, but now the Omnipresent has brought us close to serving God, as it is written: And Joshua said to all the people, "So says the EverPresent God, the God of Israel: Your ancestors lived on the other side of the river, Terach the father of Avraham and the father of Nachor, and they worshiped other gods. And I took your father, Avraham, from the other side of the river and led him through all of the land of Canaan, and I multiplied his descendants and I gave him Yitzchak, and I gave Yitzchak, Jacob and Esau, and I gave Esau the land of Seir as an inheritance, and Jacob and his sons descended to Egypt."

מִתְּחִלָּה עוֹבְדֵי עֲבוֹדָה זָרָה הָיוּ אֲבוֹתֵינוּ, וְעַכְשָׁו

קֵרְבָנוּ הַמָּקוֹם לַעֲבוֹדָתוֹ. שֶׁנֶּאֱמַר: וַיֹּאמֶר יְהוֹשֻׁעַ

אֶל־כָּל־הָעָם. כֹּה אָמַר יְיָ אֱלֹהֵי יִשְׂרָאֵל: בְּעֵבֶר

הַנָּהָר יָשְׁבוּ אֲבוֹתֵיכֶם מֵעוֹלָם, תֶּרַח אֲבִי אַבְרָהָם

וַאֲבִי נָחוֹר, וַיַּעַבְדוּ אֱלֹהִים אֲחֵרִים. וָאֶקַּח

אֶת־אֲבִיכֶם אֶת־אַבְרָהָם מֵעֵבֶר הַנָּהָר, וָאוֹלֵךְ אוֹתוֹ

בְּכָל־אֶרֶץ כְּנָעַן. וָאַרְבֶּה אֶת־זַרְעוֹ, וָאֶתֶּן לוֹ

אֶת־יִצְחָק; וָאֶתֶּן לְיִצְחָק אֶת־יַעֲקֹב וְאֶת־עֵשָׂו; וָאֶתֶּן

לְעֵשָׂו אֶת־הַר שֵׂעִיר, לָרֶשֶׁת אוֹתוֹ; וְיַעֲקֹב וּבָנָיו

יָרְדוּ מִצְרָיִם.

We said that the shame that Rav believes is the beginning of the story we should be telling is the opening statement of this paragraph: "At first our forefathers served idols." The "praise," he argues, is "but now God has brought us close to serving God." From the plain reading of the text, the ancestor to whom Rav is referring as having worshiped idols is Abraham's father, Terach. Our story of being born as a nation begins with him. Real slavery is slavery to false gods, not merely a cruel king. Unlike physical slavery, which is forced upon people, idolatry—spiritual slavery—is self-imposed and potentially even more damaging. To Rav, being the involuntary victim of a powerful political tyrant is not necessarily shameful; the voluntary choosing and serving of false gods, idolatry, is what is shameful. Thus, even on the surface, Rav provides both a historical and spiritual explanation of why the Jewish People were later enslaved in Egypt.

Similarly in explaining why the Jewish People were redeemed, what is praiseworthy for Rav is not merely that God took us out of Egypt into freedom. What is praiseworthy is that we evolved to a passionate spiritual connection with *HaMakom,* the "Ground" of the universe. For Rav, the Exodus was not merely from Egyptian slavery but from our ancestors' idolatry. Just as the story begins with the idolatry of Terach, several generations before the Jews went down to Egypt, so too does it conclude with the Jewish People's authentic spirituality several generations after they left Egypt. The story concludes only once the Jewish People succeed in settling the Land of Israel, building the Temple, and living together with the Holy One, Blessed be God.

There may be an even deeper intention behind Rav's opening words of shame: "At first our forefathers served idols," which points the finger of blame for the enslavement not solely upon the shoulders of the Egyptians (as Samuel implied), or even upon Abraham's idol-worshiping father, Terach (the plain meaning of Rav's words), but upon a different generation of our idol-worshiping ancestors: Jacob's sons, who came down to Egypt (the concluding verse of Joshua's retelling quoted in the Haggadah).

After all, why did the children of Jacob descend to Egypt in the first place? (Note: In the Torah, the term "descend" is not a mere geographic description of traveling southward, but a moral critique denoting failure to take responsibility for the other [see Gen. 38:1].)

They descended because ten of Joseph's brothers kidnapped Joseph and sold him into slavery. What prompted them to do that? Their own jealousy of Joseph's rising star within the family and their insecurity vis-à-vis his treatment of them. Jealousy and insecurity between siblings are normal, but kidnapping and enslaving a sibling are not. When jealousy and insecurity lead a person or a group of persons to degrade and deny the dignity of the other created in God's image and likeness, that is not mere sibling rivalry, that is idolatry. The brothers' mockery of Joseph's human dignity by stripping him of his clothes and throwing him naked into a pit, and their reckless disregard of his life and welfare when they sold him into a life of slavery, testified that in the youth of the "children of Israel" they were not God-fearing individuals. Indeed, "At first our forefathers served idols...."

Nor was Joseph better on this score. In fact, from reading chapter 47 of the Book of Genesis, we get the impression that Joseph, the original victim of his brothers' cruelty, may have been much worse. What did Joseph do? During the seven years of plenty, he taxed the native Egyptian people of all their surplus grain and stored it in granaries, which he had them build for that purpose. When the famine began, instead of handing out rations to the Egyptian people to get them through the famine, he sold the stored grain back to the Egyptians at prices so exorbitant that within one year he had bankrupted the entire Egyptian economy:

> Now there was no bread in all the world, for the famine was very severe; both the land of Egypt and the land of Canaan languished because of the famine. Joseph gathered in all the money that was to be found in the land of Egypt and in the land of Canaan, as payment for the rations that were being procured, and Joseph brought the money into Pharaoh's palace.
>
> Genesis 47:13–14

Having achieved a monopoly over the money supply, Joseph then sold the grain for commodities, soon giving Pharaoh control over all the livestock of Egypt:

> And when the money gave out in the land of Egypt and in the land of Canaan, all the Egyptians came to Joseph and said, "Give us bread, lest we die before your very eyes; for the money is gone!" And Joseph said, "Bring your livestock, and I will sell to you against your livestock, if the money is gone." So they brought their livestock to Joseph, and Joseph gave them bread in exchange for the horses, for the stocks of sheep and cattle, and the donkeys; thus he provided them with bread that year in exchange for all their livestock.
>
> Genesis 47:15–17

By the end of the second year, Joseph gained control over all the real estate in the country and manipulated the population to sell themselves into slavery to Pharaoh:

> And when that year was ended, they came to him the next year and said to him, "We cannot hide from my lord that, with all the money and stocks of animals consigned to my lord, nothing is left at my lord's disposal save our persons and our farmland. Let us not perish before your eyes, both we and our land. Take us and our land in exchange for bread, and we with our land will be slaves to Pharaoh; provide the seed, that we may live and not die, and that the land may not become a waste." So Joseph gained possession of all the farm land of Egypt for Pharaoh, every Egyptian having sold his field because the famine was too much for them; thus the land passed over to Pharaoh.
>
> Genesis 47:18–20

More egregious still was that Joseph engaged in massive population transfers, thereby making the Egyptians strangers in their own land:

> And he removed the population town by town, from one end of Egypt's border to the other.
>
> Genesis 47:21

The only persons who were exempt from Joseph's draconian policies were, interestingly enough, the priesthood. It should be remembered that Joseph's wife was the daughter of the priest of On:

> Only the land of the priests he did not take over, for the priests had an allotment from Pharaoh, and they lived off the allotment which Pharaoh had made to them; therefore, they did not sell their land.
>
> Genesis 47:22

Having gained ownership over all of Egypt—money, livestock, real estate, and persons—he then added insult to injury by imposing a 20 percent tax on any crops that they were able to produce, to insure a continuing stream of income into Pharaoh's coffers:

> Then Joseph said to the people, "Whereas I have this day acquired you and your land for Pharaoh, here is seed for you to sow the land. And when harvest comes, you shall give one-fifth to Pharaoh, and four-fifths shall be yours as seed for the fields and as food for you and those in your households, and as nourishment for your children."
>
> Genesis 47:23–24

Joseph was so successful in subjugating the Egyptian natives that they actually expressed gratitude to him for saving their lives. In effect, they were thanking Joseph for making them into slaves. Joseph had so succeeded in exploiting, impoverishing, and enslaving the Egyptian People that they internalized the identity of penniless slaves and did not realize the pernicious nature of Joseph's actions:

> And they said, "You have saved our lives! We are grateful to my lord, and we will be slaves to Pharaoh." And Joseph made it into a land law in Egypt, which is still valid, that a fifth should be Pharaoh's; only the land of the priests did not become Pharaoh's.
>
> Genesis 47:25–26

What could Joseph have done instead? He could have done what Franklin Delano Roosevelt did for U.S. citizens during World War II—he could have handed out ration cards to the Egyptian people to enable them to survive the famine without robbing them of all their possessions and their human dignity. After all, the grain that Joseph had gathered in Pharaoh's silos was the surplus grain that he had taxed from the Egyptian people during their years of plenty. Had he redistributed that grain in a fair and equitable manner, the people would have been eternally grateful to him and to Pharaoh. Instead, Joseph ended up breeding a bitter generation of Egyptians who were only too happy to turn the tables on Joseph's people once they had the political opportunity to do so.

What makes Joseph's actions all the more painful and shameful to read about is that while he was enslaving the Egyptians, he was unapologetically protecting his Jewish brethren in Goshen.

> Thus Israel settled in the country of Egypt, in the region of Goshen; they acquired property there, were fertile, and increased greatly.
>
> Genesis 47:27

The Israelites were unaffected by the famine and Joseph's exploitative policies. No wonder that the Torah tells us both in Genesis and again at the outset of Exodus that the Jews took hold of the land, were fertile, and increased greatly! They were living the good life while the Egyptians were surviving by the skin of their teeth.

Let me be clear: it was not wrong for Joseph to take care of his extended family. It was wrong for him to do so while he impoverished and enslaved the family of Egypt. Had he been fair and benevolent with the Egyptians, his favoring of his own family would barely have been noticed. As it was, however, his nepotism must have stood out like a sore thumb. It took a later Pharaoh "who knew not Joseph," that is, who owed Joseph no allegiance for consolidating the monarchy's power, to capitalize on the pent-up rage that the Egyptians must have felt by directing their anger against the increasingly powerful Jewish People.

Why did Joseph do this? Put in broader terms, what causes any person to enslave another, any nation to enslave another nation? A number of answers come to mind:

- An uncontrolled obsession with accumulating wealth (greed)
- An uncontrolled obsession with exercising power (control)
- Irrational fear or insecurity (paranoia)

Wealth, power, and security are, in proper proportion, desirable values for people to cultivate. It is when any or all of these values become disproportionately emphasized, so that they become infinite rather than finite goals, that they metamorphose from values into idols. When people treat other human beings like discardable chattel, when they deny the basic humanity of themselves or of other human beings in the pursuit of these values, they are denying the God who created every human being in God's image. They then, in effect, become idol worshipers. Not only what we believe about God but also the way we behave toward other human beings are the ways that Judaism knows who worships God and who serves false idols.

Why did Joseph reduce the "image of God" of the Egyptian People to purchasable property, to mere chattel? Because in doing so he was not serving the Creator of the world, the Sovereign of sovereigns, who fashioned human beings in God's own image, but rather Pharaoh, sovereign of Egypt. Whether consciously or not, and the text seems to imply that it was quite conscious, Joseph served Pharaoh, the chief idol of Egypt, and in so doing enslaved all the Egyptian People in the process. It took only a couple of small steps—Joseph's death and a new king arising over Egypt—to take the results of Joseph's misdirected service—the all-powerful, centralized government that Joseph had created—and turn it against Joseph's own people. The Jewish People, who lived free of the impoverishment and enslavement experienced by the rest of Egypt in Joseph's day, now had to experience the pernicious wrath of a new king and a vengeful population.[6]

Acknowledging Joseph's role in bolstering Pharaoh's position as Egypt's omnipotent ruler does not excuse the later Pharaoh and Egyptians from their own vile behavior toward the Jews. Even if one views the subsequent enslavement of the Jews as a "justified" comeuppance for Joseph's behavior, it did not excuse Pharaoh's decision to murder the Jewish male infants and to attempt the genocide of the Jewish people (i.e., if there were no more Jewish males, in one generation or two at the most, there would no more Jewish People). But what this explanation does do is provide the historical and political background of how and why the process of enslavement was initiated in the first place.

This may be the deeper import of Rav's "At first our forefathers served idols." Both Joseph and his brothers behaved in a shameful, idolatrous way, which led to the Jewish People's subsequent enslavement. That, for Rav, is the proper starting point if we want to understand not merely what happened to the Jewish People but why it happened.

Rav's teaching stands as a subtle warning to Jews in all generations of the dangers of exercising power to please the ruling elite at the expense of the mass of ordinary men and women. The warning is subtle, rather than explicit, in order not to give the Jewish People's current or future enemies "grist for the mill"—pretexts for the persecution of future generations of Jews, as happened all too often in Jewish history.[7]

**Baruch Shomer Havtachato LeYisrael ... Vehi She-amdah.** Having deepened our understanding of the cause, in Rav's view, for the Jewish People's enslavement, the Haggadah now suggests why they were redeemed. Despite our ancestors' mistakes in worshiping idols and the consequences that flowed from that, God had already foreseen this turn of events long before and had also promised the people's future redemption. In God's first covenant with Abraham, which took place immediately after Abraham risked his life to save his nephew Lot from captivity and where Abraham nobly refused to partake of the spoils of battle, God promised Abraham to, in effect, reward Abraham's descendants for his courageous and noble deeds by freeing them from captivity with great wealth:

> *Blessed be God, who keeps God's promise to Israel;*
> *blessed be God. The Holy One, blessed be God, predeter-*
> *mined the time for our final deliverance in order to fulfill*
> *what God had pledged to our father Abraham in a*
> *covenant, as it is written (Gen. 15:13–14): "God said to*
> *Abram, 'Your descendants will surely be strangers in a*
> *land that is not their own, and they will be enslaved and*
> *afflicted for four hundred years; however, I will punish*
> *the nation that enslaved them, and afterwards they will*
> *leave with great wealth.'"*

בָּרוּךְ שׁוֹמֵר הַבְטָחָתוֹ לְיִשְׂרָאֵל. בָּרוּךְ הוּא.
שֶׁהַקָּדוֹשׁ בָּרוּךְ הוּא חִשַּׁב אֶת־הַקֵּץ, לַעֲשׂוֹת כְּמָה
שֶׁאָמַר לְאַבְרָהָם אָבִינוּ בִּבְרִית בֵּין הַבְּתָרִים,
שֶׁנֶּאֱמַר: וַיֹּאמֶר לְאַבְרָם: יָדֹעַ תֵּדַע, כִּי־גֵר יִהְיֶה
זַרְעֲךָ בְּאֶרֶץ לֹא לָהֶם, וַעֲבָדוּם וְעִנּוּ אֹתָם אַרְבַּע
מֵאוֹת שָׁנָה, וְגַם אֶת־הַגּוֹי אֲשֶׁר יַעֲבֹדוּ דָּן אָנֹכִי.
וְאַחֲרֵי כֵן יֵצְאוּ בִּרְכֻשׁ גָּדוֹל.

The paragraph that follows this one, beginning with the words, "This promise has sustained our ancestors and us," is referring to God's promise of ultimate redemption at the covenant of the pieces (as per my translation, which follows). The anonymous author of the Haggadah is in fact saying that God in the covenantal promise to Abraham did not prognosticate that the Jews will be slaves in and redeemed only from Egypt in the year 1250 B.C.E. Rather, the covenant constituted a recurring prediction and promise of redemption for all generations of Jews. God was informing Abraham that throughout Jewish history his descendants might find themselves in dire circumstances. But even so, even if they found themselves actually or metaphorically estranged, enslaved and impoverished in lands not under their control for long periods of time, they should not lose hope.[8] Eventually they would be saved by God and redeemed with great wealth. Following on the heels of Rav's teaching, the Haggadah seems also to be conveying that this prediction/promise is valid regardless of the cause of the exile and enslavement. That is, even if the cause is idolatry, even if the Jews through errors in judgment bring the situation at least partially upon themselves, nevertheless God, out of God's loyalty and promise to Abraham, will ultimately come to their aid. This is why we so strongly assert God's abiding loyalty in *Vehi She-amdah*:

> This promise has sustained our ancestors and us. For not
> only one enemy has risen against us to annihilate us,
> but in every generation they rise against us to annihilate
> us. But the Holy One, blessed be God, saves us from
> their hand.

וְהִיא שֶׁעָמְדָה לַאֲבוֹתֵינוּ וְלָנוּ. שֶׁלֹּא אֶחָד בִּלְבָד
עָמַד עָלֵינוּ לְכַלּוֹתֵנוּ. אֶלָּא שֶׁבְּכָל דּוֹר וָדוֹר,
עוֹמְדִים עָלֵינוּ לְכַלּוֹתֵנוּ. וְהַקָּדוֹשׁ בָּרוּךְ הוּא מַצִּילֵנוּ
מִיָּדָם.

It is customary to raise the second glass of wine and to ask all the participants to join in song when reciting the *Vehi She-amdah* paragraph. In effect we are raising a toast to God for taking notice of our suffering and remembering the covenantal promise to our Patriarchs. This moment is the pivot point in the saga when God decides to intervene and halt hundreds of years of slavery and oppression, and this toast is the first kinesthetic action, the first symbolic telling, that we do during *Maggid*, the verbal telling.

Adding the kinesthetic action to the verbal telling underlines the pivotal importance of this moment. It also picks up the story from the last kinesthetic action that we performed, the hiding away of the matzah in *Yachatz*. That hiding symbolized Moses being hidden away from the Jewish People first by his mother, then by Pharaoh's daughter in the royal palace, and finally in Midian as a fugitive from Pharaoh. The sequencing of these two kinesthetic actions— hiding the matzah and raising a toast to God for remembering the covenantal promise—reflects the juxtaposition of these stories at the end of chapter 2 in the book of Exodus. The text in Exodus reads:

> Pharaoh ... sought to slay Moses. But Moses fled from the face of Pharaoh and dwelt in the land of Midian; and he sat down by a well. ... And Moses was content to dwell [there]. ... And it was in those many days that the king of Egypt died. And the children of Israel sighed because of the work and they cried out, and their screams from the labor rose to God. And God heard their groaning, and God remembered God's covenant with Abraham, with Isaac, and with Jacob, and God saw the children of Israel and God knew.
>
> Exodus 2:15–25

By offering a toast to God for remembering God's covenantal promise, we conclude Rav's explanation of the underlying reasons for our enslavement and redemption with words and actions of praise, as we are instructed by the Mishnah.

### The Anonymous Author of the Mishnah's Explanation of Why We Were Enslaved and Redeemed: Jewish Destiny and God's Empathy

As the Mishnah prescribes, the second part of the *Leimor* subsection also begins in shame, this time with the father of the Jewish People, Jacob, being persecuted and victimized. Here it is not Pharaoh, but Jacob's uncle Lavan who seeks to destroy the Jewish

People. The reference to Lavan, an earlier tormentor of the Jewish People, is a natural segue from the previous paragraph, which stated, "For not only one enemy has risen against us to annihilate us, but in every generation they rise against us."

Furthermore, if we are to tell the story of our people, "the children of Israel," and explain how and why we were enslaved in Egypt, we need to begin the story with Jacob, even before he is renamed Israel, at the point and in the place where his children, the children of Israel, are born: Aram, Assyria, the home of Lavan. "Israel's" slavery and affliction did not begin in Egypt but in the home of Lavan where Jacob/Israel expanded his family tremendously, but slaved away miserably for twenty years and where he would have been enslaved for life, or worse, been killed, had he not fled and received divine protection (Gen. 31:29–43):

Go out and learn what Lavan the Aramean sought to do to our father, Jacob. For Pharaoh issued his decree only against the males, but Lavan sought to uproot everything as it says: "My father was a fugitive from Aram...."

צֵא וּלְמַד, מַה בִּקֵשׁ לָבָן הָאֲרַמִּי לַעֲשׂוֹת לְיַעֲקֹב אָבִינוּ. שֶׁפַּרְעֹה לֹא גָזַר אֶלָּא עַל הַזְּכָרִים, וְלָבָן בִּקֵשׁ לַעֲקֹר אֶת־הַכֹּל, שֶׁנֶּאֱמַר: אֲרַמִּי אֹבֵד אָבִי...

Father Jacob/Israel and his family are the prototype of what the descendants who are named after him, the children of Israel, and their leader, Moses, will later experience. The Jewish People in Egypt also grew tremendously, only to find themselves miserably enslaved and having to flee, with God's assistance, to avoid servitude in perpetuity or, worse, death.

Theologically, the parallelism of the lives of our Patriarchs with the later experience of their descendants is referred to by our Sages as *ma'aseh avot siman levanim*, "the actions of our ancestors

are signs for their descendants." This theological position assumes
that there are certain patterns in our people's historical experience that repeat themselves. Not only, as we argued in our commentary on *Karpas* and at the beginning of *Maggid,* is the
experience of the Jewish People in Egypt paradigmatic of subsequent exilic experiences of the Jewish People, but even the experience of the Jewish People in Egypt as narrated in the Book of
Exodus was already foreshadowed and preexperienced in the
Book of Genesis by the Patriarchs and Matriarchs of our people. As
we will see, this predetermined destiny of the Jewish People will
reflect the opinion of the anonymous author of the Mishnah as to
why the Jewish People were enslaved in Egypt.

**My Father Was a Fugitive from Aram.** Aside from beginning
in shame and concluding with praise, *Mishnah Pesachim* instructs us
that in telling the story of the Exodus from Egypt, we should do
*midrash,* an exegetical analysis of the pilgrim's pronouncement in
Deuteronomy 26 upon presenting God with his first fruits.

Why is this pilgrim's formula in Deuteronomy chosen by the
anonymous author of the Mishnah to be the centerpiece of the
"saying" subsection (i.e., *Leimor*) explaining why/how we were
enslaved and redeemed? True, it is brief and succinct (containing
only four verses), which gives it a distinct advantage over reading
the entire story of the redemption from Egypt straight from the
Book of Exodus (several biblical chapters). However, since the
Mishnah instructs us to do a creative, exegetical analysis (i.e.,
*midrash*) of these verses, the brevity of the piece is lost in the expansive interpretation and proof-texts offered.

Rather, as we said before, at the Passover Seder, we ourselves
are "virtual pilgrims" journeying through time. As "pilgrims" who
are journeying through the Exodus from Egyptian bondage, it is
appropriate for us to recite the formula recited by the ancient pilgrims to Jerusalem before the late-spring holiday of Shavuot, the
festive conclusion of the Passover holiday season (referred to by
our Sages as *Atzeret,* literally "conclusion"). That pilgrims' formula,

which was brief enough for even those who were not literate to memorize and recite, recounted the reasons and the process of our ancestors' enslavement and redemption from Egypt, the very focus of *Maggid,* the verbal telling. Still, unlike the physical pilgrims to Jerusalem, who recited the formula by rote, we, as virtual pilgrims, get to interpret this formula creatively and imaginatively as befits virtual time travelers.

Another reason that the Mishnah chooses these four verses to be the centerpiece of *Leimor* is that this text is Moses's script for how future generations of Jews should retell their people's story, within Deuteronomy, which is Moses's own retelling of the Jewish People's story. Unlike the first four books of the Torah, which are written in the third person, most of the Book of Deuteronomy is in the first-person voice of Moses himself. Deuteronomy constitutes Moses's retelling of the Jewish People's story to the children of the Jews who left Egypt in the Exodus. Moses's retelling in Deuteronomy to that second generation differs in many details from the original telling in the Book of Exodus. Moses varied the story because the audience he was addressing differed from the generation who personally experienced the Exodus. While the previous generation could offer their children firsthand, eyewitness testimony to the miracles of their redemption, this second generation had to rely on "hearsay" evidence. To make sure that this generation and future generations of Israelites would not forget the story, Moses first retold the story of the Exodus to that latter generation and then provided for every subsequent generation an easy-to-remember, textual formula for retelling. After the Jewish People settled in the Land of Israel and built the Temple in Jerusalem, that formula was used by every Israelite going on the late-spring pilgrimage to conclude the Passover festival season.

Moreover, like the commandment in the Book of Exodus to retell the story of the Exodus *(Vehigadeta levinkha bayom hahu leimor...),* which is the entire basis and roadmap of *Maggid,* the pilgrim's scripted story in Deuteronomy begins with the words

*Higadeti hayom,* "I am retelling today [the story of my ancestors]" and then continues with the word *ve-amarta,* "that he [the pilgrim] should say ..." (Deuteronomy 26:5). Apparently, in addressing the next generation of Israelites in Deuteronomy, Moses was explaining God's commandment to their parents in Exodus 13:8: "And you should tell your child on that day, saying: 'Because of this, the EverPresent God did for me when I left Egypt.'"

We had asked rhetorically before who would know better than Joshua, Moses's disciple, what Moses meant when he instructed the Jewish People in the Book of Exodus to tell their children the story of the Exodus. Here the Haggadah provides the answer: Moses himself! We follow Moses's "retelling" formula in Deuteronomy, shortly before his death, to elaborate upon Moses's original instruction to "tell" the story in the Book of Exodus forty years previously.

The text from Deuteronomy reads as follows:

My ancestor was a fugitive from Aram. He went down to Egypt with a small number of people and lived there as an immigrant, and there he became a great, powerful, and numerous nation.

אֲרַמִּי אֹבֵד אָבִי, וַיֵּרֶד מִצְרַיְמָה, וַיָּגָר שָׁם בִּמְתֵי

מְעָט. וַיְהִי שָׁם לְגוֹי גָּדוֹל, עָצוּם וָרָב.

The Egyptians suspected us of evil and afflicted us; they imposed hard labor upon us.

וַיָּרֵעוּ אֹתָנוּ הַמִּצְרִים וַיְעַנּוּנוּ. וַיִּתְּנוּ עָלֵינוּ עֲבֹדָה

קָשָׁה.

We cried out to the EverPresent God, the God of our ancestors, and the EverPresent God heard our voice and saw our suffering, our toil, and our oppression.

וַנִּצְעַק אֶל־יְיָ אֱלֹהֵי אֲבֹתֵינוּ, וַיִּשְׁמַע יְיָ אֶת־קֹלֵנוּ,
וַיַּרְא אֶת־עָנְיֵנוּ, וְאֶת־עֲמָלֵנוּ, וְאֶת לַחֲצֵנוּ.

The EverPresent God brought us out of Egypt with a mighty
hand and outstretched arm, with great awe, miraculous
signs, and wonders.

וַיּוֹצִאֵנוּ יְיָ מִמִּצְרַיִם, בְּיָד חֲזָקָה, וּבִזְרֹעַ נְטוּיָה,
וּבְמֹרָא גָּדוֹל, וּבְאֹתוֹת, וּבְמֹפְתִים.

Deuteronomy 26:5–8

These four verses in Deuteronomy deal with four issues in
consecutive order: First, why did the Jewish People go down to
Egypt? Second, how were we enslaved? Third, why were we
redeemed from slavery? And finally, how were we redeemed from
slavery?

The Midrash, the rabbinic interpretation of the biblical text
cited by the anonymous author of the Mishnah, will in effect answer
these questions by doing its own "retelling." By embroidering the
four verses from Deuteronomy with other verses found throughout
the Bible, the Midrash will give expression to the rabbinic understanding of Jewish destiny, history, theology, and justice.

### Jewish Destiny: The Midrash Explains Why the Jewish People Went Down to Egypt.

> My ancestor was a fugitive from Aram. He went down to
> Egypt with a small number of people and lived there as
> an immigrant, and there he became a great, powerful,
> and numerous nation. (Deut. 26:5)

אֲרַמִּי אֹבֵד אָבִי, וַיֵּרֶד מִצְרַיְמָה, וַיָּגָר שָׁם בִּמְתֵי
מְעָט. וַיְהִי שָׁם לְגוֹי גָּדוֹל, עָצוּם וָרָב.

The Rabbis' interpretation of why we were enslaved (the first verse of the pilgrims' telling) in the midrash that follows, is fraught with a sense of divinely directed destiny notwithstanding our ancestors' human intentions:

> *"He went down to Egypt," compelled by divine decree.*

וַיֵּרֶד מִצְרַיְמָה, אָנוּס עַל פִּי הַדִּבּוּר.

In fact, everything intended by the people in the first verse turns out the opposite of how it first appears. Jacob intended only to come to Egypt for a short period of time, but his descendants ended up staying for hundreds of years:

> *"He lived there as an immigrant" implies that he did not come down to settle in Egypt but only to live there temporarily, as it is written: "They [the sons of Jacob] said to Pharaoh: 'We have come to sojourn in this land because there is no pasture for your servants' flocks, for the famine is severe in the land of Canaan. For now, though, let your servants dwell in the land of Goshen.'"*

וַיָּגָר שָׁם, מְלַמֵּד שֶׁלֹּא יָרַד יַעֲקֹב אָבִינוּ
לְהִשְׁתַּקֵּעַ בְּמִצְרַיִם, אֶלָּא לָגוּר שָׁם, שֶׁנֶּאֱמַר:
וַיֹּאמְרוּ אֶל־פַּרְעֹה, לָגוּר בָּאָרֶץ בָּאנוּ, כִּי אֵין מִרְעֶה
לַצֹּאן אֲשֶׁר לַעֲבָדֶיךָ, כִּי כָבֵד הָרָעָב בְּאֶרֶץ כְּנָעַן.
וְעַתָּה, יֵשְׁבוּ־נָא עֲבָדֶיךָ בְּאֶרֶץ גֹּשֶׁן.

Jacob came reluctantly, hoping to survive by keeping a low profile and being inconspicuous, but the Jews grew into an outstanding, powerful, and numerous nation:

*"With a small number of people," as it is written: "With seventy souls your ancestors went down to Egypt, and now the EverPresent God, your God, has made you as numerous as the stars in the sky."*

*"There he became a nation" means that they became a distinct people in Egypt.*

*"Great, powerful," as it is written: "The children of Israel were fruitful and increased greatly; they multiplied and became mighty, and the land was full of them."*

בְּמָתֵי מְעָט, כְּמָה שֶׁנֶּאֱמַר: בְּשִׁבְעִים נֶפֶשׁ יָרְדוּ אֲבֹתֶיךָ מִצְרָיְמָה. וְעַתָּה שָׂמְךָ יְיָ אֱלֹהֶיךָ כְּכוֹכְבֵי הַשָּׁמַיִם לָרֹב. וַיְהִי שָׁם לְגוֹי, מְלַמֵּד שֶׁהָיוּ יִשְׂרָאֵל מְצֻיָּנִים שָׁם. גָּדוֹל עָצוּם, כְּמָה שֶׁנֶּאֱמַר: וּבְנֵי יִשְׂרָאֵל פָּרוּ וַיִּשְׁרְצוּ וַיִּרְבּוּ וַיַּעַצְמוּ בִּמְאֹד מְאֹד, וַתִּמָּלֵא הָאָרֶץ אֹתָם.

The children of Israel's sensuality and fecundity, graphically symbolized by the blood of childbirth, which Pharaoh and the Egyptian nation viewed as a threat and tried to suppress, was seen as a blessing by God:

*"And numerous," as it is written: "I made you as populous as the plants of the field; you grew up and wore choice adornments; your breasts were firm and your hair grew long; yet, you were bare and naked. And I passed over you and saw you wallowing in your blood, and I said to you, 'Through your blood you shall live,' and I said to you, 'Through your blood you shall live.'"*

וָרֹב, כְּמָה שֶׁנֶּאֱמַר: רְבָבָה כְּצֶמַח הַשָּׂדֶה נְתַתִּיךְ,

וַתִּרְבִּי, וַתִּגְדְּלִי, וַתָּבֹאִי בַּעֲדִי עֲדָיִים - שָׁדַיִם נָכֹנוּ,

וּשְׂעָרֵךְ צִמֵּחַ, וְאַתְּ עֵרֹם וְעֶרְיָה. וָאֶעֱבֹר עָלַיִךְ

וָאֶרְאֵךְ מִתְבּוֹסֶסֶת בְּדָמָיִךְ, וָאֹמַר לָךְ: בְּדָמַיִךְ חֲיִי,

וָאֹמַר לָךְ: בְּדָמַיִךְ חֲיִי.

There is an expression in Yiddish that captures the essence of this first Midrashic exegesis: *Maan tracht un Gott lacht,* "People may plan, but God laughs at their plans and does what the Holy One intends." Unlike Rav, who sees our ancestors' worship of strange gods as the root cause for our people's descent into Egypt, the anonymous author of the Mishnah ascribes the cause of our descent into Egypt and the conditions that precipitated our enslavement to God's predetermined destiny for the Jewish People.

In the visual and kinesthetic "tellings" of the Haggadah, this section of *Maggid,* which describes our early experiences in Egypt of growth and burgeoning power, was expressed in the ritual of eating *karpas.*

**How the Jews Were Enslaved: A Multistage Process of Delegitimization and Oppression.** This section fleshes out the various dimensions of slavery and the several-stage process of enslavement. Rav had ascribed at least partial moral fault to the Jewish People for their own enslavement. Their worship of idols had led, albeit indirectly, to their descent into Egyptian slavery. The Midrash chosen by the anonymous author of the Mishnah, in contrast, places the moral blame for the enslavement of the Jewish People solely on the shoulders of the Egyptian authorities. God may have directed our people's descent into Egypt, but the Egyptians' evil cunning is what shackled the Jewish People in chains of bondage.

> *"The Egyptians suspected us of evil and afflicted us; they imposed hard labor upon us." (Deut. 26:6)*

וַיָּרֵעוּ אֹתָנוּ הַמִּצְרִים וַיְעַנּוּנוּ, וַיִּתְּנוּ עָלֵינוּ עֲבֹדָה קָשָׁה.

The Jewish People did not go from being successful, free people to impoverished, oppressed slaves overnight. First, Pharaoh undermined the Israelites' status as loyal citizens by projecting them to his advisors as a looming, potential threat:

> *"The Egyptians suspected us of evil," as it is written: "Let us deal with them wisely lest they multiply, and if we happen to be at war, they may join our enemies and fight against us and then leave the country."*

וַיָּרֵעוּ אֹתָנוּ הַמִּצְרִים, כְּמָה שֶׁנֶּאֱמַר: הָבָה נִתְחַכְּמָה לוֹ פֶּן־יִרְבֶּה, וְהָיָה כִּי־תִקְרֶאנָה מִלְחָמָה, וְנוֹסַף גַּם הוּא עַל־שֹׂנְאֵינוּ, וְנִלְחַם־בָּנוּ וְעָלָה מִן־הָאָרֶץ.

Then, Pharaoh placed a "labor tax" on the Jews to oppress them and put them into a subservient role:

> *"They imposed hard labor upon us," as it is written: "They imposed backbreaking labor upon the people of Israel; the people of Israel built Pithom and Ra'amses as storage cities for Pharaoh."*

וַיְעַנּוּנוּ, כְּמָה שֶׁנֶּאֱמַר: וַיָּשִׂימוּ עָלָיו שָׂרֵי מִסִּים,

לְמַעַן עַנֹּתוֹ בְּסִבְלֹתָם, וַיִּבֶן עָרֵי מִסְכְּנוֹת לְפַרְעֹה,

אֶת־פִּתֹם וְאֶת־רַעַמְסֵס.

Finally, "they" (apparently the Egyptian authorities now joined Pharaoh) formally enslaved the Jews with backbreaking work:

> "And afflicted us," as it is written: "They set taskmasters over them in order to oppress them with their burdens."

וַיִּתְּנוּ עָלֵינוּ עֲבֹדָה קָשָׁה, כְּמָה שֶׁנֶּאֱמַר: וַיַּעֲבִדוּ

מִצְרַיִם אֶת־בְּנֵי יִשְׂרָאֵל בְּפָרֶךְ.

Like the Nazi regime in Germany in the 1930s, Pharaoh's court engaged in a manipulative, multistage process of delegitimization with successively more onerous forms of abuse before attempting the wholesale murder of the Jewish People. Learning to recognize the first steps on this slippery slope toward genocide in order to halt that process in its tracks was then, and is again today, a necessary tool for Jewish survival.

In the visual and kinesthetic tellings of the Haggadah, this section was expressed in the rituals of the dipping in salt water or *charoset*, in the breaking of the matzah, and later on in the eating of *maror*.

### Why the Jewish People Were Redeemed from Slavery: God's Emotional Empathy with God's People.

We cried out to the EverPresent God, the God of our ancestors, and the EverPresent God heard our voice and saw our suffering, our toil, and our oppression.

Deuteronomy 26:7

וַנִּצְעַק אֶל־יְיָ אֱלֹהֵי אֲבֹתֵינוּ, וַיִּשְׁמַע יְיָ אֶת־קֹלֵנוּ,
וַיַּרְא אֶת־עָנְיֵנוּ, וְאֶת־עֲמָלֵנוּ, וְאֶת לַחֲצֵנוּ.

Why were the Jewish People redeemed? In Rav's explanation,
the focus was on God's remembering his promise to Abraham at
the covenant of the pieces to redeem his descendants. God, as the
paragon of truth and justice, keeps God's promises. Rav emphasized God's attribute of justice, what the Rabbis referred to as
*Midat HaDin,* to explain why we were redeemed from slavery. The
Midrash cited here, in contrast, while assuming that covenantal
promise, nevertheless focuses on divine concern for the suffering
of the Jewish People:

"We cried to the EverPresent God, the God of our ancestors," as it is written: "It happened in the course of those
many days that the king of Egypt died; the children of
Israel sighed because of their work and cried out; their
screams from the labor rose to God."

"And the EverPresent God heard our voice," as it is
written: "God heard their groaning; God remembered
God's covenant with Abraham, with Isaac, and with
Jacob."

"And saw our suffering," that is, the conjugal separation of husband and wife, as it is written: "God saw the
children of Israel and God knew."

"Our toil" refers to the drowning of the sons, as it is
written: "Every son that is born you shall cast into the
river, but you shall let every daughter live."

"Our oppression" means the pressure put upon
them, as it is written: "I have also seen how the
Egyptians are oppressing them."

וַנִּצְעַק אֶל־יְיָ אֱלֹהֵי אֲבֹתֵינוּ, כְּמָה שֶׁנֶּאֱמַר: וַיְהִי
בַיָּמִים הָרַבִּים הָהֵם, וַיָּמָת מֶלֶךְ מִצְרַיִם, וַיֵּאָנְחוּ
בְנֵי־יִשְׂרָאֵל מִן־הָעֲבֹדָה וַיִּזְעָקוּ. וַתַּעַל שַׁוְעָתָם
אֶל־הָאֱלֹהִים מִן־הָעֲבֹדָה.

וַיִּשְׁמַע יְיָ אֶת־קֹלֵנוּ, כְּמָה שֶׁנֶּאֱמַר: וַיִּשְׁמַע אֱלֹהִים
אֶת־נַאֲקָתָם, וַיִּזְכֹּר אֱלֹהִים אֶת־בְּרִיתוֹ אֶת־אַבְרָהָם,
אֶת־יִצְחָק, וְאֶת־יַעֲקֹב.

וַיַּרְא אֶת־עָנְיֵנוּ, זוֹ פְּרִישׁוּת דֶּרֶךְ אֶרֶץ, כְּמָה
שֶׁנֶּאֱמַר: וַיַּרְא אֱלֹהִים אֶת־בְּנֵי יִשְׂרָאֵל. וַיֵּדַע
אֱלֹהִים.

וְאֶת־עֲמָלֵנוּ, אֵלּוּ הַבָּנִים, כְּמָה שֶׁנֶּאֱמַר: כָּל־הַבֵּן
הַיִּלּוֹד הַיְאֹרָה תַּשְׁלִיכֻהוּ, וְכָל־הַבַּת תְּחַיּוּן.
וְאֶת־לַחֲצֵנוּ, זֶה הַדְּחַק, כְּמָה שֶׁנֶּאֱמַר: וְגַם־רָאִיתִי
אֶת־הַלַּחַץ אֲשֶׁר מִצְרַיִם לֹחֲצִים אֹתָם.

Our abject conditions, of which God takes cognizance, and God's emotional empathy with our suffering are what move God to save the Jewish People. For this midrash it is the compassionate side of God, what the Rabbis called *Midat HaRachamim*, that explains why the Jewish People were redeemed. God heard, saw, and felt our pain and identified with us in our suffering. This identification led God to remember God's covenant to redeem the Jewish People. In the kinesthetic Seder, this verbal telling was embodied in the "toast to God" when singing *Vehi She-amdah*.

Later on, Rabban Gamliel will offer yet a third set of reasons for why we were redeemed, which can be interpreted as focusing less on God's attributes and more on the virtues demonstrated by the Jewish People. All three explanations are in fact alluded to in the biblical text, so that the three explanations of why we were redeemed should be viewed as complementary rather than as mutually exclusive. As in most of life, the reason for our redemption was due to a multiplicity of factors. The editor of the Haggadah includes all of them but, for reasons of clarity, lays them out as three separate and distinct points of view.

### How Were the Jewish People Redeemed from Slavery? The Power of the Plagues.

> The EverPresent God brought us out of Egypt with a mighty hand and outstretched arm, with great awe, miraculous signs, and wonders.
>
> Deuteronomy 26:8

וַיּוֹצִיאֵנוּ יְיָ מִמִּצְרַיִם בְּיָד חֲזָקָה, וּבִזְרֹעַ נְטוּיָה, וּבְמֹרָא גָדֹל, וּבְאֹתוֹת, וּבְמֹפְתִים.

The fourth question and answer constitute the longest and most explicated section of *Maggid,* as it should be, and culminates in one of the most powerful symbolic actions of the entire Seder: the spilling of the ten drops of wine. This is not surprising, for how the Jewish People were redeemed—the tale of the ten plagues and the rescue of the Jewish People at the Sea of Reeds—is also the longest, most detailed, and certainly one of the most emotionally gripping sections of the Exodus story. While the process of enslavement comprises less than two chapters in the Torah, the saga of the plagues and the drowning of the Egyptian legions at the Sea comprise nearly eight full chapters. It is therefore important to look at this section of the Haggadah with its lengthy midrash on the plagues to understand their role both in the section of *Maggid* and in the Haggadah's telling of the Exodus story.

It is ironic that the story of the plagues is precisely the subsection in *Maggid* with which North American Jews feel most uncomfortable. Along with the *Shefoch Chamatkha* prayer, recited at

the Seder immediately following the Grace after Meals, the plagues
are seen to be politically incorrect. After all, punishing the
Egyptians seems so vindictive and vengeful. For American Jews who
are steeped in the liberal ethic, believing that all people are essen-
tially good, the recounting of the plagues that struck the Egyptians
seems out of character. Therefore, Haggadot published by liberal
or secular denominations of Judaism have either shortened the section describing the plagues or deleted that section altogether (as
well as the *Shefoch Chamatkha* prayer; see p. 138–141).

Why then are the plagues not only recited but elaborated
upon in such painful detail in the traditional Haggadah? First,
God's bringing of the plagues served to teach the Jewish People
that there was an intelligent force in the universe who personally
guaranteed ultimate justice and vindication. The midrash at this
point in the Haggadah goes to great lengths to make the point that
it was God, personally, who brought the plagues upon the
Egyptians and thereby freed the Jewish People from centuries of
slavery and oppression:

> "The EverPresent God brought us out of Egypt with a
> mighty hand and outstretched arm, with great awe,
> miraculous signs, and wonders."
>
> The EverPresent God brought us out of Egypt not by
> an angel, not by a seraph, not by a messenger, but by the
> Holy One, blessed be God, God-self, as it is written: "I
> will pass through the land of Egypt on that night; I will
> smite all the first-born in the land of Egypt from man
> unto beast; on all the gods of Egypt I will execute judg-
> ments; I am the EverPresent God.
>
> "I will pass through the land of Egypt on that night,
> Myself and not an angel; I will smite all the first-born in
> the land of Egypt, Myself and not a seraph; on all the gods
> of Egypt I will execute judgments, Myself and not the mes-
> senger; I am the EverPresent God, I and none other."

"Mighty hand" refers to the disease among the cattle, as it is written: "Behold the hand of the EverPresent God strikes your cattle that are in the field, the horses, the donkeys, the camels, the herds, and the flocks—a very severe pestilence."

"Outstretched arm" means the sword, as it is written: "God's drawn sword in God's hand, outstretched over Jerusalem."

"Great awe" alludes to the divine Revelation, as it is written: "Has God ever attempted to take unto God a nation from the midst of another nation by trials, miraculous signs and wonders, by war and with a mighty hand and outstretched arm and by awesome revelations, just as you saw the EverPresent God, your God, do for you in Egypt, before your eyes?"

"Miraculous signs" refers to the miracles performed with the staff of Moses, as it is written: "Take this staff in your hand, that you may perform the miraculous signs with it."

"Wonders" alludes to the plague of blood, as it is written: "I will show wonders in the sky and on the earth."

וַיּוֹצִיאֵנוּ יְיָ מִמִּצְרַיִם, לֹא עַל־יְדֵי מַלְאָךְ, וְלֹא עַל־יְדֵי שָׂרָף, וְלֹא עַל־יְדֵי שָׁלִיחַ, אֶלָּא הַקָּדוֹשׁ בָּרוּךְ הוּא בִּכְבוֹדוֹ וּבְעַצְמוֹ. שֶׁנֶּאֱמַר: וְעָבַרְתִּי בְאֶרֶץ מִצְרַיִם בַּלַּיְלָה הַזֶּה, וְהִכֵּיתִי כָל־בְּכוֹר בְּאֶרֶץ מִצְרַיִם, מֵאָדָם וְעַד בְּהֵמָה, וּבְכָל־אֱלֹהֵי מִצְרַיִם אֶעֱשֶׂה שְׁפָטִים, אֲנִי יְיָ.

וְעָבַרְתִּי בְאֶרֶץ־מִצְרַיִם בַּלַּיְלָה הַזֶּה, אֲנִי וְלֹא מַלְאָךְ. וְהִכֵּיתִי כָל בְּכוֹר בְּאֶרֶץ־מִצְרַיִם, אֲנִי וְלֹא שָׂרָף.

וּבְכָל־אֱלֹהֵי מִצְרַיִם אֶעֱשֶׂה שְׁפָטִים, אֲנִי וְלֹא
הַשָּׁלִיחַ. אֲנִי יְיָ. אֲנִי הוּא וְלֹא אַחֵר.

בְּיָד חֲזָקָה, זוֹ הַדֶּבֶר, כְּמָה שֶׁנֶּאֱמַר: הִנֵּה יַד־יְיָ
הוֹיָה בְּמִקְנְךָ אֲשֶׁר בַּשָּׂדֶה, בַּסּוּסִים בַּחֲמֹרִים
בַּגְּמַלִּים, בַּבָּקָר וּבַצֹּאן, דֶּבֶר כָּבֵד מְאֹד.

וּבִזְרֹעַ נְטוּיָה, זוֹ הַחֶרֶב, כְּמָה שֶׁנֶּאֱמַר: וְחַרְבּוֹ
שְׁלוּפָה בְּיָדוֹ, נְטוּיָה עַל־יְרוּשָׁלָיִם.

וּבְמוֹרָא גָּדוֹל, זֶה גִּלּוּי שְׁכִינָה, כְּמָה שֶׁנֶּאֱמַר: אוֹ
הֲנִסָּה אֱלֹהִים לָבוֹא לָקַחַת לוֹ גוֹי מִקֶּרֶב גּוֹי,
בְּמַסֹּת בְּאֹתֹת וּבְמוֹפְתִים וּבְמִלְחָמָה, וּבְיָד חֲזָקָה
וּבִזְרוֹעַ נְטוּיָה, וּבְמוֹרָאִים גְּדֹלִים, כְּכֹל אֲשֶׁר־עָשָׂה
לָכֶם יְיָ אֱלֹהֵיכֶם בְּמִצְרַיִם לְעֵינֶיךָ.

וּבְאֹתוֹת, זֶה הַמַּטֶּה, כְּמָה שֶׁנֶּאֱמַר: וְאֶת הַמַּטֶּה
הַזֶּה תִּקַּח בְּיָדֶךָ, אֲשֶׁר תַּעֲשֶׂה־בּוֹ אֶת־הָאֹתֹת.

וּבְמוֹפְתִים, זֶה הַדָּם, כְּמָה שֶׁנֶּאֱמַר: וְנָתַתִּי מוֹפְתִים
בַּשָּׁמַיִם וּבָאָרֶץ.

In light of this awareness that the plagues were a manifesta-
tion of God's justice in the world, we can read into the ten plagues
a "measure for measure" response to the enslavement and decree
of infanticide foisted upon the Jews by the Egyptians. This principle of "measure for measure" is the underlying principle of justice
in the legal sections of the Torah (also known as the "talion" principle, Exod. 21:23–25). This principle also operates as a key underlying motif in the narrative sections of the Torah.[9] The Torah
understood that when someone or some group of people do some-

thing wrong, it is not sufficient to punish them. The perpetrator of the wrongful act must also be taught what it was that was wrongful. That teaching is most effective when the perpetrator actually experiences in the flesh what it felt like to be the victim of the wrongful behavior. The "measure for measure" principle embodied in the plagues taught those who witnessed and experienced it what was done wrong in the first place.

Thus:

- The plague of turning the water of the Nile River into blood (#1) was a clear measure-for-measure response to the Egyptians' attempt to hide the mass murder of the Jewish infant males by drowning them in the Nile. While the Egyptians thought they could dispose of the bodies of the Jewish children without affronting their delicate sensibilities, the first plague forced them to confront their evil of making Jewish blood run like water.
- The plague of frogs (#2), while less obvious than the plague of blood, also had a measure-for-measure response. The Torah describes how the frogs infiltrated all the normally private spaces of the Egyptians—their beds, their ovens, their food, and so on. Just as the life of slaves lacks the realm of privacy, since the "master" has rights to everything connected to the slave—the slave's food, sexual privileges, and so on—so too did the frogs impinge on the private realm of the Egyptians, giving them a taste, as it were, of their own medicine.
- The plague of lice (#3) was distinguished from the plague of frogs by the fact that the lice got under the skin of their victims and left welts in their wake. One can easily imagine that this too reflects the life of a slave, whose abused body stings with the welts of slavery.
- The plague of wild animals (#4) in which the animals burst into the homes of the Egyptians was a "measure-for-measure" response to the Egyptians who behaved like wild animals by bursting into the homes of the Jews to kidnap and drown

the Jewish baby boys. To carry out Pharaoh's nefarious decree, the Egyptian people engaged in the first "pogroms" of the Jewish historical experience.

- The cattle plague (#5) was a measure-for-measure response to the Egyptians for expropriating the cattle that had formerly belonged to the Jews. God, as it were, expropriated the Egyptian cattle back through this plague, thus demonstrating that unjust enrichment would not be tolerated.
- The plague of boils (#6) left the Egyptians feeling afflicted and looking disfigured, much like a beaten and downtrodden slave feels and looks.
- The plague of hail (#7) was God hurling the stones of abuse and the fiery flames of subjugation back at the Egyptians for acting similarly toward the Jews.
- The plague of locusts (#8), which consumed all the crops of the Egyptians not destroyed by the hail, expropriated the product of Jewish slave labor in the fields of Egypt (see Exod. 1:14).
- The plague of darkness (#9) made palpable to the Egyptians for a short period of time the psychological darkness that enveloped the Jewish People during hundreds of years of slavery.
- The plague of the first-born (#10) as well as the drowning of the soldiers of the Egyptian legions at the Sea of Reeds was a payback in kind for the drowning of the Jewish males by the Egyptians (probably overseen and executed by the soldiers of the Egyptian army).

√ The ten plagues disabled the Egyptian economy and freed the Jewish people from slavery in stages. There was no more field work to do, with the fields destroyed, nor backbreaking construction work to undertake, with the economy in shambles. The poverty and suffering wrought by the plagues gave the Egyptian People a taste over the course of several months of what the Jewish People had experienced over hundreds of years.

✓ So important were the plagues and what they symbolized that the Rabbis had us perform a ritual, kinesthetic action (dipping our forefinger in the wine and spilling a drop for each plague) while we name each plague and again when we mention them in abbreviated form:

> *These are the ten plagues that the Holy One, blessed be God, brought upon the Egyptians in Egypt, namely: (1) Blood, (2) frogs, (3) lice, (4) wild animals, (5) cattle disease, (6) boils, (7) hail, (8) locusts, (9) darkness, (10) death of the first-born.*
>
> *Rabbi Judah abbreviated the ten plagues by composing three words from their Hebrew initials:* D'tzakh, Adash, B'achav.

אֵלּוּ עֶשֶׂר מַכּוֹת שֶׁהֵבִיא הַקָּדוֹשׁ בָּרוּךְ הוּא

עַל־הַמִּצְרִים בְּמִצְרַיִם, וְאֵלּוּ הֵן: דָּם. צְפַרְדֵּעַ. כִּנִּים.

עָרוֹב. דֶּבֶר. שְׁחִין. בָּרָד. אַרְבֶּה. חֹשֶׁךְ. מַכַּת בְּכוֹרוֹת.

רַבִּי יְהוּדָה הָיָה נוֹתֵן בָּהֶם סִמָּנִים: דְּצַ"ךְ עֲדַ"שׁ

בְּאַחַ"ב.

✓ This ritual of dipping our finger into the wine is probably not, as many claim, to "reduce our joy because of the suffering of the Egyptians." Were that the case, the traditional Haggadah would have toned down and given short shrift to the plagues instead of offering such ebullient, expansive descriptions. Rather, this kinesthetic marking of the plagues graphically demonstrates the point that spilling some Egyptian blood was, unfortunately, the only way to defeat that nation's tyranny. Just as we raised our cups at *Vehi She-amdah* to toast God for remembering the covenant, this demonstrative, kinesthetic action of dipping/spilling, done within

*Maggid,* the verbal telling, underscores the pivotal importance of the plagues to the story of the Exodus. Without the plagues there would have been no redemption. Negotiating with a tyrant such as Pharaoh was, and is, a waste of time. Only the exercise of over-whelming force and the "bloodletting" of the Egyptian legions, symbolized by transferring drops of wine from our cup to our plate, ultimately succeeded in freeing the Jewish People from slav-ery and saving them from annihilation at the Sea. ⟋

While the plagues themselves represented a powerful response to Egyptian evil, the Rabbis in this midrash on the plagues felt the need to multiply that powerful response four and five times so that it became overwhelming rather than merely "measure for measure." In so doing, the Rabbis in the Haggadah are teaching us that to effectively parry forces of radical evil, one needs to use overwhelming rather than merely commensurate force. While commensurate force is an important limiting factor in petty criminal law (e.g., one may not use lethal force to stop a com-mon pickpocket), in dealing criminally with heinous or potentially lethal crimes, as well as in dealing politically with radically evil regimes, one needs to exercise power that goes beyond a mere pro-portionate response to the evil perpetrated.

Overwhelming force is necessary against an evil regime for two reasons. First, the total impact of all the evil perpetrated by the individual members of the regime is greater than the mere sum of its parts. This totality of evil needs to be met with an appro-priately vigorous, even exponentially powerful response. Second, in order to create a deterrent effect, the punishment for the evildoer needs to be greater than the evil perpetrated. Thus, for instance, according to biblical law, a thief who committed the equivalent of grand larceny not only had to repay the value of the item he or she stole but also had to pay a fine over and above the value of the stolen object. In some cases (e.g., the stealing of crucial com-modities of an agrarian economy like a sheep or an ox, which was later sold or slaughtered), the thief had to pay a penalty four or five times the value of the stolen object. This latter law explains why Rabbi Yosi HaGlili, Rabbi Eliezer, and Rabbi Akiva chose to multiply the number of plagues imposed on the Egyptians four and five times.

*Rabbi Yosi the Galilean says: How does one derive that, after the ten plagues in Egypt, the Egyptians suffered fifty plagues at the Sea? Concerning the plagues in Egypt the Torah states that "the magicians said to Pharaoh, it is the finger of God." However, at the Sea, the Torah relates that "Israel saw the great hand which the EverPresent God laid upon the Egyptians, and the people revered the EverPresent God and they believed in the EverPresent God and in God's servant Moses." It reasons that if they suffered ten plagues in Egypt, they must have been made to suffer fifty plagues at the Sea.*

*Rabbi Eliezer says: How does one derive that every plague that God inflicted upon the Egyptians in Egypt was equal in intensity to four plagues? It is written: "God sent upon them God's fierce anger, wrath, fury and trouble, a band of evil messengers." Since each plague was comprised of (1) wrath, (2) fury, (3) trouble, and (4) a band of evil messengers, they must have suffered forty plagues in Egypt and two hundred at the Sea.*

*Rabbi Akiva says: How does one derive that every plague that God inflicted upon the Egyptians in Egypt was equal in intensity to five plagues? It is written: "God sent upon them God's fierce anger, wrath, fury and trouble, a band of evil messengers." Since each plague was comprised of (1) fierce anger, (2) wrath, (3) fury, (4) trouble, and (5) a band of evil messengers, they must have suffered fifty plagues in Egypt and two hundred and fifty at the Sea.*

רַבִּי יוֹסֵי הַגְּלִילִי אוֹמֵר: מִנַּיִן אַתָּה אוֹמֵר שֶׁלָּקוּ
הַמִּצְרִים בְּמִצְרַיִם עֶשֶׂר מַכּוֹת, וְעַל הַיָּם לָקוּ
חֲמִשִּׁים מַכּוֹת? בְּמִצְרַיִם מָה הוּא אוֹמֵר: וַיֹּאמְרוּ
הַחַרְטֻמִּם אֶל־פַּרְעֹה, אֶצְבַּע אֱלֹהִים הִוא. וְעַל הַיָּם
מָה הוּא אוֹמֵר? וַיַּרְא יִשְׂרָאֵל אֶת־הַיָּד הַגְּדֹלָה
אֲשֶׁר עָשָׂה יְיָ בְּמִצְרַיִם, וַיִּירְאוּ הָעָם אֶת־יְיָ, וַיַּאֲמִינוּ
בַּייָ וּבְמשֶׁה עַבְדּוֹ. כַּמָּה לָקוּ בְּאֶצְבַּע, עֶשֶׂר מַכּוֹת.
אֱמוֹר מֵעַתָּה, בְּמִצְרַיִם לָקוּ עֶשֶׂר מַכּוֹת, וְעַל־הַיָּם
לָקוּ חֲמִשִּׁים מַכּוֹת.

רַבִּי אֱלִיעֶזֶר אוֹמֵר: מִנַּיִן שֶׁכָּל־מַכָּה וּמַכָּה, שֶׁהֵבִיא
הַקָּדוֹשׁ בָּרוּךְ הוּא עַל הַמִּצְרִים בְּמִצְרַיִם, הָיְתָה
שֶׁל אַרְבַּע מַכּוֹת? שֶׁנֶּאֱמַר: יְשַׁלַּח־בָּם חֲרוֹן אַפּוֹ,
עֶבְרָה וָזַעַם וְצָרָה, מִשְׁלַחַת מַלְאֲכֵי רָעִים. עֶבְרָה
אַחַת. וָזַעַם שְׁתַּיִם. וְצָרָה שָׁלשׁ. מִשְׁלַחַת מַלְאֲכֵי
רָעִים אַרְבַּע. אֱמוֹר מֵעַתָּה: בְּמִצְרַיִם לָקוּ אַרְבָּעִים
מַכּוֹת, וְעַל הַיָּם לָקוּ מָאתַיִם מַכּוֹת.

רַבִּי עֲקִיבָא אוֹמֵר: מִנַּיִן שֶׁכָּל־מַכָּה וּמַכָּה, שֶׁהֵבִיא
הַקָּדוֹשׁ בָּרוּךְ הוּא עַל הַמִּצְרִים בְּמִצְרַיִם, הָיְתָה
שֶׁל חָמֵשׁ מַכּוֹת? שֶׁנֶּאֱמַר: יְשַׁלַּח־בָּם חֲרוֹן אַפּוֹ,
עֶבְרָה וָזַעַם וְצָרָה, מִשְׁלַחַת מַלְאֲכֵי רָעִים. חֲרוֹן
אַפּוֹ אַחַת. עֶבְרָה שְׁתַּיִם. וָזַעַם שָׁלשׁ. וְצָרָה אַרְבַּע.
מִשְׁלַחַת מַלְאֲכֵי רָעִים חָמֵשׁ. אֱמוֹר מֵעַתָּה: בְּמִצְרַיִם

לָקוּ חֲמִשִּׁים מַכּוֹת, וְעַל הַיָּם לָקוּ חֲמִשִּׁים וּמָאתַיִם
מַכּוֹת.

The plagues, which seem vindictive and excessive on the surface, actually teach us important principles of the Torah's conception
of justice in the political as well as the criminal sphere. The plagues
were not an incidental part of the Exodus saga that we should gloss
over or delete because we initially feel uncomfortable with them or
think of their tone as politically incorrect. Rather, we should think
hard about what they might teach us regarding the need of the
Jewish People to confront radical evil in an as yet unredeemed world.

Understood in this context, the expansive description of the
plagues in the Haggadah is itself a recitation of praise to God, the thematic device used throughout *Maggid* to tell the story of the Exodus.
We conclude the opinion of the anonymous author of the Mishnah
by praising the God of justice who reversed the course of nature itself
to protect the innocent and punish the guilty.

***"Dayenu": Epilogue of Praise.*** We noted in the introduction to
the Seder that the number "fifteen" is a recurring one in the
Passover Seder. There are fifteen items in the Seder, the holiday
commences on the fifteenth day of the month, and there are fifteen items for which we offer praise to God in the "Dayenu." We
linked these various "fifteens" to God's name, *Yah,* which appears
in the Song at the Sea, which in *gematria* (Jewish numerology) also
equals fifteen. "Dayenu," like the Haggadah itself, is a paean of
praise that gives expression to our people's passionate love affair
with God. Contrary to the common understanding, by saying
*Dayenu,* "It would be enough for us," we are not saying that it would
have been enough if only God had done one, three, or ten of the
fifteen items for us, the Jewish People. What we are saying is that
had God only done any one of the fifteen items, it would be sufficient cause in and of itself for us to praise God. Each of the fifteen
steps played a distinctive and important role in resurrecting the
dignity of the Jewish People and deserves our grateful thanks.

The fifteen elements that elicit our praise are an interweaving of the spiritual and the physical. While there are some elements that seem primarily spiritual, such as the gifts of Shabbat, Torah, and the Holy Temple, most of the elements are primarily physical and material in nature. This is because, as we pointed out in *U-Rechatz*, the Exodus from Egypt was not so much a tale of spiritual redemption as it was a story of our physical redemption from Egyptian bondage. Our bodies and our body-politic had to be redeemed before we could commune with God on the Shabbat, receive the Torah at Mount Sinai, or witness God's Presence descend into the sacred precincts of the Tabernacle.

*How many good steps has God bestowed upon us:*

*Had God brought us out of Egypt, and not executed judgments against the Egyptians, it would have been enough—*dayenu!

*Had God executed judgments against the Egyptians, and not their gods, it would have been enough—*dayenu!

*Had God executed judgments against their gods and not put to death their first-born, it would have been enough—*dayenu!

*Had God put to death their first-born, and not given us their riches, it would have been enough—*dayenu!

*Had God given us their riches, and not split the Sea for us, it would have been enough—*dayenu!

*Had God split the Sea for us, and not led us through it on dry land, it would have been enough—*dayenu!

*Had God led us through it on dry land, and not sunk our foes in it, it would have been enough—*dayenu!

*Had God sunk our foes in it, and not satisfied our needs in the desert for forty years, it would have been enough—dayenu!*

*Had God satisfied our needs in the desert for forty years, and not fed us the manna, it would have been enough—dayenu!*

*Had God fed us the manna, and not given us the Sabbath, it would have been enough—dayenu!*

*Had God given us the Sabbath, and not brought us to Mount Sinai, it would have been enough—dayenu!*

*Had God brought us to Mount Sinai, and not given us the Torah, it would have been enough—dayenu!*

*Had God given us the Torah, and not brought us into Israel, it would have been enough—dayenu!*

*Had God brought us into Israel, and not built the Temple for us, it would have been enough—dayenu!*

*How much more so, then, should we be grateful to God for the numerous favors that God bestowed upon us: God brought us out of Egypt, and punished the Egyptians; God smote their gods, and slew their first-born; God gave us their wealth, and split the Sea for us; God led us through it on dry land, and sunk our foes in it; God sustained us in the desert for forty years, and fed us with the manna; God gave us the Sabbath, and brought us to Mount Sinai; God gave us the Torah, and brought us to Israel; God built the Temple for us, to atone for all our sins.*

כַּמָּה מַעֲלוֹת טוֹבוֹת לַמָּקוֹם עָלֵינוּ׃

אִלּוּ הוֹצִיאָנוּ מִמִּצְרַיִם,

וְלֹא עָשָׂה בָהֶם שְׁפָטִים,  דַּיֵּנוּ.

אִלּוּ עָשָׂה בָהֶם שְׁפָטִים,

וְלֹא עָשָׂה בֵאלֹהֵיהֶם,  דַּיֵּנוּ.

אִלּוּ עָשָׂה בֵאלֹהֵיהֶם,

וְלֹא הָרַג אֶת־בְּכוֹרֵיהֶם,  דַּיֵּנוּ.

אִלּוּ הָרַג אֶת־בְּכוֹרֵיהֶם,

וְלֹא נָתַן לָנוּ אֶת־מָמוֹנָם,  דַּיֵּנוּ.

אִלּוּ נָתַן לָנוּ אֶת־מָמוֹנָם,

וְלֹא קָרַע לָנוּ אֶת־הַיָּם,  דַּיֵּנוּ.

אִלּוּ קָרַע לָנוּ אֶת־הַיָּם,

וְלֹא הֶעֱבִירָנוּ בְתוֹכוֹ בֶּחָרָבָה  דַּיֵּנוּ.

אִלּוּ הֶעֱבִירָנוּ בְתוֹכוֹ בֶּחָרָבָה,

וְלֹא שִׁקַּע צָרֵינוּ בְּתוֹכוֹ,  דַּיֵּנוּ.

אִלּוּ שִׁקַּע צָרֵינוּ בְּתוֹכוֹ,

וְלֹא סִפֵּק צָרְכֵּנוּ בַּמִּדְבָּר אַרְבָּעִים שָׁנָה,  דַּיֵּנוּ.

אִלּוּ סִפֵּק צָרְכֵּנוּ בַּמִּדְבָּר אַרְבָּעִים שָׁנָה,

וְלֹא הֶאֱכִילָנוּ אֶת־הַמָּן,  דַּיֵּנוּ.

אִלּוּ הֶאֱכִילָנוּ אֶת־הַמָּן,

וְלֹא נָתַן לָנוּ אֶת־הַשַּׁבָּת,  דַּיֵּנוּ.

אִלּוּ נָתַן לָנוּ אֶת־הַשַּׁבָּת,

וְלֹא קֵרְבָנוּ לִפְנֵי הַר סִינַי,          דַּיֵנוּ.

אִלּוּ קֵרְבָנוּ לִפְנֵי הַר סִינַי,

וְלֹא נָתַן לָנוּ אֶת־הַתּוֹרָה,          דַּיֵנוּ.

אִלּוּ נָתַן לָנוּ אֶת־הַתּוֹרָה,

וְלֹא הִכְנִיסָנוּ לְאֶרֶץ יִשְׂרָאֵל,          דַּיֵנוּ.

אִלּוּ הִכְנִיסָנוּ לְאֶרֶץ יִשְׂרָאֵל,

וְלֹא בָנָה לָנוּ אֶת־בֵּית הַבְּחִירָה,          דַּיֵנוּ.

## עַל אַחַת

כַּמָּה וְכַמָּה טוֹבָה כְפוּלָה וּמְכֻפֶּלֶת לַמָּקוֹם עָלֵינוּ:

שֶׁהוֹצִיאָנוּ מִמִּצְרַיִם,          וְעָשָׂה בָהֶם שְׁפָטִים,

וְעָשָׂה בֵאלֹהֵיהֶם, וְהָרַג אֶת־בְּכוֹרֵיהֶם,

וְנָתַן לָנוּ אֶת־מָמוֹנָם,          וְקָרַע לָנוּ אֶת־הַיָּם,

וְהֶעֱבִירָנוּ בְתוֹכוֹ בֶּחָרָבָה, וְשִׁקַּע צָרֵינוּ בְּתוֹכוֹ,

וְסִפֵּק צָרְכֵּנוּ בַּמִּדְבָּר אַרְבָּעִים שָׁנָה,

וְהֶאֱכִילָנוּ אֶת־הַמָּן,          וְנָתַן לָנוּ אֶת־הַשַּׁבָּת,

וְקֵרְבָנוּ לִפְנֵי הַר סִינַי,          וְנָתַן לָנוּ אֶת־הַתּוֹרָה,

וְהִכְנִיסָנוּ לְאֶרֶץ יִשְׂרָאֵל, וּבָנָה לָנוּ אֶת־בֵּית הַבְּחִירָה

לְכַפֵּר עַל־כָּל־עֲוֹנוֹתֵינוּ.

One of these fifteen items for which we praise God in the "Dayenu" blatantly emphasizes the material nature of our redemption: "Had God given us their riches, and not split the Sea for us, it would have been enough—*dayenu!*" A popular twentieth-century Haggadah deleted this line of praise, apparently because it smacks of crass materialism rather than ennobling spirituality. The medieval author of the traditional "Dayenu," in contrast, based himself on two sources in the Torah in attributing importance to the material enrichment of the Israelites. First, in God's promise to Abraham at the covenant of the pieces (Gen. 15), God makes a point of saying that not only would God free Abraham's descendants from (Egyptian) slavery, but would also make sure that they left Egypt materially enriched: "I will execute judgment on the nation they will serve, and afterward they will depart with great wealth" (Gen. 15:14). Second, in the days leading to the Exodus from Egypt, the Torah goes out of its way to point out God's command to the Jewish People to "borrow" silver and gold from their Egyptian neighbors and the people's acting in accordance with God's command to acquire their fair share of the Egyptian wealth:

> And God said to Moses, "... Speak now in the ears of the people, and let every man borrow from his neighbor, and every woman from her neighbor, jewels of silver, and jewels of gold." And God gave the people favor in the sight of the Egyptians.... And the people of Israel did according to the word of Moses, and they borrowed from the Egyptians jewels of silver, and jewels of gold, and garments. And God gave the people favor in the sight of the Egyptians, so that they lent them such things as they required, and they carried away the wealth of the Egyptians.
>
> Exodus 11:1–3, 12:35–36

Why does God put such emphasis on the people's acquiring wealth both in the original covenant with Abraham and immediately prior to the Exodus from Egypt? First, because God understood that just as impoverishment is an intrinsic step toward enslavement, enrichment is an essential step toward liberation and human dignity. A rabbinic statement says that "a pauper feels like a dead person" (Tractate *Nedarim* 64b; *Bereshit Rabbah* 71:6). This means that a pauper feels worthless because from an economic point of view he recognizes that he has no "net worth." Therefore at the threshold of their redemption, God commanded the people to "borrow" silver, gold, and fine clothing in order to help the Jewish People transition from being slaves caked in mud, clothed in rags, and feeling figuratively "dead" to being well clothed, adorned with valuable accessories, and feeling worthy and valued. It was these clothes and jewels with which the Jews adorned themselves at Mount Sinai, as might a prospective bride (see Exod. 33:4–6), when God publicly designated them as God's "kingdom of priests and sacred people" and "took them" (Exod. 19:6) in a sort of wedding ceremony to be God's covenantal people.

There is a second point that Genesis 15:14 implies was part of the enrichment process, and that is the concept of justice ("I will execute judgment on the nation they will serve, and afterward they will depart with great wealth"). After providing free labor for the Egyptians for generations, it would have been neither right nor just for the Jewish People to exit Egypt without first receiving fair compensation for their services. Just as the Egyptians enslaved the Jewish People with cunning (Exod. 1:10), using as the medium of enslavement the pretense of building store cities for their leader, Pharaoh, so too does God instruct the people to extract their compensation with commensurate cunning: "borrowing" the Egyptians' gold, silver, and fine clothing on the pretense of being properly adorned for their festive worship of the Jewish People's leader, God.

This process of just enrichment, which God considered important enough to include in the original covenant of the pieces contracted with Abraham in Genesis 15 (see *Baruch Shomer Havtachato LeYisrael*, pp. 75–78), and to which the Torah devotes several additional verses in Exodus, was for the author of the "Dayenu" an indispensable step in the redemption process and one certainly worthy of praise.

Although the "Dayenu" was a medieval addition to the Haggadah and is not included in the twelfth-century Haggadah of Maimonides, nevertheless it serves as a wonderful tool to sum up the second section of *Leimor*. By taking us from the beginning of the process of redemption to the building of God's Temple in the Land of Israel, this section points us toward the consummation of the entire Haggadah, which concludes with the building of God's chosen house, the Temple in Jerusalem (see *Nirtzah*, pp. 155–163). Finally, "Dayenu" concludes the second subsection of *Leimor* with a sort of "epilogue of abundant praise," as per the Mishnah's thematic prescription throughout *Maggid* of "beginning in shame and concluding with praise."

## Rabban Gamliel's Opinion of Why the Jewish People Were Redeemed: "We Earned It"

> *"And you should tell your child on that day, saying: 'Because of this, the EverPresent God did for me when I left Egypt.'" (Exod. 13:8)*

וְהִגַּדְתָּ לְבִנְךָ בַּיּוֹם הַהוּא לֵאמֹר: בַּעֲבוּר זֶה עָשָׂה
יְיָ לִי, בְּצֵאתִי מִמִּצְרָיִם.

What is the "this" to which the parent points in explaining why God redeemed the Jewish People from Egypt? Rabban Gamliel states that there are three things that must be spoken about and pointed to in order to fulfill one's biblical obligation to "tell" the story of the Exodus and explain why we were redeemed. They are *pesach*, matzah, and *maror*. Each of these three items in the Seder is followed by the word *zeh*, "this"—this *pesach*, this matzah, and this *maror*—to pick up on the language of why we were redeemed in the biblical verse of Exodus 13:8, *ba'avur zeh*, "because of this." (After the destruction of the Temple, the word *zeh*, "this," was deleted after *pesach*, the Passover sacrifice offering, because the Passover sacrifice could no longer be offered and eaten as part of the Seder meal.)

For Rabban Gamliel, the reason for the Jewish People being redeemed by God is not only because God remembered the covenantal promise to Abraham, as Rav's opinion implied; nor was it merely God's empathy with the suffering of the Jewish People, as the anonymous author of the Mishnah implies. Those were necessary but not sufficient reasons for our liberation. For Rabban Gamliel, there had to be virtues in the Jewish People, God's covenantal partner, that caused them to merit divine intervention and redemption. Those virtues are symbolized by the three foods that made up the first Seder in Jewish history: the Passover sacrifice, matzah, and *maror.*

> *Rabbi Gamliel used to say: Anyone who has not discussed [literally: said] these three things on Passover has not fulfilled his duty, namely:* pesach, *the Passover offering;* matzah, *the unleavened bread;* maror, *the bitter herbs.*

רַבָּן גַּמְלִיאֵל הָיָה אוֹמֵר: כָּל שֶׁלֹא אָמַר שְׁלשָׁה

דְבָרִים אֵלוּ בַּפֶּסַח, לֹא יָצָא יְדֵי חוֹבָתוֹ, וְאֵלוּ הֵן:

פֶּסַח מַצָּה וּמָרוֹר.

Rabban Gamliel explains that we ate the Passover sacrifice in Temple times because God passed over the houses of the Jewish People when God smote the Egyptian first-born. But why *did* God pass over the Jewish houses and redeem the Jewish People from Egypt the very next day? Because the head of every Jewish household had the courage to set aside and slaughter a sheep, which was worshiped by the Egyptians as a God; then, in an act of brave defiance toward their former taskmasters, the Jews painted their doorways with the blood of the slaughtered sheep. Every Jewish household engaging in this ritual demonstrated that they would henceforth be engaged in serving God rather than in serving Pharaoh and their former Egyptian masters. Because of the courage of the Jewish People did God hover over the Jewish homes and spare their first-born while striking down the Egyptian first-born.

*Why did our ancestors eat the Passover offering during
the period of the Temple? It is because the Holy One,
blessed be God, passed over the houses of our ancestors
in Egypt, as it is written: "You shall say: It is the
Passover offering for the EverPresent God, who passed
over the houses of the children in Egypt when God smote
the Egyptians and spared our houses. The people knelt
and bowed down."*

פֶּסַח שֶׁהָיוּ אֲבוֹתֵינוּ אוֹכְלִים בִּזְמַן שֶׁבֵּית הַמִּקְדָּשׁ
הָיָה קַיָּם, עַל שׁוּם מָה? עַל שׁוּם שֶׁפָּסַח הַקָּדוֹשׁ
בָּרוּךְ הוּא עַל בָּתֵּי אֲבוֹתֵינוּ בְּמִצְרַיִם, שֶׁנֶּאֱמַר:
וַאֲמַרְתֶּם זֶבַח פֶּסַח הוּא לַיָי, אֲשֶׁר פָּסַח עַל בָּתֵּי
בְנֵי יִשְׂרָאֵל בְּמִצְרַיִם, בְּנָגְפּוֹ אֶת־מִצְרַיִם וְאֶת־בָּתֵּינוּ
הִצִּיל, וַיִּקֹּד הָעָם וַיִּשְׁתַּחֲווּ.

Rabban Gamliel explains that we eat matzah because God
redeemed the Jewish People with such suddenness that the people had no time to prepare provisions. But to say this, is to credit
not only the swiftness of God's redemption but the Jewish
People's leap of faith in following Moses out of Egypt into the barren desert without having made adequate preparations or provisions for the journey. The Jewish People's desire to be free and
their trust in God overcame their fear of the unknown. As God,
through the prophet Jeremiah, later commented on this generation's faithfulness and unquestioning devotion: "I remember your
loving-kindness, the love of your days as a bride, when you followed me in the desert, in a land unsown" (Jer. 2:2). Because of
the people's faith and trust in God were they redeemed from
Egypt.

*Why do we eat this matzah? It is because the Sovereign of sovereigns, the Holy One, revealed God's self to our ancestors and redeemed them before their dough had time to ferment, as it is written: "They baked the dough that they had brought out of Egypt into unleavened cakes; for they were driven out of Egypt and could not delay, nor had they prepared any provisions for their journey."*

מַצָּה זוֹ שֶׁאָנוּ אוֹכְלִים, עַל שׁוּם מָה? עַל שׁוּם שֶׁלֹּא הִסְפִּיק בְּצֵקָם שֶׁל אֲבוֹתֵינוּ לְהַחֲמִיץ, עַד שֶׁנִּגְלָה עֲלֵיהֶם מֶלֶךְ מַלְכֵי הַמְּלָכִים, הַקָּדוֹשׁ בָּרוּךְ הוּא, וּגְאָלָם, שֶׁנֶּאֱמַר: וַיֹּאפוּ אֶת־הַבָּצֵק אֲשֶׁר הוֹצִיאוּ מִמִּצְרַיִם, עֻגֹת מַצּוֹת, כִּי לֹא חָמֵץ, כִּי גֹרְשׁוּ מִמִּצְרַיִם, וְלֹא יָכְלוּ לְהִתְמַהְמֵהַּ, וְגַם צֵדָה לֹא עָשׂוּ לָהֶם.

For Rabban Gamliel, why do the Jews eat *maror*, bitter herbs, at the Passover Seder? Because the Jewish People had the fortitude to remain a distinct people in Egypt and to keep up their hope despite the excruciatingly bitter lives, symbolized by the *maror*, that they led in Egypt. Because of their collective resilience and hope were the Jewish people redeemed from Egypt.

*Why do we eat this bitter herb? It is because the Egyptians embittered the lives of our ancestors in Egypt, as it is written: "They made life bitter for them with hard labor, with clay and bricks, and with all kinds of labor in the field; whatever work tasks they performed were backbreaking."*

מָרוֹר זֶה שֶׁאָנוּ אוֹכְלִים, עַל שׁוּם מָה? עַל שׁוּם
שֶׁמֵּרְרוּ הַמִּצְרִים אֶת־חַיֵּי אֲבוֹתֵינוּ בְּמִצְרָיִם, שֶׁנֶּאֱמַר:
וַיְמָרְרוּ אֶת־חַיֵּיהֶם בַּעֲבֹדָה קָשָׁה, בְּחֹמֶר וּבִלְבֵנִים,
וּבְכָל־עֲבֹדָה בַּשָּׂדֶה, אֵת כָּל־עֲבֹדָתָם אֲשֶׁר עָבְדוּ
בָהֶם, בְּפָרֶךְ.

What Rabban Gamliel is saying in emphatic terms is that the Jewish People's own strength of character and initiative were responsible for their redemption. So important were these three symbols of *pesach,* matzah, and *maror* and what they stood for that anyone who did not speak of them on the night of the Seder had not told the complete story of the Exodus. The "this" in "because of *this* God did for me when I left Egypt" is pointing to what the Seder items represent, to their symbolism, rather than to the items themselves. In this understanding, the items point to a meaning beyond themselves, which is why they have to be "said," that is, explained, in order to tell the story of the Seder.

## An Alternative Reading of *Ba'avur Zeh*

*"And you should tell your child on that day, saying: 'This is because of what the EverPresent God did for me when I left Egypt.'" (Exod. 13:8)*

וְהִגַּדְתָּ לְבִנְךָ בַּיּוֹם הַהוּא לֵאמֹר: בַּעֲבוּר זֶה עָשָׂה
יְיָ לִי, בְּצֵאתִי מִמִּצְרָיִם.

Another way to read this section, one that alters the plain meaning of the words in the Bible but that is more consistent with the context in which this verse originally appears in Exodus, is that the verse is not pointing symbolically to why the Jews were redeemed ("because of this, the EverPresent God did for me when I left Egypt"). That had already been addressed by Rav and the anonymous author of the Mishnah. Rather, Rabban Gamliel is explaining why we are supposed to consume the three central foods of the Seder meal that will imminently be eaten: the Passover sacrifice (or its substitute, the *afikoman*, today), matzah, and *maror* ("this [i.e., the *afikoman*, matzah, and *maror*] is because of what God did for me when I left Egypt"). According to this interpretation of these words, when we point at the items and say "this matzah" or "this *maror*," we are not pointing to what these items represent but to the items themselves. We are saying that our ingesting of these items tonight is because our people were commanded to partake of these very same items on the night of their Exodus from Egypt. Since we are totally identifying with our ancestors, we too consciously consume these items on this night.

## *Asah Hashem Li:* In "Every Generation ..."

> *"And you should tell your child on that day, saying: 'Because of this, the EverPresent God did for me when I left Egypt.'" (Exod. 13:8)*

וְהִגַּדְתָּ לְבִנְךָ בַּיּוֹם הַהוּא לֵאמֹר: בַּעֲבוּר זֶה עָשָׂה
יְיָ לִי, בְּצֵאתִי מִמִּצְרָיִם.

The *Maggid* section began by stating that had God not redeemed us from Egypt, we and all our descendants would still be slaves to Pharaoh in Egypt. In the middle of the *Maggid* section *(Vehi She-amdah)*, the Haggadah told us that in every generation the enemies of the Jews have tried to eliminate our people and we have been saved because of the covenantal promise given to Abraham by the Holy One, blessed be God. Now, near the conclusion of the *Maggid* section, the author of the Haggadah spells out what each of these previous statements have implied: that every Jew in every

generation ought to perceive him- or herself as having been personally redeemed from Egypt:

> *In every generation it is a person's duty to regard him- or*
> *herself as though he or she personally had come out of*
> *Egypt, as it is written: "And you should tell your child on*
> *that day, saying: 'Because of this, the EverPresent God*
> *did for me when I left Egypt.'" It was not only our ances-*
> *tors whom the Holy One redeemed from slavery; we, too,*
> *were redeemed with them, as it is written: "God took us*
> *out from there so that God might take us to the land that*
> *God had sworn to our ancestors."*

בְּכָל־דּוֹר וָדוֹר חַיָּב אָדָם לִרְאוֹת אֶת־עַצְמוֹ כְּאִלּוּ

הוּא יָצָא מִמִּצְרַיִם, שֶׁנֶּאֱמַר: וְהִגַּדְתָּ לְבִנְךָ בַּיּוֹם

הַהוּא לֵאמֹר: בַּעֲבוּר זֶה עָשָׂה יְיָ לִי, בְּצֵאתִי

מִמִּצְרָיִם. לֹא אֶת־אֲבוֹתֵינוּ בִּלְבָד גָּאַל הַקָּדוֹשׁ בָּרוּךְ

הוּא, אֶלָּא אַף אוֹתָנוּ גָּאַל עִמָּהֶם, שֶׁנֶּאֱמַר: וְאוֹתָנוּ

הוֹצִיא מִשָּׁם, לְמַעַן הָבִיא אֹתָנוּ, לָתֶת לָנוּ

אֶת־הָאָרֶץ אֲשֶׁר נִשְׁבַּע לַאֲבֹתֵינוּ.

Indeed this is the whole point of the entire Seder: to so completely identify with our ancestors that, for the night of Passover,
we become them; to totally experience and believe that *we* are
being redeemed from slavery and therefore break out in a spontaneous toast and songs of praise to the Cosmic Source of our
redemption.

We begin a protracted toast to the Redeemer of our people,
by raising our cup of wine and chanting an effusive paean that
both praises God and explains why we praise God on this night of
our deliverance:

*Therefore it is our duty to thank and praise, pay tribute and glorify, exalt and honor, bless and acclaim the One who performed all these miracles for our ancestors and for us. God took us out of slavery into freedom, out of grief into joy, out of mourning into a festival, out of darkness into a great light, out of slavery into redemption. We will recite a new song before God! Hallelujah!*

לְפִיכָךְ אֲנַחְנוּ חַיָּבִים לְהוֹדוֹת, לְהַלֵּל, לְשַׁבֵּחַ,
לְפָאֵר, לְרוֹמֵם, לְהַדֵּר, לְבָרֵךְ, לְעַלֵּה וּלְקַלֵּס, לְמִי
שֶׁעָשָׂה לַאֲבוֹתֵינוּ וְלָנוּ אֶת־כָּל־הַנִּסִּים הָאֵלּוּ.
הוֹצִיאָנוּ מֵעַבְדוּת לְחֵרוּת, מִיָּגוֹן לְשִׂמְחָה, וּמֵאֵבֶל
לְיוֹם טוֹב, וּמֵאֲפֵלָה לְאוֹר גָּדוֹל, וּמִשִׁעְבּוּד לִגְאֻלָּה.
וְנֹאמַר לְפָנָיו שִׁירָה חֲדָשָׁה. הַלְלוּיָהּ׃

Having explained why we praise God, we set down the cup of wine to launch into the singing of Psalms 113 and 114, the first two psalms of *Hallel*, praising God.

### *Betzeiti MiMitzrayim: Halleluyah ... Betzeit Yisrael MiMitzrayim*

*"And you should tell your child on that day, saying: 'Because of this, the EverPresent God did for me when I left Egypt.'" (Exod. 13:8)*

וְהִגַּדְתָּ לְבִנְךָ בַּיּוֹם הַהוּא לֵאמֹר׃ בַּעֲבוּר זֶה עָשָׂה
יְיָ לִי, בְּצֵאתִי מִמִּצְרָיִם.

The final section of *Maggid,* the verbal telling of the Exodus story, is composed of Psalms 113 and 114, which poetically describe our leaving Egypt.

Psalm 113:5–9 states: "Who is like the EverPresent God, our God, enthroned on high looking down upon heaven and earth? God raises the poor out of the dirt and lifts the needy out of the garbage heaps [presumably scavenging for food], to seat them with nobles, with the nobility of God's people. God turns the barren keeper of the household into a happy mother of children. Hallelujah!"

These poetic verses from the psalm resonate with the story of the Exodus from Egypt in the Book of Exodus. God looking down upon the people with commiseration and empathy recalls the verses in Exodus 2:23–25 when God heard their suffering, saw their misery, and remembered the covenantal promise. Raising the poor from the dust and garbage heaps and seating them with nobility recall the third and fourth questions of the *Mah Nishtanah.* As stated previously, God restored not only our ancestors' freedom but also their wealth and dignity when God redeemed them from Egypt. Finally, the transformation of the barren keeper of the household into the happy mother of children recalls the reward God bestowed upon the Hebrew midwives for defying Pharaoh by bestowing "houses" on them. More significantly, it reminds us of the prolific fertility and heroic courage of the Jewish women who built their own households and the "house of Israel" despite Pharaoh's cruel intentions and nefarious decrees.

### Psalm 113

*Hallelujah! Praise, you servants of the EverPresent God, praise the name of the EverPresent God. Blessed be the name of the EverPresent God from this time forth and forever. From the rising of the sun to its setting, the EverPresent God's name is to be praised. High above all nations is the EverPresent God; above the heavens is God's glory. Who*

*is like the EverPresent God, our God, enthroned on high,
looking down upon heaven and earth? God raises the
poor out of the dust and lifts the needy one out of the
garbage heaps, to seat them with nobles, with the
nobility of God's people. God turns the barren wife into
a happy mother of children. Hallelujah!*

הַלְלוּיָהּ. הַלְלוּ עַבְדֵי יְיָ, הַלְלוּ אֶת־שֵׁם יְיָ, יְהִי שֵׁם

יְיָ מְבֹרָךְ מֵעַתָּה וְעַד עוֹלָם: מִמִּזְרַח שֶׁמֶשׁ עַד

מְבוֹאוֹ מְהֻלָּל שֵׁם יְיָ: רָם עַל־כָּל־גּוֹיִם יְיָ, עַל

הַשָּׁמַיִם כְּבוֹדוֹ. מִי כַּיְיָ אֱלֹהֵינוּ הַמַּגְבִּיהִי לָשָׁבֶת,

הַמַּשְׁפִּילִי לִרְאוֹת בַּשָּׁמַיִם וּבָאָרֶץ? מְקִימִי מֵעָפָר

דָּל, מֵאַשְׁפֹּת יָרִים אֶבְיוֹן, לְהוֹשִׁיבִי עִם־נְדִיבִים, עִם

נְדִיבֵי עַמּוֹ. מוֹשִׁיבִי עֲקֶרֶת הַבַּיִת,

אֵם הַבָּנִים שְׂמֵחָה. הַלְלוּיָהּ!

Psalm 114 begins with the words *Betzeit Yisrael miMitzrayim,*
"when Israel left Egypt." Since there is a complete identification by
the participant of the Seder with the Jewish People who left Egypt,
singing this, our people's psalm of praise to God, is tantamount to
singing one's own song of praise to God for being personally
redeemed, *Betzeiti miMitzrayim,* "when I left Egypt," the final two
words of Exodus 13:8—the verse that provides the roadmap of
*Maggid.* (Note: In the Hebrew, by taking the first word of Psalm
114, *Betzeit,* and appending to that word the first letter of the second word, the *yod* of *Yisrael,* we end up with the exact wording of
Exodus 13:8, *Betzeiti miMitzrayim.*)

Needless to say, by concluding *Betzeiti miMitzrayim,* with this
psalm we are also following the motif prescribed by the Mishnah of
"beginning in shame and concluding with praise."

**Psalm 114**

> *When Israel went out of Egypt, Jacob's household from a people of strange speech, Judah became God's sanctuary, Israel, God's kingdom. The sea saw it and fled; the Jordan turned backward. The mountains skipped like rams, and the hills like lambs. Why is it, sea, that you flee? Why, O Jordan, do you turn backward? You mountains, why do you skip like rams? You hills, why do you leap like lambs? O earth, tremble at God's presence, at the presence of the God of Jacob, who turns the rock into a pond of water, the flint into a flowing fountain.*

בְּצֵאת יִשְׂרָאֵל מִמִּצְרָיִם, בֵּית יַעֲקֹב מֵעַם לֹעֵז,

הָיְתָה יְהוּדָה לְקָדְשׁוֹ, יִשְׂרָאֵל מַמְשְׁלוֹתָיו. הַיָּם רָאָה

וַיָּנֹס, הַיַּרְדֵּן יִסֹּב לְאָחוֹר, הֶהָרִים רָקְדוּ כְאֵילִים,

גְּבָעוֹת כִּבְנֵי־צֹאן. מַה־לְּךָ הַיָּם כִּי תָנוּס, הַיַּרְדֵּן

תִּסֹּב לְאָחוֹר, הֶהָרִים תִּרְקְדוּ כְאֵילִים, גְּבָעוֹת

כִּבְנֵי־צֹאן. מִלִּפְנֵי אָדוֹן חוּלִי אָרֶץ, מִלִּפְנֵי אֱלוֹהַּ

יַעֲקֹב, הַהֹפְכִי הַצּוּר אֲגַם־מָיִם, חַלָּמִישׁ

לְמַעְיְנוֹ־מָיִם.

Having interrupted our toast to God in order to sing God's praises for redeeming us from Egypt and from the peril at the Sea, we now conclude our final toast to God in *Maggid*. We raise our cup of wine in prayer and blessing that we actualize our ultimate vision of redemption—joyfully communing with God in the rebuilt Temple in Jerusalem:

*Blessed are You, EverPresent God, our God, Sovereign of the universe, who has redeemed us and our fathers from Egypt and enabled us to reach this night that we may eat matzah and maror. So EverPresent God, our God and God of our ancestors, enable us to reach also the forthcoming holidays and festivals in peace, rejoicing in the rebuilding of Zion Your city, and joyful at Your service. There we will eat of the offerings and Passover sacrifices that will be accepted upon Your altar. We will sing a new hymn of praise to You for our redemption and for our liberation. Blessed are You, EverPresent God, Redeemer of Israel.*

בָּרוּךְ אַתָּה יְיָ, אֱלֹהֵינוּ מֶלֶךְ הָעוֹלָם, אֲשֶׁר גְּאָלָנוּ
וְגָאַל אֶת־אֲבוֹתֵינוּ מִמִּצְרַיִם, וְהִגִּיעָנוּ הַלַּיְלָה הַזֶּה,
לֶאֱכָל־בּוֹ מַצָּה וּמָרוֹר. כֵּן, יְיָ אֱלֹהֵינוּ וֵאלֹהֵי
אֲבוֹתֵינוּ, יַגִּיעֵנוּ לְמוֹעֲדִים וְלִרְגָלִים אֲחֵרִים, הַבָּאִים
לִקְרָאתֵנוּ לְשָׁלוֹם, שְׂמֵחִים בְּבִנְיַן עִירֶךָ וְשָׂשִׂים
בַּעֲבוֹדָתֶךָ, וְנֹאכַל שָׁם מִן הַזְּבָחִים וּמִן הַפְּסָחִים
אֲשֶׁר יַגִּיעַ דָּמָם עַל קִיר מִזְבַּחֲךָ לְרָצוֹן, וְנוֹדֶה לְךָ
שִׁיר חָדָשׁ עַל גְּאֻלָּתֵנוּ וְעַל פְּדוּת נַפְשֵׁנוּ. בָּרוּךְ
אַתָּה יְיָ, גָּאַל יִשְׂרָאֵל.

# Eating the Meal of Freedom in the House of Slavery

## Are We Free Yet?

Two events concluded *Maggid:* first, Psalm 114 told the story of the splitting of the Sea; then, the blessing that followed and wrapped up *Maggid* asked God to enable us to experience God's redemption and acceptance of our offerings *(LeRatzon)* in the rebuilt Temple in Jerusalem. Since *Maggid* is the verbal microcosm of the whole Seder, those same two elements will consummate the kinesthetic telling of the Seder in *Hallel* and *Nirtzah,* as well as the visual telling of the Seder with the *zeroa (netuyah)* and *betzah* on the Seder plate.

As we transition from *Maggid,* the verbal telling, to the second cup of wine, which will launch us into the kinesthetic reenactment of the last meal in Egypt, there is an intentional ambivalence built into the structure of the Haggadah as to where we are in the Exodus story. Put simply: as we sit down to eat our meal, are we free yet? After all, in *Maggid,* we have verbally told the entire story of our transformation from slavery and infanticide to freedom and redemption. Yet, as we sit down to eat our meal, we are still physically in Egypt, the house of bondage. What kind of freedom is that?

Actually it is a type of freedom. Although the Jewish People

121

were still physically in Egypt, the plagues had unfettered them from the rigor of their previous workload. For instance, the Torah had told us that the onerous labor through which the Jews were enslaved consisted of "all sorts of work in the field" (Exod. 1:14). After the plagues of hail and locusts, which obliterated the entire agricultural output of the country, there were no more crops for the Jews to tend in the fields (Exod. 10:15). Nor was there straw for them to pick to build Pharaoh's store-cities (Exod. 5:7ff). In other words, while the Jewish People were formally still slaves, they no longer had to perform the most burdensome types of slave labor. This is what God had promised Moses in the first term of redemption: "I will take you out from under the burden/suffering of Egypt" (Exod. 6:6).

Psychologically as well, as the Jews were preparing to sit down to eat their Passover sacrifices, they felt less dread of their Egyptian masters. After all, the commandment for each family to slaughter a lamb, one of the idols worshiped by the Egyptians, and smear the blood on their doorposts and lintels "in the face" of their Egyptian masters was an act of political defiance and, to some degree, of psychic freedom. Through their actions they were replacing their servitude to the Egyptians with their service of God. And yet having said all this … they were still slaves, surrounded by their Egyptian tormentors, who, they knew, certainly did not harbor warm feelings toward them. And yes, they were still somewhat afraid—a fear that would become manifest when they reached the shores of the Sea of Reeds.

This tension between being both free and not free at this point in the Seder is expressed in a difference in opinion in the Talmud (*Pesachim* 116b) as to when *Maggid* ends. Beit Shammai says it ends with the first psalm of the *Hallel*, Psalm 113, which begins *Halleluyah*, "Praise God." Beit Hillel says that we end *Maggid* with the second psalm, Psalm 114, which begins *Betzeit Yisrael miMitzrayim*, "When Israel left Egypt." The *Tosefta* (*Pesachim* 10:6 cited in *Talmud Yerushalmi, Pesachim* 10:5) articulates Beit Shammai's reasoning for prescribing that the latter paragraph not be included in *Maggid* and be recited only after the meal: "Have the (Israelites) already left Egypt that we speak of the Exodus from

Egypt in the past tense?" Apparently, Beit Shammai felt that the second psalm, which praises God for the splitting of the Sea, should be recited only after we have reenacted the final dinner in Egypt through the eating of our Passover meal. It was only after the Israelites consumed their Passover meal, left Egypt, arrived at the Sea of Reeds, and saw their former Egyptian oppressors drowned in the Sea that they sang a joyous song of praise to God. Similarly, we should first eat our Passover meal, symbolically cross the Sea of Reeds to freedom, and only then sing our song of praise to God for splitting the Sea—that is, Psalm 114 (and the rest of *Hallel*). In other words, according to Beit Shammai, the verbal telling should follow the kinesthetic reexperiencing of the Jewish People's journey out of Egypt into total freedom—formal and informal. Beit Hillel, in contrast, argued that the entire story of the Exodus—including the splitting of the Sea and the acceptance by God of the Jewish People symbolized by the resting of the Divine Presence in the Tabernacle—should be verbally told in *Maggid* and then kinesthetically retold and relived after the meal. For Beit Hillel, as the Jews prepared to sit down at the Seder, they were already "free enough." Our Haggadot follow the opinion of Beit Hillel.

The tension between the Jews being both free and not free, between the asymmetry of the verbal telling (in which the splitting of the Sea and the worship in the Tabernacle/Temple have already been communicated before the upcoming meal) and the kinesthetic telling of the Seder (in which the splitting of the Sea and the worship in the Tabernacle/Temple will be symbolically reenacted only after the meal) underlies another difference of opinion in the Talmud. This argument concerns whether and when one should recline in drinking the four cups of wine, the second cup of which we are about to consume.

*Mishnah Pesachim* 10:1 states that even a pauper should recline when eating in order to demonstrate his status as a free person. The Talmud (Tractate *Pesachim* 108a) then records a difference of opinion as to whether one is required to recline, not when eating, but when drinking the four cups of wine. There were two traditions cited in the name of Rabbi Nachman. According to one tradition, Rabbi Nachman required that one recline while drinking the four cups of wine, while according to another tradition, he did not require that one recline when drinking the four cups of wine. The Talmud then reconciles the two traditions by saying that both traditions are correct; however, one tradition refers to two of the cups, while the other tradition refers to the other two cups. There remains, however, a difference of opinion as to which tradition applies to which cups. One opinion is that Rabbi Nachman required that we recline to symbolize our freedom only for the first two cups, since we achieve freedom during the verbal telling of *Maggid* in between these two cups. The second opinion argues that we lean as a symbol of our freedom only for the last two cups, since in the kinesthetic Seder, we are not freed until after we recite *Barekh,* the Grace after Meals, which concludes the final meal in Egypt and the commencement of our journey out of Egypt. Only after being freed from Egypt can we recline when drinking the third and fourth cups. Apparently, this latter opinion reflects the interpretation of this book, that the order of the kinesthetic Seder mirrors the order of the experience of the Jewish People in Egypt. According to this latter interpretation of Rabbi Nachman, since we are not totally liberated until we physically exit Egypt, the first two cups, drunk while we are still in Egypt, should not be drunk in a relaxed, reclining position.

Practically, because the Talmud is unable to definitively determine Rabbi Nachman's opinion, and because of the proclivity of the Rabbis to be as inclusive as possible in regard to differing opinions regarding the Seder, the Talmud resolves the argument by ruling that we lean to the left for all four cups.

## The Second Cup:
## Setting the Stage for the Meal of Freedom

We toasted God for remembering the covenant and heeding our suffering at the commencement of the redemptive narrative in the middle of *Maggid;* we toasted God again as we approached the conclusion of the redemptive narrative, the end of *Maggid.* The blessing over the second cup of wine concludes the toast, focusing our minds to that moment when the Jewish People were poised, after hundreds of years of Egyptian domination and control, to eat their last meal in Egypt and begin, at last, their journey of freedom.

At the outset of the Passover Seder we suggested that each of the four cups of wine served as "time machines," helping to focus our consciousness on a different point in time of the Exodus narrative and corresponding to the four progressive promises of redemption that God spoke to Moses in Exodus 6:6–8:

> "Therefore say to the Jewish People, I am God, and I will take you out from under the suffering of Egypt and I will rescue you from their enslavement, and I will redeem you with an outstretched arm and with great judgments. And I will take you for Me as a people, and I will be for you as God, and you will know that I am God, your God, who takes you out from under the suffering of Egypt."

The first cup chronicled the history of the Jewish People from the time they descended to Egypt, through their enslavement and God's bringing of the ten plagues; it corresponded to the first promise of redemption: taking them out from under the suffering of Egypt.

We are now transported with the second cup to the final hours of the Jewish People's stay in Egypt, their and our partaking of the last meal in Egypt, which corresponds to the second promise of redemption: rescuing the people from slave labor. As the Jewish people ate their meal of freedom on the last night of their sojourn in Egypt, their slavery was relegated to a memory. Never again, they hoped, would they be enslaved to their Egyptian taskmasters.

We raise the second cup of wine and bless God, who has created the fruit of the vine and brought us to the final meal in Egypt:

> *Blessed are You, EverPresent God, our God, Sovereign of the universe, who creates the fruit of the vine.*

בָּרוּךְ אַתָּה יְיָ, אֱלֹהֵינוּ מֶלֶךְ הָעוֹלָם, בּוֹרֵא פְּרִי הַגָּפֶן.

The next eight items in the Seder, from *Rochtzah* to *Barekh*, are a virtual reenactment of the momentous final meal of the Jewish People in Egypt.

## *Rochtzah*/רָחְצָה

Unlike the second item of the Seder, *U-Rechatz,* in which we washed our hands without a blessing to symbolically prepare our bodies to enter sacred space, the sixth item of the Seder, *Rochtzah,* prepares us to eat the matzah and the Passover meal. Since bread, even poor man's bread, is the "staff of life," we ritually wash our hands and recite the appropriate blessing to help focus our consciousness on the precious gift of life that bread symbolizes.

> *Blessed are You, EverPresent God, our God, Sovereign of the universe, who has sanctified us with Your commandments, and commanded us concerning the washing of the hands.*

בָּרוּךְ אַתָּה יְיָ, אֱלֹהֵינוּ מֶלֶךְ הָעוֹלָם, אֲשֶׁר קִדְּשָׁנוּ בְּמִצְוֹתָיו, וְצִוָּנוּ עַל נְטִילַת יָדָיִם.

## *Motzi, Matzah*/מַצָּה .מוֹצִיא

When God conveys the commandments to Moses and Aaron regarding the eating of the final meal of the Jewish People in Egypt, God says:

"They shall eat the meat [of the Passover sacrifice] during that night, roasted over fire; with matzot on bitter herbs shall they eat it."

Exodus 12:8

Since our meal on Passover night is the reenactment of the final dinner in Egypt and since at that meal the matzot were mentioned before the bitter herbs, we begin the meal by reciting the blessing over bread. Whether matzah is the bread of poverty or the bread of freedom, it is still a form of bread, the staff of life.

> *Blessed are You, EverPresent God, our God, Sovereign of the universe, who brings forth bread from the earth.*

בָּרוּךְ אַתָּה יְיָ, אֱלֹהֵינוּ מֶלֶךְ הָעוֹלָם, הַמּוֹצִיא לֶחֶם מִן הָאָרֶץ.

This is followed immediately by the blessing over the specific commandment to eat matzah.

> *Blessed are You, EverPresent God, our God, Sovereign of the universe, who has sanctified us with Your commandments, and commanded us concerning the eating of matzah.*

בָּרוּךְ אַתָּה יְיָ, אֱלֹהֵינוּ מֶלֶךְ הָעוֹלָם, אֲשֶׁר קִדְּשָׁנוּ בְּמִצְוֹתָיו וְצִוָּנוּ עַל אֲכִילַת מַצָּה.

Although the Jewish People were still in Egypt, the house of bondage, as they sat down to eat this meal, the slave labor of the Jewish people had ceased. Therefore, as we sit down in solidarity with our ancestors to eat our meal, the matzah is eaten in a reclining position as a symbol of our freedom from slavery.

## Maror/מָרוֹר

Next in the biblical verse commanding the Jewish People to feast on the Passover sacrifice (Exod. 12:8) is the mentioning of eating the *maror*, bitter herbs. In the first chapter of the Book of Exodus, we were told, *Vayemareru et chayeihem baavodah kashah, bechomer uvilveinim uvekhol avodah basadeh*, "And [the Egyptians] embittered the [Jewish People's] lives, with mortar and bricks and all the work of the fields" (Exod. 1:14). Since the embitterment took place within the context of their work in "mortar and bricks," we dip the bitter herbs, representing the embitterment, into the *charoset*, representing their toil in the mortar. We recite the blessing over the eating of the bitter herbs but do not recline while eating the *maror*, since it reminds us of our bitter toil rather than our freedom.

> *Blessed are You, EverPresent God, our God, Sovereign of the universe, who has sanctified us with Your commandments, and commanded us concerning the eating of the bitter herbs.*

בָּרוּךְ אַתָּה יְיָ, אֱלֹהֵינוּ מֶלֶךְ הָעוֹלָם, אֲשֶׁר קִדְּשָׁנוּ בְּמִצְוֹתָיו וְצִוָּנוּ עַל אֲכִילַת מָרוֹר.

## Korekh/כּוֹרֵךְ

The biblical verse that instructed the Jewish People in Egypt to bring the Passover sacrifice stated that the sacrifice was to be eaten on matzot and *maror* (Exod. 12:8). Although this instruction might have been interpreted loosely as meaning that they should eat the Passover sacrifice along with matzot and *maror*, the rabbinic sage Hillel, who lived over a thousand years after the Exodus, during the Second Temple period in Jerusalem, interpreted this verse literally to mean that these elements should be mounted on top of each other in sandwich-like fashion: *korekh* means "sandwiching."

As we saw during the *Maggid* section and as we will see again during the *Hallel* section, the Haggadah took an inclusive approach and tried to incorporate divergent opinions into their ritual practice and lore. Although there are no sacrifices today and therefore no meat eaten in this sandwich, in order to include Hillel's opinion the Haggadah instructs us to take two pieces of matzah (the Torah speaks of matzah in the plural), place bitter herbs dipped in *charoset* between them, and verbally recall Hillel's interpretation before biting into the Hillel sandwich. Since *Korekh* combines the matzah, now a symbol of freedom, with *maror*, a symbol of bitter toil, and since the Exodus story is about the triumph of freedom over slavery, *Korekh* is eaten in a reclining position. We declare the following statement:

> To remind us of the Temple, we do as Hillel did in Temple times; he combined matzah and maror in a sandwich and ate them together, to fulfill what is written in the Torah: "They shall eat it on unleavened bread and bitter herbs."

זֵכֶר לְמִקְדָּשׁ כְּהִלֵּל, כֵּן עָשָׂה הִלֵּל בִּזְמַן שֶׁבֵּית הַמִּקְדָּשׁ הָיָה קַיָם. הָיָה כּוֹרֵךְ פֶּסַח מַצָּה וּמָרוֹר וְאוֹכֵל בְּיַחַד, לְקַיֵּם מַה שֶׁנֶּאֱמַר: עַל־מַצּוֹת וּמְרוֹרִים יֹאכְלֻהוּ.

## *Shulchan Orekh*/שֻׁלְחָן עוֹרֵךְ

In the Book of Exodus, for their last meal in Egypt the families of Israel were instructed to feast on the Passover sacrifice:

> "Speak to the community of Israel and say ... every man must take a lamb for each extended family, a lamb for each household.... The lamb shall be a flawless, one-year-old male.... The entire community will slaughter the animals.

They will take some of the blood and place it on the door-posts and on the lintel above the door of the houses in which they will eat the sacrifices. And they will eat the meat during the night, roasted over fire, with matzot and *maror....* This is the Passover offering to God. And I will cross through the land of Egypt on that night and I will slay every first-born in the land of Egypt, man and beast ... I God. But the blood will be a sign for you on the houses in which you are staying, and I will see the blood and I will pass over you; so there will not be any plague among you when I strike Egypt."

Exodus 12:3–13

The Passover sacrifice was the first time that the Jewish People were instructed to offer and partake of an animal sacrifice. The word "sacrifice" in Hebrew is *korban,* which is better translated as meaning "closeness offering." The function of the *korban* was to do just that: to engender a closer relationship between the person bringing the offering and God. The *korban* did that in two ways: first, by the life of the animal acting as a surrogate offering to God for the life of the person bringing the offering; second, by acting as a gift expressing the emotions and feelings that the person bringing the gift wished to communicate to God, the gift's recipient.

The Jewish People in Egypt did not yet have a Tabernacle or a Temple to which they could bring their "closeness offering" or an altar on which they could offer it. Instead, God instructed them to transform their physical homes into mini-temples and symbolically make the entrance to their homes substitute altars. In the Tabernacle, when someone brought an animal sacrifice, the blood of the sacrifice would be sprayed on the corners of the altar to symbolize that their lifeblood belonged to God. The sacrifice would then be consumed and/or eaten within the precincts of the Temple, sharing an intimate meal with God, as it were, at God's own table. So too, for this Passover offering, the heads of each

Jewish household sprayed the blood on the four corners of the entrance to their homes to communicate to God that the lifeblood of everyone in their homes belonged to God. The blood of the Passover sacrifice therefore served as a surrogate for their own lives and spared them from the deadly plague that afflicted the Egyptians. They then sat down that evening and ate the Passover offering in their homes, symbolically sharing their family meal with God at God's makeshift table.

The Passover offerings brought in Egypt by the Jewish People were also a type of gift, a way of prospectively expressing the gratitude they were feeling for their pending redemption from Egypt. In the Temple, such a gratitude offering was designated generically with the name *korban todah,* "a closeness offering of thanksgiving." Like the Passover sacrifice in Egypt, these gratitude offerings were also offered with matzot and were accompanied by the singing of *Hallel,* psalms of praise. Later on in Temple times, in addition to the Passover offering, the families of Israel also feasted at their Seders on the *korban chagigah,* the special pilgrimage sacrifice brought in honor of the holiday.

In our time, we embrace the spirit of the meal eaten on the Jewish People's final night in Egypt and later in Temple times by embarking on a sumptuous feast at this juncture in the Seder. The Mishnah insists that two cooked foods, of whatever sort, be eaten— one to remind us of the Passover offering and one to remind us of the holiday offering (according to Rav Yosef's rationale for the Mishnah's opinion offered in Tractate *Pesachim* 114b). Since eating the main course of our meal presumably reenacts the eating of the Passover offering, some people have the custom of eating a hard-boiled egg at this point to reenact the consumption of the holiday sacrifice (see also my notes on the *zeroa* [p. 12] and on the *betzah,* the roasted egg, on the Seder plate). Regardless of which cooked foods one eats, what is mandated is that the meal that concludes with the *afikoman* be satiating, presumably to recall the final dinner in Egypt, which was one of the few satiating meals that the Jews ate in Egypt's house of bondage.

## Tzafun/צָפוּן

We now remove the "hidden one," the broken slice of matzah that was wrapped up, and we break it into small pieces and eat it. This matzah represents the revelation of Moses as the redeemer of Israel who is about to lead his people out of Egypt. Moses is revealed only now because it is only at this point that Moses can accomplish God's mission: to physically lead the Jewish people out of Egypt. To partake of this matzah is to ingest Moses's spirit of leadership and redemption. In eating of the matzah each of us becomes empowered to contribute to the redemption of Israel.

What are some of Moses's qualities that we try to symbolically assimilate through the eating of the matzah of *Tzafun?* What made his leadership so remarkable? First, his deep empathy and emotional identification with his Israelite brethren: slaying the Egyptian overseer who was beating one of his brothers to death even though he was a protected Egyptian prince at the time. Second, his passion for justice: intervening in a quarrel between two Jews to stop the aggressor, and rescuing the daughters of Jethro from a gang of bullying shepherds. Third, his courage to speak truth to power, no matter the potential consequences: confronting Pharaoh over and over again to free his people, confronting the Jewish People with their sin of the Golden Calf, and confronting even God when God wished to destroy the Jewish People after that event. Fourth, his spiritual vision and intimate relationship with God: the only person in the Bible to whom God spoke "face to face as a person speaks with his friend" (Exod. 3:11), and the one who received the Ten Commandments and the Torah at Mount Sinai. Fifth, his inspiring oratory despite his apparent speech impediment: leading the Jewish People in song after the splitting of the Sea, inspiring the Jewish People to keep God's Torah, and delivering the amazing soliloquy that constitutes the Book of Deuteronomy. Sixth, his passionate prayers on behalf of the Jewish People at the shore of the Sea of Reeds and on his sister's behalf when she was stricken with leprosy even after she had personally maligned him. Seventh, his perseverance, fortitude, and follow-through in the difficult and complex task of not only getting the Jews out of Egypt but getting Egypt out of the Jews—devoting the last forty years of his life to shepherding his people through the desert despite the people's frequent lack of gratitude. Finally, his personal humility and selflessness, knowing when it was time for him to step aside and graciously grooming a capable successor, Joshua, to lead the people after he was gone. No wonder that the "Yigdal," a liturgical poem recited daily in traditional morning services, states, *Lo kam beYisrael keMosheh od,* "Never again will one arise like Moses." While none of us can ever be quite like him, we aspire to internalize his many redeeming qualities by partaking of the matzah of *Tzafun.*[1]

After the destruction of the Temple, when the Passover sacrifice could no longer be brought, the Rabbis designated this broken piece of matzah to be a substitute for the Passover sacrifice. Since the Rabbis were intent on keeping Moses hidden in the Haggadah, the Rabbis projected onto the broken matzah the symbol of the Passover sacrifice, the next most potent symbol, aside from Moses, of the Exodus redemption. Eating this matzah became the surrogate for eating the Passover sacrifice. For post-Temple Rabbinic Judaism, the broken state of the matzah may have also symbolized God's "broken house" (the destroyed Temple), in which the Passover sacrifice could no longer be offered.

*Mishnah Pesachim* 10:4 states that "one should not eat anything after the Passover sacrifice *afikoman,*" meaning by going out after the meal to visit one's neighbors and revel in the night. A likely reason for the Mishnah's ruling is to identify the participants at our own Seders with the Jews in Egypt, who were not permitted to leave their homes on the night of Passover, lest they be struck down with the plague of the first-born. Since the matzah of *Tzafun* is the last item of food eaten at the Seder, the *Tzafun,* by association with the Passover sacrifice and the word *afikoman,* has become known colloquially as "the *afikoman,*" about as strange a naming etymology as one could imagine! The name *afikoman* stuck and is now universally used to denote the *Tzafun.*

## Barekh/בָּרֵךְ

With the meal completed, the Grace after Meals *(Birkat HaMazon)* is recited. This too has a source in the biblical narrative. After the Jewish People completed their final meal in Egypt, Pharaoh came running to Moses and Aaron and said:

> "Get up, and get out from among my people—you and the children of Israel! Go and worship God as you spoke. Take your sheep and cattle, as you said, and go! And bless [*u'veirachtem*] me too!"
>
> (Exod. 12:31–32)

Since Pharaoh is asking Moses and the Jewish People to bless him too, it indicates that the Jews were blessing someone else—undoubtedly God, their Protector from the plague of the first-born and their Redeemer from Egyptian slavery.

Hence, we too reenact this part of the Exodus story by blessing and praising God in *Birkat HaMazon,* the "Blessing after Meals." Although the Blessing after Meals on Passover night is nearly indistinguishable from the blessing of the rest of the year, nevertheless the words that thank God for "taking us out … from the land of Egypt and redeeming us from the house of bondage" (from the second paragraph of the Grace after Meals) resonate with a powerful immediacy as we recite them on the night of the Exodus.

Having concluded the final dinner with the recitation of Grace after Meals, it is time for us to exit Egypt and move on to the next stop in our journey. Although the third cup of wine is ritually linked in the Mishnah to the conclusion of Grace after Meals, symbolically, the third cup sets the stage for the events at the Sea of Reeds.

# Reenacting the Saga at the Sea

## The Third Cup/כּוֹס שְׁלִישִׁית

After the Jewish People left Egypt, the next milestone on their journey was God's showdown with the Egyptian army at the Sea of Reeds. The Jewish people may have assumed that having left the house of bondage they were now free of their Egyptian tormentors, but events were soon to challenge their assumption. The reason for this challenge was quite simple: Moses never asked Pharaoh to let the Jews go free! Contrary to the "Let my people go!" line that Charlton Heston, playing Moses, uttered to Yul Brenner, playing Pharaoh, in the movie *The Ten Commandments,* the biblical Moses said to Pharaoh in God's name: "Let My people go on a three-day journey into the desert that they may worship Me" (Exod. 5:1–3). Never, in all of Moses's subsequent confrontations and negotiations with Pharaoh, did Moses deviate from that relatively modest request for a three-day journey to offer religious worship. Pharaoh's expectation, when he came running to Moses after the plague of the first-born and told him to take his people out, was that they would all be returning after they finished their religious holiday: "Go and *worship* God *as you spoke*" (Exod. 12:32).

But after several days passed without the Jewish people heading back toward Egypt, Pharaoh got wind of the fact that the Jewish People were not just going for a three-day pilgrimage in the desert to worship their Deity, as Moses had repeatedly requested. Suddenly he realized that when the Jewish People left Egypt they intended to leave forever—the people had escaped (Exod. 14:5)! Feeling deceived, Pharaoh gathered his 600 finest chariots and horsemen in the lead and, along with the rest of his legions, went in hot pursuit of the fleeing Israelites. Little did he know that he was being deceived yet again—walking right into a trap deliberately set by God (Exod. 14:1–9). The third cup of wine takes us to the final confrontation between God and Moses on one side and Pharaoh and his army on the other at the Sea of Reeds.

Once more the Haggadah connects us to the four promises of redemption that God made to Moses in Exodus 6:6–8:

> "Therefore say to the Jewish People, I am God, and I will take you out from under the suffering of Egypt and I will rescue you from their enslavement, and I will redeem you with an outstretched arm and with great judgments. And I will take you for Me as a people, and I will be for you as God, and you will know that I am God, your God, who takes you out from under the suffering of Egypt."

The first cup corresponded to the first promise of redemption: taking them out from under the suffering of Egypt. The second cup, we said, corresponded to the Jewish people's final meal in Egypt and God's second promise of redemption: rescuing the people from slave labor on the night that their slavery was relegated to a memory.

The third cup now comes along and transports us in our time machines to the confrontation at the Sea. It corresponds to the promise of being "redeemed with an outstretched arm and with great judgments." Why does this promise refer to the miracles at the Sea? Because the miracles were done before the eyes of the Jewish People with Moses acting as God's extension, as God's "extended arm." In fact, twice in the story of the splitting of the Sea, God tells Moses to stretch out his arm to perform the miracles, and twice more the Torah tells us that Moses extended his arm to perform God's miracles:

> And God said to Moses, "...Lift up your rod and stretch out your arm over the sea and split it so that the Israelites may march into the sea bed on dry ground...." And Moses extended his arm over the sea and God drove back the sea with a strong east wind all night and transformed the sea to dry ground and split the sea."
>
> Exodus 14:15–16, 14:21

> And God said to Moses, "Stretch out your arm over the sea and return the waters on the Egyptians, on their chariots and cavalry." And Moses stretched out his arm over the sea, and the sea returned to its normal condition toward dawn.
>
> Exodus 14:26–27

Moses extending his arm with God's staff, the physical embodiment of God's extended arm, redeemed the Jewish People from the fear and panic of being reenslaved by Pharaoh's army. In the process, it brought a "measure-for-measure" judgment on the Egyptians, who had "extended their arms" to seize, throw, and drown the Jewish male infants in their sea. In God's world of justice, the punishment perfectly fit the crime.

We raise the third cup and bless God for creating the fruit of the vine and transporting us to the shores of the Sea:

*Blessed are You, EverPresent God our God, Sovereign of the universe, who creates the fruit of the vine.*

בָּרוּךְ אַתָּה יְיָ, אֱלֹהֵינוּ מֶלֶךְ הָעוֹלָם, בּוֹרֵא פְּרִי הַגָּפֶן.

## Shefoch Chamatkha

One of the most uncomfortable texts for North American Jews to recite in the Passover Haggadah is the paragraph that begins with the words *Shefoch Chamatkha,* "Pour out Your wrath." The wording of the paragraph sounds politically incorrect and vindictive, to say the least. Coming in between the grateful blessings of the Grace after Meals and the recitation of psalms of praise from the *Hallel,* its angry tone seems strangely out of place.

Oddly combined with the vengeful and angry nature of the prayer is the mysterious invisible appearance of Elijah the Prophet, for whom we fill the cup of Elijah and open the door at this point in the Seder. (Elijah the Prophet, it will be recalled, lived in the Land of Israel several hundred years after the Exodus during the reign of King Ahab and Queen Jezebel.) What are this furious prayer and Elijah the Prophet doing here? Finally, why are we opening the door for him at this point in the Seder?

To understand the significance and placement of this prayer at this point in the Seder, we must return to the story of the Exodus on the Jewish People's last night in Egypt. The Jewish People had been forbidden by Moses to leave their homes all night in order not to be struck down in the plague of the first-born. After enduring the tenth plague, Pharaoh finally relents to Moses's demands and urges Moses and Aaron to immediately lead the Jews out of Egypt. On one level, the opening of the door is simply the symbol of the Jewish People being given permission to leave their homes and exit the Land of Egypt at noon on the fifteenth day of the Hebrew month of Nisan.

The Jewish People, exiting Egypt and traveling for several days in the desert, are then told by God to change direction. By doing so, they feign being lost in the wilderness and signal to Pharaoh's spies that they are lost and confused, ripe to be recaptured by an angry, recalcitrant Pharaoh. Pharaoh falls for God's trap and goes racing with his entire army after the Jews, pinning them against the Sea of Reeds, where they are camping on the beach. Beholding Pharaoh's forces descending upon them, the Jewish People go into a panic:

> The people said to Moses: "Were there a lack of graves in Egypt that you took us to die in the desert? What have you done to us, taking us out of Egypt? Is this not the very thing that we said to you in Egypt, 'Let us be, and we will serve the Egyptians, for it is better for us to serve the Egyptians than to die in the desert!'" But Moses said to the people, "Have no fear! Stand by and watch the deliverance that the EverPresent God will do for you today; for the Egyptians whom you see today you will never see again. The EverPresent God will battle for you. You hold your peace!"
>
> Then the EverPresent God said to Moses, "Why do you [singular] cry out to me? Just tell the Israelites to go forward. And you, lift up your rod and stretch out your arm over the sea and split it, so that the Israelites may march into the sea bed on dry ground."
>
> Exodus 14:11–16

The Israelites are understandably frightened. Moses tries to calm them down by telling them to stand still and assuring them that God will do the fighting for them. That is all well and good, but God has promised nothing of the sort! On the parchment in the actual Torah scroll, however, there then appears a blank space following Moses's words to the people, "The EverPresent God will battle for you. You hold your peace!" and prior to God's response to Moses, "Why do you [singular] cry out to me?"

Apparently, in the moment represented by this blank space, Moses turned to God and cried out in prayer that God make good on Moses's promise. Although the Torah does not tell us exactly what Moses said to God, he was clearly engaged in some sort of intensely passionate prayer, because God interrupts him in a reproving tone: "What are you crying out to me for? Go speak to the people and tell them to start moving!"

What was Moses's prayer? The Torah does not tell us, but the prayer of *Shefoch Chamatkha* seems to be an awfully good, imaginary fit.

The prayer, composed of disparate verses from Psalms 79:6–7 and 69:25 and Lamentations 3:66, does not appear uniformly in Haggadot until early medieval times, although variations of it appear earlier. Its placement at this point of the Haggadah is nevertheless strikingly appropriate to the saga at the Sea of Reeds. *Shefoch Chamatkha* begins with the word "pour," a verb that is used a second time in the same five-line prayer. The Torah tells us twice in the biblical narrative that when God split the sea, the waters stood at attention as walls on the left and on the right. Anticipating the miracle that God was going to do, the Haggadah has Moses, in effect, asking God to "pour" the two walls of waters over the Egyptians.

> *"Pour out Your wrath upon the nations that do not know You and upon the kingdoms that do not call out in Your name. For they have devoured Jacob and have desolated God's abode. Pour out Your rage upon them and let Your fury overtake them. Pursue them in anger and annihilate them from under the heavens of the EverPresent God."*

שְׁפֹךְ חֲמָתְךָ אֶל־הַגּוֹיִם אֲשֶׁר לֹא יְדָעוּךָ,

וְעַל־מַמְלָכוֹת אֲשֶׁר בְּשִׁמְךָ לֹא קָרָאוּ. כִּי אָכַל

אֶת־יַעֲקֹב, וְאֶת־נָוֵהוּ הֵשַׁמּוּ. שְׁפָךְ־עֲלֵיהֶם זַעְמֶךָ,

וַחֲרוֹן אַפְּךָ יַשִּׂיגֵם. תִּרְדֹּף בְּאַף וְתַשְׁמִידֵם מִתַּחַת

שְׁמֵי יְיָ.

How do we know it is the ancient Egyptians, the tormentors of the Jews, toward whom this furious prayer is directed? Note how the enemy is described: "... upon the nations that do not know You and upon the kingdoms that do not call out in Your name." Recall that when Moses first approached Pharaoh with the message from God that the king of Egypt should free the Jewish People for a three-day holiday to serve God, Pharaoh's dismissive response was, "Who is the EverPresent God whose voice I should heed and let Israel go? I do not know the EverPresent God, and I will not let Israel go!" (Exod. 5:2). The one who did not know God was Pharaoh, the king of the Egyptian nation. It was Pharaoh and his people who devoured Jacob by drowning the baby boys and enslaving the entire nation. It was Pharaoh who devastated this glorious abode, the homes of the Jewish people among whom God dwelled. (See also Psalm 91:15, "I am with him in his suffering.")

There are also striking similarities between the words used in the *Shefoch Chamatkha* and the subsequent Song at the Sea. For instance, in the Song at the Sea, the Egyptians say, "I will pursue [*erdof*], I will capture, I will divide up the spoils" (Exod. 15:9). In the *Shefoch Chamatkha*, we use the same verb to pray that God will preempt their intentions with a measure-for-measure response, "Pursue [*tirdof*] them in anger and annihilate them." In the Song at the Sea, the Jewish People proclaim, "This is my God and I will glorify [*ve-anveihu*] God" (Exod. 15:2). In *Shefoch Chamatkha*, we say, "And God's glorious abode [*naveihu*] they made desolate." In both the Song at the Sea and the *Shefoch Chamatkha* the words *charon* and *apcha* are used to denote or to pray for God's fury against the Egyptian legions. Apparently, then, the *Shefoch Chamatkha* prayer was placed here to read between the lines of the biblical text and give expression to Moses's emotional supplication to God at the shores of the Sea.

## Why Elijah?

So why has Jewish folklore brought Elijah into the story at this point in the Seder? Why do we open the door for him and fill his cup with wine? The reason is that the figure of Elijah is another "front" for the real, albeit hidden, hero of the Exodus: Moses. Like

Moses, Elijah was an outsider to his people. Like Moses, Elijah stood up before the evil monarchs of his age and spoke truth to power. Like Moses, who stood upon Mount Sinai and confronted the idolatrous worship by the Jewish People at the Golden Calf, Elijah stood upon Mount Carmel and confronted the idolatrous prophets of Baal. Like Moses, Elijah received a personal revelation from God on Mount Sinai after a forty-day and forty-night trek in the desert as a political fugitive (I Kings 18–19).

In the narrative of the Torah, Moses was so powerful a spiritual figure that he literally had to don a mask to enable him to communicate with the Jewish People. While Moses could not see God's face (Exod. 33:20), the Jewish People in the Torah could not see Moses's face; it was so radiant that it would have blinded the people (Exod. 34:30–35). Hence, the Haggadah's "masking" of Moses in the guise of Elijah the Prophet, his typological clone, should come as no surprise to us.

Elijah is Moses in disguise. We open the door and summon him to the Seder because, like Moses, he is the jealous prophet of God and defender of the Jewish People who prayed to God and caused the destruction of the radical evildoers of his time. Without the destruction of radical evil there is no possibility for God's Presence to be manifest and for the experience of redemption. This was true for Moses, who had to squash the rebellion of the Golden Calf before God's Redemptive Presence could come and dwell among the Jewish People; it was true for Elijah, who first defeated the false prophets of the Canaanite god Baal before experiencing God's personal revelation at Mount Sinai; and it is true in our time as well. Only when those who seek to destroy us are conclusively defeated are our people able to breathe the air of freedom and redemption. What better surrogate for the hidden Moses than Elijah, who faced down the radical evildoers of his time and whom we invite to drink from the cup of deliverance and redemption that God now brings to the Jewish People?

# Hallel/הַלֵּל

Just as *Shefoch Chamatkha* represents Moses's prayer for revenge and redemption at the Sea, the *Hallel* represents Moses's and the Jewish People's song of praise at the Sea. The Talmud asks: Who were the first ones to recite *Hallel,* praise to God? Rabbi Yosi says in the name of his son, Elazar: "Moses and the Jewish People when they emerged from the split sea" (Tractate *Pesachim* 117a). *Hallel* is a reenactment of the song of praise with which the Jewish People burst forth when God destroyed their Egyptian tormentors before their very eyes. For this reason, this entire section, or as much as possible, should be sung.[1]

Why did God feel compelled to stage the entire chain of events that led to the drowning of the Egyptian legions at the Sea of Reeds? What was the point of performing yet another miracle that punished the Egyptians? And why did the Jewish People, and we in solidarity with them, burst forth in song? The point of the splitting of the Sea was to free the Jewish People not from the land of Egypt, but from their fear of the Egyptian tormentors. While the Jewish People may have witnessed the aftermath of the ten plagues, they did not witness the actual plagues as they were taking place. During the ten plagues they were sequestered in Goshen, and for the tenth plague they were further confined in their own homes. Since "seeing is believing," the Jewish People did not yet believe—not in God, not in Moses, and not fully in their own freedom, as their panic on the shore of the Sea makes clear. It was only after they witnessed Pharaoh's legions drowned in the Sea before their very eyes that they came to trust God and Moses and believe in the reality of their own freedom. Their song at the Sea can be seen as their cathartic expression of their newfound sense of freedom:

> The EverPresent God saved the Jewish People on that day from the hand of the Egyptians, and the Jews saw the Egyptians dead on the shores of the Sea. And the Jewish People saw the powerful hand that the EverPresent God

had used against the Egyptians, and the People saw [literally: were in awe of] the EverPresent God, and they believed in the EverPresent God and in Moses, God's servant. Then Moses and the Jewish People sang this song....

Exodus 14:30–15:1

If *Hallel* represents the Israelites' cathartic Song at the Sea, why do we not simply sing the Song at the Sea at this point in our Passover Seders, as we do in the traditional morning service every day of the year? The answer is found in the very first verse of the Song at the Sea: "Then Moses and the Jewish People sang this song...." Since the Song at the Sea was composed and conducted by Moses, whose role is purposefully and consistently hidden throughout the Haggadah, the Song at the Sea, which glaringly begins with Moses's name, has to be cloaked in the guise of another song praising God sung at the Sea, the *Hallel.* Hence, our spirited singing of the *Hallel* becomes a fitting substitute for the Jewish People's emotional song at the shore of the Sea of Reeds.

## Why So Many *Hallels?*

The Mishnah states that at this point in the Seder we "complete the *Hallel*" (which we began before the meal) and, in addition, recite over it "the Blessing of the Song." The Talmud then cites the opinion of Rabbi Tarfon that besides the *Hallel* and the Blessing of the Song we also recite "the Great *Hallel.*" Hence, since the time of the Talmud, there are three elements that compose the *Hallel* section of the Passover Haggadah:

- Psalms 115–118: the remainder of the *Hallel* found in our liturgy, recited when the New Moon appears and on the Jewish Pilgrimage festivals.
- Psalm 136: what is referred to by Rabbi Tarfon in the Talmud as "the Great *Hallel.*"
- *Nishmat Kol Chai*, "The Soul of Every Living Creature": according to the sage Rabbi Yochanan, this is the prayer

that the Mishnah had in mind when it mandated that we conclude the *Hallel* section with *Birkat HaShir,* "the Blessing of the Song."

These three elements were not chosen arbitrarily as the surrogates for singing the Song at the Sea. Each of them is reminiscent in some way of that song. And each of them gives expression not only to our ancestors' spontaneous song of praise, but also because we have gone back in time to the shores of the Sea, to our own song. That we sing all three testifies, again, to the Haggadah's preference for inclusivity, attempting to satisfy all rabbinic opinions, whenever possible, in the performance of Jewish rituals. Just as we already saw how this penchant for inclusivity was manifested in the *Maggid* and in the double eating of *maror,* we will now examine the spectrum of rabbinic opinion regarding the singing of *Hallel* as well.

## The Regular *Hallel*

We sing Psalms 115–118 because these psalms echo many of the same themes contained in the Song at the Sea: the rescue of God's servants from distress, *meitzar* in Hebrew, which shares its root with the Hebrew word for Egypt, *Mitzrayim;* the difference between the false gods of the enemy and the trustworthy God of Israel; the praising of God's name by the Jewish People, God's devoted servants, and the spreading of God's fame among all the nations. Therefore, *Mishnah Pesachim* 10:7 prescribes that at this point in the Seder we conclude the singing of these psalms of the liturgical *Hallel* (the first two psalms, Psalms 113 and 114, were recited before the meal) and thereby offer joyful praise to God for the salvation of God's people and, because we completely identify with our ancestors, of us from distress.

## The Great *Hallel*

Following the singing of the *Hallel,* we sing another song to remind us of the Song at the Sea: Psalm 136, which Rabbi Tarfon in the

Talmud labels "the Great *Hallel*" (*Pesachim* 8a). This psalm is a series of twenty-six couplets all praising God's works. Its center-piece is a group of four refrains that specifically praise God for the miracles at the Sea:

> *With strong hand and outstretched arm,*
>     *Chorus: God's kindness endures forever;*
> *To God who parted the Sea of Reeds,*
>     *Chorus: God's kindness endures forever;*
> *And caused Israel to pass through it,*
>     *Chorus: God's kindness endures forever;*
> *And threw Pharaoh and his legions into the Sea of Reeds,*
>     *Chorus: God's kindness endures forever.*

בְּיָד חֲזָקָה וּבִזְרוֹעַ נְטוּיָה, כִּי לְעוֹלָם חַסְדּוֹ.

לְגֹזֵר יַם סוּף לִגְזָרִים, כִּי לְעוֹלָם חַסְדּוֹ.

וְהֶעֱבִיר יִשְׂרָאֵל בְּתוֹכוֹ, כִּי לְעוֹלָם חַסְדּוֹ.

וְנִעֵר פַּרְעֹה וְחֵילוֹ בְיַם סוּף, כִּי לְעוֹלָם חַסְדּוֹ.

The fourth of these, which offers thanksgiving to God for throwing Pharaoh and his legions into the Sea, is the psalm's fifteenth refrain, the Hebrew numerical equivalent in *gematria* of *Yah*—one of God's appellations in the Song at the Sea. The pivotal nature of this fifteenth verse also reminds us of the Song at the Sea, which has fifteen steps in the center column of the Torah scroll (see pp. 16–18, "What's in a Number?"). Also, like the Song at the Sea, which was sung responsively amid the multitudes of the Jewish People, the Great *Hallel* is also designed to be sung respon-sively among the multitudes, albeit in the precincts of the Temple in Jerusalem or at our own well-attended Seder tables. Apparently, for these reasons, Rabbi Tarfon argued that this psalm should be included in the Mishnah's prescription of "completing the *Hallel*."

We follow his opinion and sing it here, immediately following the conclusion of the liturgical *Hallel* as a second surrogate for the Song at the Sea.

## The Blessing of the Song

*Mishnah Pesachim* 10:7 states that in the *Hallel* section of the Haggadah, one does not only recite the *Hallel* but also recites *Birkat HaShir*, "the Blessing of the Song." There is a difference of opinion in the Talmud as to what precisely constitutes the Blessing of the Song. Rabbi Judah says it refers to the final paragraph of the regular *Hallel*, which concludes with a blessing; hence the title "The blessing of the Song (that concludes the *Hallel*)":

> All Your works praise You, EverPresent God, our God; Your pious followers perform Your will; and all Your people, the house of Israel, praise, thank, bless, glorify, extol, exalt, revere, sanctify, and coronate Your name, our Sovereign. To You it is fitting to give thanks, and to Your name it is proper to sing praises, for You are God eternal. Blessed are You, EverPresent God, Sovereign of abundant praise.

יְהַלְלוּךְ יְיָ אֱלֹהֵינוּ כָּל מַעֲשֶׂיךָ, וַחֲסִידֶיךָ צַדִּיקִים

עוֹשֵׂי רְצוֹנֶךָ, וְכָל עַמְּךָ בֵּית יִשְׂרָאֵל בְּרִנָּה יוֹדוּ

וִיבָרְכוּ וִישַׁבְּחוּ וִיפָאֲרוּ וִירוֹמְמוּ וְיַעֲרִיצוּ וְיַקְדִּישׁוּ

וְיַמְלִיכוּ אֶת שִׁמְךָ מַלְכֵּנוּ, כִּי לְךָ טוֹב לְהוֹדוֹת

וּלְשִׁמְךָ נָאֶה לְזַמֵּר, כִּי מֵעוֹלָם וְעַד עוֹלָם אַתָּה אֵל.

בָּרוּךְ אַתָּה יְיָ, מֶלֶךְ מְהֻלָּל בַּתִּשְׁבָּחוֹת.

Paradoxically, although in accordance with Rabbi Judah's opinion we include this final paragraph of the regular, liturgical *Hallel*, we delete the concluding blessing of "Blessed are You, EverPresent God, Sovereign of abundant praise." The deletion of the final blessing is due to another rabbinic principle at work: *Saffek berachot l'kula*, that is, when there is doubt as to whether one should recite a blessing or not, we choose not to recite the blessing to avoid possibly using God's name in vain (the prohibition found in the third of the Ten Commandments). Therefore we include Rabbi Judah's opinion but drop the blessing that concludes the *Hallel*.

Rabbi Yochanan, on the other hand, argues that the Blessing of the Song refers not to the last paragraph of the liturgical *Hallel*, but to a separate piece of liturgy altogether: to the poem colloquially known by its first words, *Nishmat Kol Chai*. The latter, one of the most beautiful and moving prayers of divine praise in all of Jewish liturgy, recited every Sabbath and festival in traditional synagogues, alludes to the Song at the Sea and the Exodus from Egypt. It also identifies our experience with the experience of our ancestors' redemption, the operating principle of the entire Passover Haggadah:

> *If our mouths were as full of song as the sea, and our tongues were as joyous as its waves ... we would not be able to sufficiently praise EverPresent God, our God and the God of our ancestors and to bless Your name for the myriad of good things You have done for our ancestors and for us: from Egypt, EverPresent God, our God, You redeemed us and from the house of bondage You ransomed us ... and from the sword You saved us....*

אִלּוּ פִינוּ מָלֵא שִׁירָה כַּיָּם, וּלְשׁוֹנֵנוּ רִנָּה כַּהֲמוֹן
גַּלָּיו ... אֵין אֲנַחְנוּ מַסְפִּיקִים לְהוֹדוֹת לְךָ, יְיָ
אֱלֹהֵינוּ וֵאלֹהֵי אֲבוֹתֵינוּ, וּלְבָרֵךְ אֶת שְׁמֶךָ, עַל אַחַת
מֵאֶלֶף אַלְפֵי אֲלָפִים וְרִבֵּי רְבָבוֹת פְּעָמִים הַטּוֹבוֹת
שֶׁעָשִׂיתָ עִם אֲבוֹתֵינוּ וְעִמָּנוּ. מִמִּצְרַיִם גְּאַלְתָּנוּ יְיָ
אֱלֹהֵינוּ, וּמִבֵּית עֲבָדִים פְּדִיתָנוּ ... מֵחֶרֶב הִצַּלְתָּנוּ ...

Beyond the *Nishmat* prayer's specific references to the redemption of the Jewish People during the period of the Exodus, the *Nishmat* prayer is also—even primarily—a song of universal praise, "The souls of all living creatures will bless the name of God." This universal praise in awe of God's greatness mirrors the second half of the Song at the Sea, where Moses and the Israelites recognize that the defeat of the Egyptian legions has more far-reaching implications:

> Nations heard and shuddered; terror gripped the inhabitants of Philistia. Edom's chiefs then panicked; Moab's heroes were seized with trembling; Canaan's residents melted away; fear and dread fell upon them. At the greatness of Your arm they are still as stone.
>
> Exodus 15:14–16

Whether because of the *Nishmat*'s specific allusions to the redemption of the Jewish People in the Exodus, which mirrors the first half of the Song at the Sea, or because of its more universal emphasis, which mirrors the second half of the Song at the Sea, or perhaps because of the combination of both the particular and the universal, Rabbi Yochanan insisted that this prayer of *Nishmat* be sung at the Seder as the coda to *Hallel*. We follow the opinion of Rabbi Yochanan and sing the *Nishmat Kol Chai*, which concludes with the blessing of God, "who delights in melodious song" ("the Blessing of the Song").

## The Folk *Hallel:* Traditional Folksongs of Praise

Since the essence of the *Hallel* section of the Passover Seder is to reenact the singing by the Jewish People of God's praises at the Sea, the custom has arisen in Ashkenazic Haggadot since medieval times, and Sephardic Haggadot over the past two hundred years, to include various folksongs praising God toward the end of the Seder—songs like "Adir Hu," "Who Knows One?" and "Chad Gadya." These songs, which are later additions to the Haggadah but have become a sort of "Folk *Hallel*" over the generations, are variations on the theme of Passover. Like Psalms 115–118, Psalm 136, and the *Nishmat,* the three components of the formal *Hallel* section of the Haggadah, these folksongs give expression to the spontaneous outpouring of praise with which the Jewish People thanked God for their deliverance at the Sea. These folk compositions deal with the stroke of midnight in Jewish history when the Egyptian first-born were slain ("Vayehi Bachatzi Halayla"—"It Came to Pass at Midnight"), the Passover offering that saved the Jewish first-born ("VaAmartem Zevach Pesach"—"And They Said a Passover Offering"); with God's manifold praiseworthy attributes ("Ki Lo Na-eh"—"To Him Praise Is Due"); with the building of the Temple, which is foretold in the Song at the Sea ("Adir Hu"—"He Is Mighty"); with a recounting of Jewish tradition ("Echad Mi Yodei-a"—"Who Knows One?"); and with the metaphoric cycle of history in which God emerges at the end as the ultimate Sovereign ("Chad Gadya"—"One Kid"). "Chad Gadya" is, of course, a playful parody on the word Haggadah and a clever retelling of the story of the Passover Seder (i.e., God as the ultimate Sovereign and Judge of history).

Because these folksongs are informal additions, modern Haggadot typically include them after *Nirtzah,* as an appendix to the Seder. But this, the conclusion of the *Hallel,* is the more logical place to insert these folksongs of praise. A minority of Haggadot do print these songs at this point in the Seder, following the custom of the great rabbinic leader and liturgist of the thirteenth century, the Maharam of Rotenberg, who used to sing these folksongs immediately after the Blessing of the Song and prior to the fourth cup of wine.[2] With the addition of these folksongs, the *Hallel* section of the Seder becomes the vehicle to spontaneously sing praises to God both formally and informally, as did our ancestors at the Sea of Reeds.

# *Nirtzah—* "Acceptance"

## *Sefirat HaOmer:* Prologue to Acceptance

Following the *Hallel* and prior to the fourth cup of wine and *Nirtzah,* some Haggadot insert the counting of the Omer. Why is the counting of the Omer, recited at the Seder by those in the Diaspora who celebrate a second night of Passover, inserted at this point in the Haggadah text? Because the counting of the Omer is an expression of thanks to God for feeding us with the manna during the forty years in which the Jewish People wandered in the desert. The manna began to fall one month after the Jewish People left Egypt. God provided exactly one omer of manna for each Jew in the desert "according to the count of the People" (Exod. 16:16). Since this incredible miracle, which sustained and nurtured the Jewish People, commenced after the splitting of the Sea *(Hallel)* and prior to their reaching Mount Sinai *(Nirtzah),* we count the Omer, which commemorates the miracle of the manna, at this point in the Seder.

The manna was also a prologue to God's acceptance of the Jewish People embodied in *Nirtzah.* When the Jewish People came to Moses demanding food, God did not rebuke them despite their

151

adversarial tone, but rather responded promptly to their need for physical sustenance:

> And the whole congregation of the people of Israel began to complain against Moses and Aaron in the wilderness. And the people of Israel said to them, "If only we had died by the EverPresent God's hand in Egypt! There, we sat by the pots of meat and ate bread till we were full; but now you have brought us into this desert, to kill this whole community through starvation!" The EverPresent God said to Moses, "I will rain bread for you from heaven and the people shall go out and gather enough for each day...."
>
> Exodus 16:2–4

God understood the place of insecurity from which this group of former slaves came. Despite the onerous conditions under which the Jews labored in Egypt, the Jewish slaves were at least able to rely on their Egyptian taskmasters to provide them with enough nourishment to continue their slave labor. Now they suddenly found themselves in a barren desert without food, their provisions of matzot having run out, with no idea where their next meal would come from.

It was out of this understanding and acceptance of the people that God brought them the gift of the manna. Not only would the people have enough food to satiate each and every member of the community, but the food would be served each morning on a platter of moist dew and delivered to their doorstep. The heavenly bread that fell each morning symbolized God's acceptance of and loving-kindness toward the people throughout their journey in the desert. It also came to represent the people's trust and acceptance of God as the One who would provide them with what they needed to continue their journey toward the Promised Land. As such, it serves as the fitting prologue to the final item in the Seder, *Nirtzah,* "mutual acceptance."

On the second night of Passover we first recite the blessing and then count the first of the forty-nine days of the Omer:

> *Blessed are You, EverPresent God, our God, Sovereign of the universe, who has sanctified us with your commandments, and commanded us regarding the counting of the Omer.*
>
> *Today is the first day of the Omer.*

בָּרוּךְ אַתָּה יְיָ, אֱלֹהֵינוּ מֶלֶךְ הָעוֹלָם, אֲשֶׁר קִדְּשָׁנוּ בְּמִצְוֹתָיו וְצִוָּנוּ עַל סְפִירַת הָעֹמֶר.

הַיּוֹם יוֹם אֶחָד לָעֹמֶר.

## The Fourth Cup/כּוֹס רְבִיעִית

As we stated at the outset, each of the four cups of wine acts as a time machine, helping us to reenact the Exodus journey of our people. The first cup took us back to Egypt at the beginning of the Jewish People's residence there. The second cup took us to the night of the Exodus as we reenacted the eating of the final meal in Egypt. The third cup took us to the shores of the Sea as Moses prayed to God for deliverance and we sang a song of praise to God for rescuing us from the Egyptian legions. Now the fourth cup corresponds to the fourth promise of redemption that God spoke to Moses in Exodus 6:6–8: "And I will take you for Me as a people, and I will be for you as God, and you will know that I am the EverPresent God, your God, who takes you out from under the suffering of Egypt." It will transport us to the Jewish People standing at the foot of Mount Sinai where "God took them to be God's people" (Exod. 19:4–6) and revealed God's self as the EverPresent God, their God, who took them out of Egypt: "I am the EverPresent God, your God, who took you out from the land of Egypt from the house of bondage" (Exod. 20:2).

We raise the fourth cup of wine and bless God for creating the fruit of the vine and transporting us to Mount Sinai:

> *Blessed are You, EverPresent God, our God, Sovereign of the universe, who creates the fruit of the vine.*

בָּרוּךְ אַתָּה יְיָ, אֱלֹהֵינוּ מֶלֶךְ הָעוֹלָם, בּוֹרֵא פְּרִי הַגָּפֶן.

After the fourth cup, we thank God for the cups of wine with the traditional blessing following the drinking of wine.

> *Blessed, are You, EverPresent God our God, Sovereign of the universe, for the vine and its fruit, and for the produce of the field, for the beautiful and spacious land that You gave to our fathers as a heritage to eat of its fruit and to enjoy its goodness. Have mercy, EverPresent God, our God, on Israel Your people, on Jerusalem Your city, on Zion the abode of Your glory, on Your altar and Your Temple. Rebuild Jerusalem, the sacred city, speedily in our days. Bring us there and cheer us with its restoration; may we eat of its fruit and enjoy of its goodness; may we bless You for it in holiness and purity, and grant us happiness on this Feast of Matzot; for You, EverPresent God, are good and beneficent to all, and we thank You for the land and the fruit of the vine. Blessed are You, EverPresent God, for the land and the fruit of the vine.*

בָּרוּךְ אַתָּה יְיָ, אֱלֹהֵינוּ מֶלֶךְ הָעוֹלָם, עַל הַגֶּפֶן וְעַל פְּרִי הַגֶּפֶן, וְעַל תְּנוּבַת הַשָּׂדֶה, וְעַל אֶרֶץ חֶמְדָּה טוֹבָה וּרְחָבָה, שֶׁרָצִיתָ וְהִנְחַלְתָּ לַאֲבוֹתֵינוּ, לֶאֱכוֹל מִפִּרְיָהּ וְלִשְׂבּוֹעַ מִטּוּבָהּ. רַחֵם נָא, יְיָ אֱלֹהֵינוּ, עַל יִשְׂרָאֵל עַמֶּךָ, וְעַל יְרוּשָׁלַיִם עִירֶךָ, וְעַל צִיּוֹן מִשְׁכַּן

כְּבוֹדֶךָ, וְעַל מִזְבַּחֶךָ וְעַל הֵיכָלֶךָ. וּבְנֵה יְרוּשָׁלַיִם עִיר
הַקֹּדֶשׁ בִּמְהֵרָה בְיָמֵינוּ, וְהַעֲלֵנוּ לְתוֹכָהּ, וְשַׂמְּחֵנוּ
בְּבִנְיָנָהּ, וְנֹאכַל מִפִּרְיָהּ, וְנִשְׂבַּע מִטּוּבָהּ, וּנְבָרֶכְךָ
עָלֶיהָ בִּקְדֻשָּׁה וּבְטָהֳרָה. וְשַׂמְּחֵנוּ בְּיוֹם חַג הַמַּצּוֹת
הַזֶּה, כִּי אַתָּה יְיָ טוֹב וּמֵטִיב לַכֹּל, וְנוֹדֶה לְּךָ עַל
הָאָרֶץ וְעַל פְּרִי הַגָּפֶן. בָּרוּךְ אַתָּה יְיָ, עַל הָאָרֶץ
וְעַל פְּרִי הַגָּפֶן.

This blessing, with its prayer for the return of the Jewish people to the Land of Israel, to Jerusalem and the restored Temple, serves as a segue to *Nirtzah*.

## *Nirtzah*/נִרְצָה

The word *Nirtzah* means "acceptance." When did the Jewish People finally feel accepted by God? And when was God firmly accepted by the Jewish people?

To understand when and how this mutual acceptance occurred, it is helpful to ask ourselves what was the ultimate purpose of the Exodus. The purpose of the Exodus was not merely to free the Jews from the slavery of Egypt. Were it only a story of freedom from oppression that the Torah was telling us and that the Haggadah was retelling us, then the Book of Exodus would have ended with the Song at the Sea of Reeds (Exod. 15) and the Haggadah would have concluded with the section that parallels the Song at the Sea, the *Hallel;* or perhaps the Book of Exodus might have ended with the defeat of Amalek, an oppressor who appears shortly after the Jews left Egypt (Exod. 17), and the Haggadah could have concluded with the counting of the Omer, blessing God for sustaining the Jewish People on their journey. The fact that the Book of Exodus continues until chapter 40 and that the Haggadah concludes with *Nirtzah* tells us that there is another important element in the Jewish People's master story. In fact, two more elements remain before we can reach resolution: the attainment of a passionate, intimate relationship with God, and the arrival in a stable home where God and the Jewish People can dwell permanently together.

## *Nirtzah* as Relationship

The divine promises of redemption (Exodus 6:6–9) that parallel the four cups describe a process that did not end once the Jews were out of Egypt and the Egyptian people and army had received their comeuppance. The process of redemption continued with the fourth promise, the acceptance by God of the people and the people's acceptance of God: "And I will take you to be My people, and I will be your God."

This mutual acceptance was supposed to occur before, during, and immediately following God's Revelation of the Ten Commandments at Mount Sinai. In the preamble to the Ten Commandments, God tells Moses:

> "So shall you say to the house of Jacob and tell to the children of Israel: 'You have seen what I did to Egypt and how I carried you on the wings of eagles and brought you to Me. Now, if you really listen to My voice and guard My covenant … then you will be a treasure to Me from among all the nations, even though the whole earth is mine. And you will be for Me a kingdom of priests and a sacred nation'; these are the words that you should say to the Jewish People." Moses came and called all the elders of the people and placed before them all these words that the EverPresent God had commanded him. All the people responded in unison, saying, "Everything that the EverPresent God said we will do."
>
> Exodus 19:3–8

At this point in the people's journey, God was about to fulfill his promise of redemption to take them to be God's people and to be their God by "marrying" them, as it were, at Mount Sinai. The covenant was to be the "marriage contract" sealing the courtship between God and God's people. The people were going to hear the first commandment, which would let them "know" (see Gen. 4:1) the God who took them out of Egypt to be God's spouse in history: "I am the EverPresent God, your God, who took you out of the land of Egypt, the house of bondage" (Exod. 20:2). After the Revelation of the Ten Commandments, the people enthusiastically reiterated their acceptance of God's kingship and of the terms of the marriage covenant: "We will do and obey all that the EverPresent God has declared" (Exod. 24:7). This was supposed to be *Nirtzah,* the mutual acceptance of the Jewish People by God and of God by the Jewish people, to be, as it were, husband and wife.

However, just forty days after the Revelation of the Ten Commandments, while Moses was up on Mount Sinai getting final architectural and interior design instructions for their new, shared home, the Tabernacle, the Jewish People betrayed their divine bridegroom at the incident of the Golden Calf:

> And the people saw that Moses was delayed in coming down from the mountain, and the people ganged up on Aaron and said to him, "Get up and make us a god who will lead us, because the whereabouts of that Moses man, who took us up from the land of Egypt, is unknown to us." ... So [Aaron] made them a molten calf, and they said, "This is your god, O Israel, who brought you up from the land of Egypt!" ... And they awoke the next day and they offered up sacrifices ... and the people sat down to eat and drink and arose to revel.
>
> Exodus 32:1–6

Instead of recognizing God as "the One who took you out of the land of Egypt, the house of bondage" (the opening line of the Ten Commandments), the people ascribed the miracle of the Exodus to an Egyptian deity, a golden calf, a blatant violation of the exclusive relationship with God expressed in the first commandment. They then proceeded to violate the second commandment, their commitment to exclusive devotion and service to their divine spouse, by fashioning and orgiastically worshiping the molten calf, a replica of the Egyptian deity Apis. Although Moses finally persuades God not to destroy the people, God refuses to accompany the people any longer. God feels betrayed by his newly-wed bride. In effect God tells Moses, "If the people do not want Me, then I will not be with them. You, Moses, lead them into the land I promised them" (Exod. 33:1–3).

The people's sincere remorse for their actions, which follows their hearing of God's abandonment of them, together with Moses putting his own relationship on the line and prevailing upon God to reconcile with his wayward spouse and accompany the people, causes God to reconsider and agree to rejoin the people on their journey after all:

> Moses said to the EverPresent God, "You have told me to bring up this people [to the Promised Land], yet You did not tell me whom You will send with me. You have said, 'I know you by name,' and You are pleased with me. Now therefore, I beg You, if I have indeed pleased You, show me now Your ways that I may know how I may continue to be pleasing to You and see that this nation is Your people." And God said, "My Presence shall go with you and lead you [singular]." [Moses] said to God, "If Your Presence does not accompany [all of] us, do not bring us up from here! For where shall it be known here that I and Your people have been pleasing to You? Is it not by Your accompanying us, I and Your people, and thereby distinguishing us from all the peoples that are upon the face of the earth?" The EverPresent God said to Moses, "Since you have been pleasing to me and I know you by name, I will also fulfill this request of yours."
>
> Exodus 33:12–17

Nevertheless, despite Moses's audacious request and God's verbal agreement here in Exodus 33, God's Presence only returns to the Jewish People in the final five verses of Exodus 40. It is only after the Jewish People complete God's Tabernacle, God's home, which will now house both God's commandments, the terms of the marriage agreement engraved on the stone tablets, and God's visible Presence, that God returns to live among God's People:

> And the cloud covered the Tent of Meeting, and the Presence of the EverPresent God filled the Tabernacle. Moses was unable to enter the Tent of Meeting because the cloud rested upon it and the Presence of the EverPresent God filled the Tabernacle. And when the cloud lifted from over the Tabernacle, the Jewish People would travel in all their journeys. And if the cloud did not lift, they would not travel until the day that it did lift. Because the cloud of the EverPresent God was over the Tabernacle by day and a fire would be on it by night, before the eyes of all the house of Israel throughout all their journeys.
>
> Exodus 40:34–38

Only when God's visible and palpable Presence, symbolized by the cloud, descends from the heavens on high to dwell in the finite, earthly abode that the people have built for God has God finally accepted the Jewish People, flaws and all. When God literally and metaphorically "cohabits" with the Jewish People, when God's Presence fills them with God's love, God validates and confirms God's acceptance of them. Likewise, the people wholeheartedly accept and confirm their devotion to God by building and fully furnishing the "home" to house God's Presence in their midst, and then journeying forward and resting only at God's initiative. When God moves, they move; when God rests, they rest. God leads, and the people accompany God. Always. This mutual, confirmed acceptance *(Nirtzah)* by God and the Jewish People fulfilled the fourth promise of redemption and the ultimate purpose, albeit not the final destination, of the Jewish People's journey.

In these concluding verses of the Book of Exodus, the redemption of the Jewish People reaches its apogee. There is a direct, unmitigated, spousal relationship between God and the Jewish People. The intensity and exclusivity of that relationship mean that Moses cannot enter God's hearth and home—Moses, who led the people out of Egypt; Moses, who passionately prayed for the people at the Sea; Moses, who patiently shepherded them to Sinai; Moses, who saved the people from God's wrath after the Golden Calf and who persuaded God to rejoin the people on their journey. No matter; Moses is unable to enter the Tabernacle just as he had to remain hidden in the Haggadah. By bringing God and the people together, Moses has done his job and must now fade into the background. It is God and the Jewish People who are locked in an exclusive, passionate, eternal embrace for all generations in all the Jewish People's journeys. *Nirtzah.*

## *Nirtzah* as Destination

The purpose of the Exodus has been achieved. The Jewish People reach their spiritual potential by communing with God in the concluding verses of the Book of Exodus and in *Nirtzah* during the Passover Seder. Yet, there is still an unfulfilled promise and an unreached destination left hanging in the air throughout the Book of Exodus and, indeed, throughout the remainder of the entire Torah. The promised destination follows the first four promises of redemption in Exodus that we have been tracking throughout the Seder:

> "And I will bring you to the Land that I swore to Abraham, Isaac, and Jacob that I would give it [to their descendants]; and I will indeed give it to you as a perpetual inheritance, I, the EverPresent God."
>
> Exodus 6:8

When God appeared to Moses at the Burning Bush, God did not merely tell him to lead the Jews out of Egypt to worship God on Mount Sinai; God told him to lead them toward the land flowing with milk and honey. When God promised Moses that God would free and redeem the Jewish People, God did not stop with the promise to take them to be God's people; God told Moses that God would bring them to the Land and give the people that land as an eternal inheritance. Finally, when Moses and the Jewish People sang the song of praise to God at the Sea of Reeds, they did not conclude the song with the drowning of the Egyptian legions, but with God bringing and planting them on the "mountain of [God's] heritage," the Temple of God where God would be their Sovereign permanently and forever (Exod. 15:17–18).

The ultimate dream of the Jewish People was to enshrine their passionate, exclusive relationship of redemption with God in a stable, solid, permanent home. Living in tents or other temporary dwellings, even one as beautiful and meticulously furnished as the biblical Sanctuary, was fine while the people were journeying on the road to the Promised Land. Ultimately, though, ceaseless journeying makes one weary and leaves one feeling vulnerable (see Deut. 25:18). Even when traveling with one's beloved, as the Jewish people journeyed with God, or perhaps especially when traveling with one's beloved, there is a yearning to come home and nest, to settle down and sink roots into a permanent place. The Promised Land, the city of Jerusalem, and even more specifically the Temple, God's House in Jerusalem, was the ultimate destination where God and the Jewish People were to finally "settle down" to a steady life of shared values, passionate engagement, and devoted service.

Yet the Book of Exodus—indeed the Five Books of Moses— conclude with God's promise and the Jewish People's Song at the Sea not yet fulfilled. The people are living with God, but they are journeying together in a temporary, mobile dwelling, the biblical Sanctuary. The final lines of *Nirtzah* in the Haggadah capture the tension of this as-yet-unfulfilled divine promise of permanence in the Torah:

*We have completed the order of the Passover journey*
*With all its traditions and symbols of history.*
*Just as we were privileged to enact this order tonight*
*So may we be granted to reenact it again.*

*Pure One, whose Presence dwells in God's abode,*
*Establish us as a community of people who are*
*innumerable.*
*Speedily lead Your planted seedlings,*
*As a redeemed nation to Zion with joyous song.*

*Next year in the rebuilt Jerusalem!*

חֲסַל סִדּוּר פֶּסַח כְּהִלְכָתוֹ

כְּכָל מִשְׁפָּטוֹ וְחֻקָּתוֹ.

כַּאֲשֶׁר זָכִינוּ לְסַדֵּר אוֹתוֹ,

כֵּן נִזְכֶּה לַעֲשׂוֹתוֹ.

זָךְ שׁוֹכֵן מְעוֹנָה,

קוֹמֵם קְהַל עֲדַת מִי מָנָה,

בְּקָרוֹב נַהֵל נִטְעֵי כַנָּה,

פְּדוּיִים לְצִיּוֹן בְּרִנָּה.

לְשָׁנָה הַבָּאָה בִּירוּשָׁלַיִם הַבְּנוּיָה!

By praying that God return God's "planted seedlings," God's people, as a "redeemed" nation to "Zion," a word used variously in the Bible to designate the Land of Israel, the city of Jerusalem, and the Temple Mount, the Haggadah turns our attention toward the

Jewish People's final, but yet unattained destination. That destination is not merely Israel or even Jerusalem, but a rebuilt Temple in Jerusalem *(Yerushalayim Habenuyah)*, where the Jewish People can live with God's visible, palpable, loving Presence in their very midst. For the Jewish People to return "redeemed to Zion" means not only that they return to the Land of Israel (the Zionist dream), but that God returns with them. To return to Zion redeemed means that, like the conclusion of the Book of Exodus, the people will be filled with God's pervasive love, and God's spirit will be with them, cohabiting with them in their shared, permanent home. The fact that the Jewish People pray for this acknowledges that such a blessed state of affairs has not yet come to pass.

The presence on the table of the fifth cup, which is customarily thought of as the cup of Elijah, may also be symbolic of this, as yet unfulfilled, promise of permanent redemption. Like this fifth cup of redemption, which sits in the center of our table but is not drunk, God's promise of the rebuilt Temple in the Land of Israel remains central to our people's ultimate vision of redemption but remains to be fulfilled. Yet, just as God has fulfilled the first four promises of redemption, the presence of the cup and the text of the Haggadah before us express our hope that God will soon fulfill the remaining promise. Hence the culminating proclamation in the Haggadah: Next year in the rebuilt Jerusalem!

9

# The Triple Helix:
# What It All Means

The Haggadah is a retelling of the Book of Exodus from the first seven verses, when the Jewish People descend into the land of Egypt, to the final five verses, when God's Presence descends to dwell among the Jewish People. Along the way we experience incredible growth at the outset, followed by the bitterness of enslavement and infanticide, followed by God's wondrous miracles in Egypt and at the Sea, and concluding with God's speaking to us at Sinai, coming to dwell with us in the Tabernacle, and promising to ultimately bring us to and join us in our permanent home in the Land of Israel. This story is the master story of our people. It is the spiritual pilgrimage that we lead, and through which the Jewish People journey, on Passover night.

But our master story is not just a story of our biblical past that we retell and reexperience in the present. This story is also a metaphor of our people's journey throughout history and of our own individual life's journey. In the *Maggid* section of the Seder, the Haggadah uses the expression "in each and every generation" only two times: once concerning the historical experience of the Jewish people and once concerning each individual's personal life experience. Regarding the historical experience of the Jewish People, the Haggadah tells us:

*This promise [of redemption] has sustained our ancestors and us. For not only one enemy has risen against us to annihilate us, rather in each and every generation men rise against us to annihilate us. But the Holy One, blessed be God, saves us from their hand.*

Regarding our own individual life experience, the Haggadah states:

*In each and every generation it is a person's duty to regard him- or herself as though he or she personally had come out of Egypt.... It was not only our ancestors whom the Holy One redeemed from slavery; we, too, were redeemed with them, as it is written: "God took us out from there so that God might take us to the land that God had sworn to our ancestors."*

Together, these two paragraphs are telling us that the biblical story of our ancestors' Exodus from Egypt has a valuable lesson to teach both each and every generation of Jews and each and every individual human being. The first message is sobering: that our paths and our journeys, no matter how successful at the start, no matter how well planned or prepared, can often take detours into dangerous, uncharted, and unanticipated territory. Any of us may wake up one day and find ourselves in a totally transformed environment where we suddenly experience oppressive bondage and an urgent threat to our own or our family's/people's very existence. Evil is a reality that can erupt without a moment's notice. That has been the recurring experience of the Jewish People throughout our existence, and that is the existential human condition of each and every human being since time immemorial.

What keeps our people and each of us sane in such a potentially dangerous and absurd world is our relationship with God and with our master story of redemption. Our trust that God oversees a just world, that over the course of generations—if not in any single given lifetime—the wicked get their just desert and the righteous receive their deserved reward, keeps us going even when the reality around us seems to shout otherwise.

If the Haggadah's first message is sobering, its second message is inspiring: reliving our ancestors' biblical experience, as we do each and every year at the Seder, reminds us that despite the evil all around us, redemption too can come in the blink of an eye. Even when the odds seem stacked against us, our situation can undergo a radical change for the better. The world is not only dark; it is also full of light. God's promises to God's people of ultimate redemption and our internalization of our people's remarkable story of the Exodus instill in us the hope and the courage to go forward even when chaos and darkness seem poised to engulf us.

Those who have suffered a terrifying experience in their own life or in the lives of their community and have survived to tell the tale and live a vital and vibrant life again have led a personal version of the Passover journey. Those of our ancestors, like my own parents, who lost their families during the period of the Holocaust and yet survived and came to the shores of America to raise families and build meaningful new lives as American Jews, have traveled the Passover road from slavery to freedom; those of us from the New York or Washington, D.C., area who were directly affected by the events of September 11, 2001, or who witnessed the tragic events in Israel of the past several years, and who have resolutely chosen to continue to live their lives to the fullest have retold in their own souls the essence of the Passover story; and others, who have had to fight a battle against a life-threatening disease and have been fortunate enough to be given a second lease on life, or who have had to overcome personal tragedies or deep, interpersonal disappointments to begin life anew, know in their very flesh and blood of this journey from oppression to redemption that the Seder teaches us.

The Jewish People's journey from slavery and oppression to freedom and redemption is the journey we are all destined to travel in one way or another in our lives on this planet. Like our biblical ancestors, we too often struggle to free ourselves from those physical, relational, or psychological forces that try to enslave and hurt us, to defeat them so that they no longer constitute a threat to us or to our loved ones, and then seek to find the type of personal meaning, interpersonal relationship, and permanence of place that our people call redemption. The biblical story, our people's story, and our own personal stories are one story—the story of "slavery to freedom, grief to joy … darkness to light, and oppression to redemption." Together, they form a *chut hameshulash*, a "triple helix," which King Solomon teaches us "does not easily unravel" (Eccles. 4:12). May our stories and journeys bring hope for our generation and meaning for the generations that preceded us, and light the path for the generations that follow, until the final redemption of God's people and God's world.

# Notes

## Chapter Two: Understanding the
## Order of the Seder

1. See, for example, *Nitei Gavriel—Hilchot Pesach, Chelek Bet* (New York: Moriah Press, 1989), which contains ten different arrangements.

2. See Richard Bandler and John Grinder, *Frogs into Princes* (Moab, Utah: Real People Press, 1979), for neuro-linguistic programming's three representational senses: the visual, audial, and kinesthetic.

3. According to one contemporary scholar's interpretation of Rabbi Yochanan in the Babylonian Talmud (Tractate *Pesachim* 8a), these fifteen psalms are to be recited as part of *Hallel*, the fourteenth item in the Seder. According to this interpretation, Rabbi Yochanan apparently viewed these psalms as part of the fifteen-step process of encountering the Divine Presence. Also, see Nachman Cohen, *The Historical Haggadah* (Yonkers, N.Y.: Torah Lishmah Institute, 2001), p. 3.

4. It is interesting to note that the Babylonian Talmud in discussing the elements of the Seder (Tractate *Pesachim* 7a) focuses on *Yah*, the particular appellation for God that equals fifteen. The editor of the Talmud was undoubtedly aware of the connection of the saga of the Exodus to the number fifteen. This name for God

is, in any event, one of the names used by the Jewish People at the Song of the Sea (Exodus 15), one of the climactic episodes of the Jewish People's redemption from Egypt.

## Chapter Three: Traveling Back to Sacred Time and Sacred Space

1. In contrast to the *Kiddush* we recite on Passover, the *Kiddush* recited on Shabbat reminds us of two moments in time: God's creation of the universe *(zikaron lema'aseh vereishit)* and God's liberating us from Egypt *(zecher litziat Mitzrayim)*. On Passover and the other Festivals we remind ourselves only of the Exodus, since the Exodus is the starting point of our people's collective experience that the biblical Festivals commemorate.

## Chapter Five: The Narrative of Redemption

1. I first came across this deciphering of the general order of *Maggid* in a brilliant introductory essay by Rav Naftali Maskil LeAison (1829–97) to an English translation of the *Malbim Haggadah* (New York: Targum Press/Feldheim Publishers, 1993, pp. V–XXVI). Although my analysis also follows the order of the verse in Exodus 13:8, it parses the verse differently in two instances: separating the words *vehigadeta* from *levinkha*, since the Haggadah treats them as distinct topics; and combining *Leimor* with *ba'avur zeh*, since that entire subsection of *Maggid* deals with the causes of the enslavement and redemption. For a similar, more recent, yet equally insightful treatment of this verse to explain *Maggid*, see Menachem Liebtag, *Understanding Maggid,* Yeshivat Gush Etzion, Tanakh Study Center Archives, www.Tanakh.org/arch 2003.

2. See Mordechai Breuer, *Pirkei Moadot*, 3rd ed. (Jerusalem: Horev Press, 1993), vol. 1, p. 182.

3. See Babylonian Talmud, Tractate *Berachot* 5a–b for a discussion of this issue.

4. Some scholars have attempted to argue that Egyptian slavery was an example of state-imposed slavery rather than an instance of individualized master-slave abuse as in pre–Civil War America.

Nevertheless, the overwhelming concern of the Torah with modifying the individualized master-slave relationship rather than with abolishing state slavery indicates that, at the very least, the abuse of the slave and the slave's family by the slave owner was a significant part of the Jewish People's experience of slavery in Egypt.

5. Utilizing this reasoning, the eighteenth-century Gaon of Vilna cautioned traditional Jews against reciting the Haggadah on the afternoon of Shabbat HaGadol, the Shabbat preceding Passover, despite the prevalent custom in his day and ours. See the *biur halacha* on the gloss of Rabbi Moshe Isserles in *Shulchan Arukh*, Laws of Passover, 430:1.

6. For an even more sweeping censure of Joseph's role, see Aaron Wildavsky, *Assimilation Versus Separation: Joseph the Administrator and the Politics of Religion* (Somerset, N.J.: Transaction Press, 1986).

7. See, for instance, the Martyrology section of the Yom Kippur liturgy recording Hadrian's slaying of the ten leading Jewish sages of his time for the "unpunished crime" of the ten brothers' selling Joseph into slavery fifteen hundred years earlier.

8. Four hundred years is not meant to be literal but simply constitutes "a very long time"; see also the use of the number 400 in Genesis 32:7. Note that the letter *tav,* the last letter of the Hebrew alphabet, is equivalent to 400, the largest number in *gematria,* Jewish numerology.

9. See, for instance, Robert Alter, "Joseph and His Brothers," *Commentary,* November 1980; *The Art of Biblical Narrative* (New York: Basic Books, 1981).

## Chapter Six: Eating the Meal of Freedom in the House of Slavery

1. It is not surprising that a central part of Mass in the Christian tradition is the ingesting of the wafer, symbolizing the body of the Christian redeemer; many aspects of Christian ritual are a conscious transfiguration of traditional Jewish practice. See

also Lawrence A. Hoffman's insightful article "A Symbol of Salvation in the Passover Haggadah," *Worship* 53 (1979): 6.

## Chapter Seven: Reenacting the Saga at the Sea

1. See *Shulchan Arukh* 487:4 and *Biur Hagra*, ad. loc.

2. Cited by Rabbi Shimshon Bar Tzadok in *Tashbatz*, as quoted by Daniel Goldschmidt, *The Passover Haggadah: Its Sources and History* (Jerusalem: Bialik, 1977), p. 96.

# Suggestions for Further Reading

## Bible Translations

Berlin, Adele, and Marc Zvi Brettler, eds. *The Jewish Study Bible.* Oxford, UK: Oxford University Press, 2004.

Fox, Everett, trans. and annotation. *The Five Books of Moses.* New York: Schocken Books, 1997.

Kaplan, Aryeh, trans. and annotation. *The Living Torah.* Brooklyn, NY: Moznaim Publishers, 1981.

## Bible Commentaries

Eisen, Arnold M. *Taking Hold of Torah.* Bloomington, IN: Indiana University Press, 1999.

Leibowitz, Nehama. *Studies in* Shemot / *Exodus.* Translated and adapted by Aryeh Newman. Jerusalem: Department for Torah Education and Culture in the Diaspora, 1996.

Nachmanides. *Nachmanides' Commentary on the Bible: The Book of Exodus,* translated by Charles B. Chavel. New York: Shilo Publishing, 1971.

Silber, David. *The Joseph Narrative: Reconstruction of a Family* (8-CD set). New York: Drisha Institute, 2002.

Walzer, Michael. *Exodus and Revolution.* New York: Basic Books, 1985.

Wildavsky, Aaron. *Assimilation versus Separation: Joseph the Administrator and the Politics of Religion in Biblical Israel.* Somerset, NJ: Transaction Press, 1986.

## Haggadot of Passover

Goldschmidt, Daniel. *The Passover Haggadah: Its Sources and History.* Jerusalem: Bialik Publishers, 1977 (Hebrew).

Rabinowicz, Rachel Anne. *The Feast of Freedom Haggadah.* New York: United Synagogue Books, 1982.

Safrai, Shmuel, and Ze'ev Safrai. *Haggadah of the Sages: The Passover Haggadah.* Jerusalem: Carta Press, 1998 (Hebrew).

Shaw, Yisroel, and Jonathon Taub, trans. *The Malbim Haggadah.* New York: Targum Press/Feldheim Publishers, 1993.

Tabory, Yosef. *The Passover Ritual throughout the Generations.* Tel Aviv: Hakibbutz Hameuchad Publishing, 1996 (Hebrew).

## Jewish Holidays and Literacy

Bloch, Abraham P. *The Biblical and Historical Background of the Jewish Holy Days.* New York: Ktav Publishing, 1978.

Greenberg, Blu. *How to Run a Traditional Jewish Household.* New York: Fireside Publishing, 1985.

Greenberg, Irving. *The Jewish Way: Living the Holidays.* Lanham, MD: Jason Aronson, 1998.

Telushkin, Joseph. *Jewish Literacy.* New York: William Morrow Publishers, 1991.

## Jewish Thought

Besdin, Abraham. *Reflections of the Rav: Lessons in Jewish Thought Adapted from the Lectures of Rabbi Joseph B. Soloveitchik,* vol. 1. Jersey City, NJ: Ktav Publishing, 1993.

Buber, Martin. *I and Thou.* Translated by Walter Kaufmann. New York: Free Press, 1971.

Gordis, Daniel. *God Was Not in the Fire: The Search for a Spiritual Judaism.* New York: Touchstone Press, 1997.

Harav, Shiurei. *A Conspectus of the Public Lectures of Rabbi Joseph B. Soloveitchik.* Edited by Joseph Epstein. Jersey City, NJ: KTAV Press, 1994.

Hartman, David. *A Living Covenant: The Innovative Spirit in Traditional Judaism.* Woodstock, VT: Jewish Lights, 1998.

Wyschograd, Michael. *The Body of Faith: Judaism as Corporeal Election.* San Francisco: Harper and Row, 1983.

## Selected Further Readings from Jewish Lights

Anisfeld, Sharon Cohen, Tara Mohr, and Catherine Spector, eds. *The Women's Seder Sourcebook: Rituals and Readings for Use at the Passover Seder* and *The Women's Passover Companion: Women's Reflections on the Festival of Freedom.* Woodstock, VT: Jewish Lights Publishing, 2003.

Cohen, Norman J. *The Way Into Torah.* Woodstock, VT: Jewish Lights Publishing, 2004.

Gillman, Neil. *The Way Into Encountering God in Judaism.* Woodstock, VT: Jewish Lights Publishing, 2004.

Goldstein, Elyse, ed. *The Women's Haftarah Commentary: New Insights from Women Rabbis on the 54 Weekly Haftarah Portions, the Five* Megillot, *and Special* Shabbatot. Woodstock, VT: Jewish Lights Publishing, 2004.

———. *The Women's Torah Commentary: New Insights from Women Rabbis on the 54 Weekly Torah Portions.* Woodstock, VT: Jewish Lights Publishing, 2000.

Green, Arthur. *These Are the Words: A Vocabulary of Jewish Spiritual Life.* Woodstock, VT: Jewish Lights Publishing, 2000.

Hoffman, Lawrence A. *The Way Into Jewish Prayer.* Woodstock, VT: Jewish Lights Publishing, 2004.

Hoffman, Lawrence A., ed. *My People's Prayer Book: Traditional Prayers, Modern Commentaries* Series. Woodstock, VT: Jewish Lights Publishing, 1997–.

Kushner, Lawrence. *The Way Into Jewish Mystical Tradition.* Woodstock, VT: Jewish Lights Publishing, 2004.

Wolfson, Ron. *Passover, 2nd Edition: The Family Guide to Spiritual Celebration.* Woodstock, VT: Jewish Lights Publishing, 2003.

# Index

# About the Author

Nathan Laufer is senior fellow at the Shalem Center in Jerusalem, a research institute for Jewish and Israeli social thought, and president emeritus of the Wexner Heritage Foundation. The foundation educates Jewish leaders in the traditions, history, thought, and contemporary challenges of the Jewish people. In his seventeen years of leadership, Rabbi Laufer brought the foundation's program to thirty-one cities across North America, educating over thirteen hundred of its most influential lay leaders. Rabbi Laufer wrote this book while on sabbatical at the Shalom Hartman Institute in Jerusalem as a Wexner Heritage Scholar.

Before joining the Wexner Heritage Foundation in 1986, Rabbi Laufer was the director of East Coast Educational Programs for the Simon Wiesenthal Center and director of Legal Affairs and Community Education for the Coalition to Free Soviet Jews. A graduate of the Rabbi Isaac Elchanan Theological Seminary of Yeshiva University and the Fordham University School of Law, he writes, teaches, and lectures across North America and Israel regarding issues of leadership, Jewish identity and meaning, and the future of North American Jewry.

Rabbi Laufer, a member of the New York Board of Rabbis and the New York State Bar Association, is married to Sharon Laufer and is the father of four children, including triplets.

# Bar/Bat Mitzvah

**The Bar/Bat Mitzvah Memory Book**
An Album for Treasuring the Spiritual Celebration
*By Rabbi Jeffrey K. Salkin and Nina Salkin*
A unique album for preserving the spiritual memories of the day, and for recording plans for the Jewish future ahead. Contents include space for creating or recording family history; teachings received from rabbi, cantor, and others; mitzvot and *tzedakot* chosen and carried out, etc.
8 x 10, 48 pp, Deluxe Hardcover, 2-color text, ribbon marker, ISBN 1-58023-111-X **$19.95**

**Bar/Bat Mitzvah Basics:** A Practical Family Guide to Coming of Age Together
Edited by Helen Leneman. Foreword by Rabbi Jeffrey K. Salkin.
6 x 9, 240 pp, Quality PB, ISBN 1-58023-151-9 **$18.95**

**For Kids—Putting God on Your Guest List:** How to Claim the Spiritual Meaning
of Your Bar or Bat Mitzvah By Rabbi Jeffrey K. Salkin
6 x 9, 144 pp, Quality PB, ISBN 1-58023-015-6 **$14.95** For ages 11–12

**Putting God on the Guest List, 3rd Edition:** How to Reclaim the Spiritual
Meaning of Your Child's Bar or Bat Mitzvah By Rabbi Jeffrey K. Salkin
6 x 9, 224 pp, Quality PB, ISBN 1-58023-222-1 **$16.99**; Hardcover, ISBN 1-58023-260-4 **$24.99**

**Tough Questions Jews Ask:** A Young Adult's Guide to Building a Jewish Life
By Rabbi Edward Feinstein 6 x 9, 160 pp, Quality PB, ISBN 1-58023-139-X **$14.95** For ages 13 & up
Also Available: **Tough Questions Jews Ask Teacher's Guide**
8½ x 11, 72 pp, PB, ISBN 1-58023-187-X **$8.95**

# Bible Study/Midrash

**Hineini in Our Lives:** Learning How to Respond to Others through 14 Biblical Texts,
and Personal Stories By Norman J. Cohen
6 x 9, 240 pp, Hardcover, ISBN 1-58023-131-4 **$23.95**

**Ancient Secrets:** Using the Stories of the Bible to Improve Our Everyday Lives
By Rabbi Levi Meier, Ph.D. 5½ x 8½, 288 pp, Quality PB, ISBN 1-58023-064-4 **$16.95**

**Moses—The Prince, the Prophet:** His Life, Legend & Message for Our Lives
By Rabbi Levi Meier, Ph.D. 6 x 9, 224 pp, Quality PB, ISBN 1-58023-069-5 **$16.95**

**Self, Struggle & Change:** Family Conflict Stories in Genesis and Their Healing Insights
for Our Lives By Norman J. Cohen 6 x 9, 224 pp, Quality PB, ISBN 1-879045-66-4 **$18.99**

**Voices from Genesis:** Guiding Us through the Stages of Life By Norman J. Cohen
6 x 9, 192 pp, Quality PB, ISBN 1-58023-118-7 **$16.95**

# Congregation Resources

**Becoming a Congregation of Learners:** Learning as a Key to Revitalizing
Congregational Life By Isa Aron, Ph.D. Foreword by Rabbi Lawrence A. Hoffman.
6 x 9, 304 pp, Quality PB, ISBN 1-58023-089-X **$19.95**

**Finding a Spiritual Home:** How a New Generation of Jews Can Transform the
American Synagogue By Rabbi Sidney Schwarz
6 x 9, 352 pp, Quality PB, ISBN 1-58023-185-3 **$19.95**

**Jewish Pastoral Care, 2nd Edition:** A Practical Handbook from Traditional &
Contemporary Sources Edited by Rabbi Dayle A. Friedman
6 x 9, 464 pp, Hardcover, ISBN 1-58023-221-3 **$40.00**

**The Self-Renewing Congregation:** Organizational Strategies for Revitalizing
Congregational Life By Isa Aron, Ph.D. Foreword by Dr. Ron Wolfson.
6 x 9, 304 pp, Quality PB, ISBN 1-58023-166-7 **$19.95**

# Children's Books

## What You Will See Inside a Synagogue
*By Rabbi Lawrence A. Hoffman and Dr. Ron Wolfson; Full-color photos by Bill Aron*
A colorful, fun-to-read introduction that explains the ways and whys of Jewish worship and religious life. Full-page photos; concise but informative descriptions of the objects used, the clergy and laypeople who have specific roles, and much more. For ages 6 & up.
8½ x 10½, 32 pp, Full-color photos, Hardcover, ISBN 1-59473-012-1 **$17.99** *(A SkyLight Paths book)*

## Because Nothing Looks Like God
*By Lawrence and Karen Kushner*
What is God like? Introduces children to the possibilities of spiritual life. Real-life examples of happiness and sadness invite us to explore, together with our children, the questions we all have about God.
11 x 8½, 32 pp, Full-color illus., Hardcover, ISBN 1-58023-092-X **$16.95** *For ages 4 & up*

Also Available: **Because Nothing Looks Like God Teacher's Guide**
8½ x 11, 22 pp, PB, ISBN 1-58023-140-3 **$6.95** *For ages 5–8*

**Board Book Companions to *Because Nothing Looks Like God***
5 x 5, 24 pp, Full-color illus., SkyLight Paths Board Books, **$7.95** each *For ages 0–4*

**What Does God Look Like?** ISBN 1-893361-23-3
**How Does God Make Things Happen?** ISBN 1-893361-24-1
**Where Is God?** ISBN 1-893361-17-9

## The 11th Commandment: Wisdom from Our Children
*by The Children of America*
"If there were an Eleventh Commandment, what would it be?" Children of many religious denominations across America answer in their own drawings and words.
8 x 10, 48 pp, Full-color illus., Hardcover, ISBN 1-879045-46-X **$16.95** *For all ages*

## Jerusalem of Gold: Jewish Stories of the Enchanted City
*Retold by Howard Schwartz. Full-color illus. by Neil Waldman.*
A beautiful and engaging collection of historical and legendary stories for children. Based on Talmud, midrash, Jewish folklore, and mystical and Hasidic sources.
8 x 10, 64 pp, Full-color illus., Hardcover, ISBN 1-58023-149-7 **$18.95** *For ages 7 & up*

## The Book of Miracles: A Young Person's Guide to Jewish Spiritual Awareness
*By Lawrence Kushner. All-new illustrations by the author.*
6 x 9, 96 pp, 2-color illus., Hardcover, ISBN 1-879045-78-8 **$16.95** *For ages 9–13*

## In Our Image: God's First Creatures
*By Nancy Sohn Swartz*
9 x 12, 32 pp, Full-color illus., Hardcover, ISBN 1-879045-99-0 **$16.95** *For ages 4 & up*

Also Available as a Board Book: **How Did the Animals Help God?**
5 x 5, 24 pp, Board, Full-color illus., ISBN 1-59473-044-X **$7.99** *For ages 0–4 (A SkyLight Paths book)*

# *From* SKYLIGHT PATHS PUBLISHING

## Becoming Me: A Story of Creation
*By Martin Boroson. Full-color illus. by Christopher Gilvan-Cartwright.*
Told in the personal "voice" of the Creator, a story about creation and relationship that is about each one of us.
8 x 10, 32 pp, Full-color illus., Hardcover, ISBN 1-893361-11-X **$16.95** *For ages 4 & up*

## Ten Amazing People: And How They Changed the World
*By Maura D. Shaw. Foreword by Dr. Robert Coles. Full-color illus. by Stephen Marchesi.*
Black Elk • Dorothy Day • Malcolm X • Mahatma Gandhi • Martin Luther King, Jr. • Mother Teresa • Janusz Korczak • Desmond Tutu • Thich Nhat Hanh • Albert Schweitzer.
8½ x 11, 48 pp, Full-color illus., Hardcover, ISBN 1-893361-47-0 **$17.95** *For ages 7 & up*

## Where Does God Live? *By August Gold and Matthew J. Perlman*
Helps young readers develop a personal understanding of God.
10 x 8½, 32 pp, Full-color photo illus., Quality PB, ISBN 1-893361-39-X **$8.99** *For ages 3–6*

# Children's Books
## by Sandy Eisenberg Sasso

### Adam & Eve's First Sunset: God's New Day
Engaging new story explores fear and hope, faith and gratitude in ways that will delight kids and adults—inspiring us to bless each of God's days and nights.
9 x 12, 32 pp, Full-color illus., Hardcover, ISBN 1-58023-177-2 **$17.95** *For ages 4 & up*

### But God Remembered
#### Stories of Women from Creation to the Promised Land
Four different stories of women—Lillith, Serach, Bityah, and the Daughters of Z—teach us important values through their faith and actions.
9 x 12, 32 pp, Full-color illus., Hardcover, ISBN 1-879045-43-5 **$16.95** *For ages 8 & up*

### Cain & Abel: Finding the Fruits of Peace
Shows children that we have the power to deal with anger in positive ways. Provides questions for kids and adults to explore together.
9 x 12, 32 pp, Full-color illus., Hardcover, ISBN 1-58023-123-3 **$16.95** *For ages 5 & up*

### God in Between
If you wanted to find God, where would you look? This magical, mythical tale teaches that God can be found where we are: within all of us and the relationships between us.
9 x 12, 32 pp, Full-color illus., Hardcover, ISBN 1-879045-86-9 **$16.95** *For ages 4 & up*

### God's Paintbrush: Special 10th Anniversary Edition
Wonderfully interactive, invites children of all faiths and backgrounds to encounter God through moments in their own lives. Provides questions adult and child can explore together.
11 x 8½, 32 pp, Full-color illus., Hardcover, ISBN 1-58023-195-0 **$17.95** *For ages 4 & up*

### Also Available: God's Paintbrush Teacher's Guide
8½ x 11, 32 pp, PB, ISBN 1-879045-57-5 **$8.95**

### God's Paintbrush Celebration Kit
A Spiritual Activity Kit for Teachers and Students of All Faiths, All Backgrounds
Additional activity sheets available:
8-Student Activity Sheet Pack (40 sheets/5 sessions), ISBN 1-58023-058-X **$19.95**
Single-Student Activity Sheet Pack (5 sessions), ISBN 1-58023-059-8 **$3.95**

### In God's Name
Like an ancient myth in its poetic text and vibrant illustrations, this award-winning modern fable about the search for God's name celebrates the diversity and, at the same time, the unity of all people.
9 x 12, 32 pp, Full-color illus., Hardcover, ISBN 1-879045-26-5 **$16.99** *For ages 4 & up*

### Also Available as a Board Book: What Is God's Name?
5 x 5, 24 pp, Board, Full-color illus., ISBN 1-893361-10-1 **$7.99** *For ages 0–4 (A SkyLight Paths book)*

### Also Available: In God's Name video and study guide
Computer animation, original music, and children's voices. 18 min. **$29.99**

### Also Available in Spanish: El nombre de Dios
9 x 12, 32 pp, Full-color illus., Hardcover, ISBN 1-893361-63-2 **$16.95** *(A SkyLight Paths book)*

### Noah's Wife: The Story of Naamah
When God tells Noah to bring the animals of the world onto the ark, God also calls on Naamah, Noah's wife, to save each plant on Earth. Based on an ancient text.
9 x 12, 32 pp, Full-color illus., Hardcover, ISBN 1-58023-134-9 **$16.95** *For ages 4 & up*

### Also Available as a Board Book: Naamah, Noah's Wife
5 x 5, 24 pp, Full-color illus., Board, ISBN 1-893361-56-X **$7.95** *For ages 0–4 (A SkyLight Paths book)*

### For Heaven's Sake: Finding God in Unexpected Places
9 x 12, 32 pp, Full-color illus., Hardcover, ISBN 1-58023-054-7 **$16.95** *For ages 4 & up*

### God Said Amen: Finding the Answers to Our Prayers
9 x 12, 32 pp, Full-color illus., Hardcover, ISBN 1-58023-080-6 **$16.95** *For ages 4 & up*

# Current Events/History

**The Story of the Jews:** A 4,000-Year Adventure—A Graphic History Book
*Written & illustrated by Stan Mack*
Through witty, illustrated narrative, we visit all the major happenings from biblical times to the twenty-first century. Celebrates the major characters and events that have shaped the Jewish people and culture.
6 x 9, 288 pp, illus., Quality PB, ISBN 1-58023-155-1 **$16.95**

**The Jewish Prophet:** Visionary Words from Moses and Miriam to Henrietta Szold and A. J. Heschel   *By Rabbi Michael J. Shire*
6½ x 8½, 128 pp, 123 full-color illus., Hardcover, ISBN 1-58023-168-3 **Special gift price $14.95**

**Shared Dreams:** Martin Luther King, Jr. & the Jewish Community
*By Rabbi Marc Schneier. Preface by Martin Luther King III.*
6 x 9, 240 pp, Hardcover, ISBN 1-58023-062-8 **$24.95**

**"Who Is a Jew?":** Conversations, Not Conclusions  *By Meryl Hyman*
6 x 9, 272 pp, Quality PB, ISBN 1-58023-052-0 **$16.95**

# Ecology

**Ecology & the Jewish Spirit:** Where Nature & the Sacred Meet
*Edited by Ellen Bernstein*  6 x 9, 288 pp, Quality PB, ISBN 1-58023-082-2 **$16.95**

**Torah of the Earth:** Exploring 4,000 Years of Ecology in Jewish Thought
Vol. 1: Biblical Israel: One Land, One People; Rabbinic Judaism: One People, Many Lands
Vol. 2: Zionism: One Land, Two Peoples; Eco-Judaism: One Earth, Many Peoples
*Edited by Rabbi Arthur Waskow*
Vol. 1: 6 x 9, 272 pp, Quality PB, ISBN 1-58023-086-5 **$19.95**
Vol. 2: 6 x 9, 336 pp, Quality PB, ISBN 1-58023-087-3 **$19.95**

# Grief/Healing

**Against the Dying of the Light:** A Parent's Story of Love, Loss and Hope
*By Leonard Fein*
In this unusual exploration of heartbreak and healing, Leonard Fein chronicles the sudden death of his 30-year-old daughter and shares the hard-earned wisdom that emerges in the face of loss and grief.
5½ x 8½, 176 pp, Hardcover, ISBN 1-58023-110-1 **$19.95**

**Grief in Our Seasons:** A Mourner's Kaddish Companion  *By Rabbi Kerry M. Olitzky*
4½ x 6½, 448 pp, Quality PB, ISBN 1-879045-55-9 **$15.95**

**Healing of Soul, Healing of Body:** Spiritual Leaders Unfold the Strength & Solace in Psalms  *Edited by Rabbi Simkha Y. Weintraub, C.S.W.*
6 x 9, 128 pp, 2-color illus. text, Quality PB, ISBN 1-879045-31-1 **$14.95**

**Jewish Paths toward Healing and Wholeness:** A Personal Guide to Dealing with Suffering  *By Rabbi Kerry M. Olitzky. Foreword by Debbie Friedman.*
6 x 9, 192 pp, Quality PB, ISBN 1-58023-068-7 **$15.95**

**Mourning & Mitzvah, 2nd Edition:** A Guided Journal for Walking the Mourner's Path through Grief to Healing  *By Anne Brener, L.C.S.W.*
7½ x 9, 304 pp, Quality PB, ISBN 1-58023-113-6 **$19.95**

**The Perfect Stranger's Guide to Funerals and Grieving Practices**
A Guide to Etiquette in Other People's Religious Ceremonies  *Edited by Stuart M. Matlins*
6 x 9, 240 pp, Quality PB, ISBN 1-893361-20-9 **$16.95**  (*A SkyLight Paths book*)

**Tears of Sorrow, Seeds of Hope:** A Jewish Spiritual Companion for Infertility and Pregnancy Loss  *By Rabbi Nina Beth Cardin*
6 x 9, 192 pp, Hardcover, ISBN 1-58023-017-2 **$19.95**

**A Time to Mourn, A Time to Comfort, 2nd Edition:** A Guide to Jewish Bereavement and Comfort  *By Dr. Ron Wolfson*
7 x 9, 336 pp, Quality PB, ISBN 1-58023-253-1 **$19.99**

**When a Grandparent Dies:** A Kid's Own Remembering Workbook for Dealing with Shiva and the Year Beyond  *By Nechama Liss-Levinson, Ph.D.*
8 x 10, 48 pp, 2-color text, Hardcover, ISBN 1-879045-44-3 **$15.95**  *For ages 7–13*

# Abraham Joshua Heschel

**The Earth Is the Lord's:** The Inner World of the Jew in Eastern Europe
5½ x 8, 128 pp, Quality PB, ISBN 1-879045-42-7 **$14.95**

**Israel:** An Echo of Eternity *New Introduction by Susannah Heschel*
5½ x 8, 272 pp, Quality PB, ISBN 1-879045-70-2 **$19.95**

**A Passion for Truth:** Despair and Hope in Hasidism
5½ x 8, 352 pp, Quality PB, ISBN 1-879045-41-9 **$18.99**

# Holidays/Holy Days

**Reclaiming Judaism as a Spiritual Practice:** Holy Days and Shabbat
*By Rabbi Goldie Milgram*
Provides a framework for understanding the powerful and often unexplained intellectual, emotional, and spiritual tools that are essential for a lively, relevant, and fulfilling Jewish spiritual practice. 7 x 9, 272 pp, Quality PB, ISBN 1-58023-205-1 **$19.99**

**7th Heaven:** Celebrating Shabbat with Rebbe Nachman of Breslov
*By Moshe Mykoff with the Breslov Research Institute*
Based on the teachings of Rebbe Nachman of Breslov. Explores the art of consciously observing Shabbat and understanding in-depth many of the day's traditional spiritual practices. 5⅛ x 8¼, 224 pp, Deluxe PB w/flaps, ISBN 1-58023-175-6 **$18.95**

**The Women's Passover Companion**
Women's Reflections on the Festival of Freedom
*Edited by Rabbi Sharon Cohen Anisfeld, Tara Mohr, and Catherine Spector*
Groundbreaking. A provocative conversation about women's relationships to Passover as well as the roots and meanings of women's seders.
6 x 9, 352 pp, Hardcover, ISBN 1-58023-128-4 **$24.95**

**The Women's Seder Sourcebook**
Rituals & Readings for Use at the Passover Seder
*Edited by Rabbi Sharon Cohen Anisfeld, Tara Mohr, and Catherine Spector*
Gathers the voices of more than one hundred women in readings, personal and creative reflections, commentaries, blessings, and ritual suggestions that can be incorporated into your Passover celebration as supplements to or substitutes for traditional passages of the haggadah.
6 x 9, 384 pp, Hardcover, ISBN 1-58023-136-5 **$24.95**

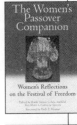

**Creating Lively Passover Seders:** A Sourcebook of Engaging Tales, Texts & Activities
*By David Arnow, Ph.D.* 7 x 9, 416 pp, Quality PB, ISBN 1-58023-184-5 **$24.99**

**Hanukkah, 2nd Edition:** The Family Guide to Spiritual Celebration
*By Dr. Ron Wolfson. Edited by Joel Lurie Grishaver.*
7 x 9, 240 pp, illus., Quality PB, ISBN 1-58023-122-5 **$18.95**

**The Jewish Family Fun Book:** Holiday Projects, Everyday Activities, and Travel Ideas
with Jewish Themes *By Danielle Dardashti and Roni Sarig. Illus. by Avi Katz.*
6 x 9, 288 pp, 70+ b/w illus. & diagrams, Quality PB, ISBN 1-58023-171-3 **$18.95**

**The Jewish Gardening Cookbook:** Growing Plants & Cooking for
Holidays & Festivals *By Michael Brown* 6 x 9, 224 pp, 30+ illus., Quality PB, ISBN 1-58023-116-0 **$16.95**

**The Jewish Lights Book of Fun Classroom Activities:** Simple and Seasonal
Projects for Teachers and Students *By Danielle Dardashti and Roni Sarig*
6 x 9, 240 pp, Quality PB, ISBN 1-58023-206-X **$19.99**

**Passover, 2nd Edition:** The Family Guide to Spiritual Celebration
*By Dr. Ron Wolfson with Joel Lurie Grishaver* 7 x 9, 352 pp, Quality PB, ISBN 1-58023-174-8 **$19.95**

**Shabbat, 2nd Edition:** The Family Guide to Preparing for and Celebrating the Sabbath
*By Dr. Ron Wolfson* 7 x 9, 320 pp, illus., Quality PB, ISBN 1-58023-164-0 **$19.95**

**Sharing Blessings:** Children's Stories for Exploring the Spirit of the Jewish Holidays
*By Rahel Musleah and Michael Klayman*
8½ x 11, 64 pp, Full-color illus., Hardcover, ISBN 1-879045-71-0 **$18.95** *For ages 6 & up*

# Inspiration

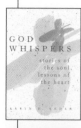

## God in All Moments
Mystical & Practical Spiritual Wisdom from Hasidic Masters
*Edited and translated by Or N. Rose with Ebn D. Leader*
Hasidic teachings on how to be mindful in religious practice and cultivating every-day ethical behavior—*hanhagot*. 5½ x 8½, 192 pp, Quality PB, ISBN 1-58023-186-1 **$16.95**

## Our Dance with God: Finding Prayer, Perspective and Meaning in the
Stories of Our Lives *By Karyn D. Kedar*
Inspiring spiritual insight to guide you on your life journeys and teach you to live and thrive in two conflicting worlds: the rational/material and the spiritual.
6 x 9, 176 pp, Quality PB, ISBN 1-58023-202-7 **$16.99**

Also Available: **The Dance of the Dolphin** (Hardcover edition of *Our Dance with God*)
6 x 9, 176 pp, Hardcover, ISBN 1-58023-154-3 **$19.95**

## The Empty Chair: Finding Hope and Joy—Timeless Wisdom from a Hasidic Master,
Rebbe Nachman of Breslov *Adapted by Moshe Mykoff and the Breslov Research Institute*
4 x 6, 128 pp, 2-color text, Deluxe PB w/flaps, ISBN 1-879045-67-2 **$9.95**

## The Gentle Weapon: Prayers for Everyday and Not-So-Everyday Moments—
Timeless Wisdom from the Teachings of the Hasidic Master, Rebbe Nachman of Breslov
*Adapted by Moshe Mykoff and S. C. Mizrahi, together with the Breslov Research Institute*
4 x 6, 144 pp, 2-color text, Deluxe PB w/flaps, ISBN 1-58023-022-9 **$9.95**

## God Whispers: Stories of the Soul, Lessons of the Heart *By Karyn D. Kedar*
6 x 9, 176 pp, Quality PB, ISBN 1-58023-088-1 **$15.95**

## An Orphan in History: One Man's Triumphant Search for His Jewish Roots
*By Paul Cowan. Afterword by Rachel Cowan.* 6 x 9, 288 pp, Quality PB, ISBN 1-58023-135-7 **$16.95**

## Restful Reflections: Nighttime Inspiration to Calm the Soul, Based on Jewish Wisdom
*By Rabbi Kerry M. Olitzky & Rabbi Lori Forman* 4½ x 6½, 448 pp, Quality PB, ISBN 1-58023-091-1 **$15.95**

## Sacred Intentions: Daily Inspiration to Strengthen the Spirit, Based on Jewish Wisdom
*By Rabbi Kerry M. Olitzky and Rabbi Lori Forman* 4½ x 6½, 448 pp, Quality PB, ISBN 1-58023-061-X **$15.95**

# Kabbalah/Mysticism/Enneagram

## Seek My Face: A Jewish Mystical Theology
*By Dr. Arthur Green*
This classic work of contemporary Jewish theology, revised and updated, is a profound, deeply personal statement of the lasting truths of Jewish mysticism and the basic faith claims of Judaism. A tool for anyone seeking the elusive presence of God in the world. 6 x 9, 304 pp, Quality PB, ISBN 1-58023-130-6 **$19.95**

## Zohar: Annotated & Explained
*Translation and annotation by Dr. Daniel C. Matt. Foreword by Andrew Harvey*
Offers insightful yet unobtrusive commentary to the masterpiece of Jewish mysticism that explains references and mystical symbols, shares wisdom of spiritual masters, and clarifies the *Zohar*'s bold claim: We have always been taught that we need God, but in order to manifest in the world, God needs us.
5½ x 8½, 160 pp, Quality PB, ISBN 1-893361-51-9 **$15.99** *(A SkyLight Paths book)*

## Cast in God's Image: Discover Your Personality Type Using the Enneagram and Kabbalah
*By Rabbi Howard A. Addison*
7 x 9, 176 pp, Quality PB, Layflat binding, 20+ journaling exercises, ISBN 1-58023-124-1 **$16.95**

## Ehyeh: A Kabbalah for Tomorrow *By Dr. Arthur Green*
6 x 9, 224 pp, Quality PB, ISBN 1-58023-213-2 **$16.99;** Hardcover, ISBN 1-58023-125-X **$21.99**

## The Enneagram and Kabbalah: Reading Your Soul *By Rabbi Howard A. Addison*
6 x 9, 176 pp, Quality PB, ISBN 1-58023-001-6 **$15.95**

## Finding Joy: A Practical Spiritual Guide to Happiness *By Dannel I. Schwartz with Mark Hass*
6 x 9, 192 pp, Quality PB, ISBN 1-58023-009-1 **$14.95;** Hardcover, ISBN 1-879045-53-2 **$19.95**

## The Gift of Kabbalah: Discovering the Secrets of Heaven, Renewing Your Life on Earth
*By Tamar Frankiel, Ph.D.*
6 x 9, 256 pp, Quality PB, ISBN 1-58023-141-1 **$16.95;** Hardcover, ISBN 1-58023-108-X **$21.95**

## The Way Into Jewish Mystical Tradition *By Lawrence Kushner*
6 x 9, 224 pp, Quality PB, ISBN 1-58023-200-0 **$18.99;** Hardcover, ISBN 1-58023-029-6 **$21.95**

# Life Cycle
## Marriage / Parenting / Family / Aging

**Jewish Fathers:** A Legacy of Love
*Photographs by Lloyd Wolf. Essays by Paula Wolfson. Foreword by Harold S. Kushner.*
Honors the role of contemporary Jewish fathers in America. Each father tells in his own words what it means to be a parent and Jewish, and what he learned from his own father. Insightful photos. 9½ x 9⅞, 144 pp with 100+ duotone photos, Hardcover, ISBN 1-58023-204-3 **$30.00**

**The New Jewish Baby Album:** Creating and Celebrating the Beginning of a Spiritual Life—A Jewish Lights Companion
*By the Editors at Jewish Lights. Foreword by Anita Diamant. Preface by Sandy Eisenberg Sasso.*
A spiritual keepsake that will be treasured for generations. More than just a memory book, *shows you how—and why it's important*—to create a Jewish home and a Jewish life. 8 x 10, 64 pp, Deluxe Padded Hardcover, Full-color illus., ISBN 1-58023-138-1 **$19.95**

**The Jewish Pregnancy Book:** A Resource for the Soul, Body & Mind during Pregnancy, Birth & the First Three Months
*By Sandy Falk, M.D., and Rabbi Daniel Judson, with Steven A. Rapp*
Includes medical information on fetal development, pre-natal testing and more, from a liberal Jewish perspective; prenatal *Aleph-Bet* yoga; and prayers and rituals for each stage of pregnancy. 7 x 10, 208 pp, Quality PB, b/w illus., ISBN 1-58023-178-0 **$16.95**

**Celebrating Your New Jewish Daughter:** Creating Jewish Ways to Welcome Baby Girls into the Covenant—New and Traditional Ceremonies
*By Debra Nussbaum Cohen* 6 x 9, 272 pp, Quality PB, ISBN 1-58023-090-3 **$18.95**

**The New Jewish Baby Book, 2nd Edition:** Names, Ceremonies & Customs—A Guide for Today's Families *By Anita Diamant* 6 x 9, 336 pp, Quality PB, ISBN 1-58023-251-5 **$19.99**

**Parenting As a Spiritual Journey:** Deepening Ordinary and Extraordinary Events into Sacred Occasions *By Rabbi Nancy Fuchs-Kreimer* 6 x 9, 224 pp, Quality PB, ISBN 1-58023-016-4 **$16.95**

**Embracing the Covenant:** Converts to Judaism Talk About Why & How
*Edited and with introductions by Rabbi Allan Berkowitz and Patti Moskovitz*
6 x 9, 192 pp, Quality PB, ISBN 1-879045-50-8 **$16.95**

**The Guide to Jewish Interfaith Family Life:** An InterfaithFamily.com Handbook
*Edited by Ronnie Friedland and Edmund Case* 6 x 9, 384 pp, Quality PB, ISBN 1-58023-153-5 **$18.95**

**Introducing My Faith and My Community**
The Jewish Outreach Institute Guide for the Christian in a Jewish Interfaith Relationship
*By Rabbi Kerry M. Olitzky* 6 x 9, 176 pp, Quality PB, ISBN 1-58023-192-6 **$16.99**

**Making a Successful Jewish Interfaith Marriage:** The Jewish Outreach Institute Guide to Opportunities, Challenges and Resources
*By Rabbi Kerry M. Olitzky with Joan Peterson Littman* 6 x 9, 176 pp, Quality PB, ISBN 1-58023-170-5 **$16.95**

**How to Be a Perfect Stranger, 3rd Edition:** The Essential Religious Etiquette Handbook *Edited by Stuart M. Matlins and Arthur J. Magida*
The indispensable guide to the rituals and celebrations of the major religions and denominations in North America from the perspective of an interested guest of any other faith. 6 x 9, 432 pp, Quality PB, ISBN 1-893361-67-5 **$19.95** *(A SkyLight Paths book)*

**The Creative Jewish Wedding Book:** A Hands-On Guide to New & Old Traditions, Ceremonies & Celebrations *By Gabrielle Kaplan-Mayer*
Provides the tools to create the most meaningful Jewish traditional or alternative wedding by using ritual elements to express your unique style and spirituality.
9 x 9, 288 pp, b/w photos, Quality PB, ISBN 1-58023-194-2 **$19.99**

**Divorce Is a Mitzvah:** A Practical Guide to Finding Wholeness and Holiness When Your Marriage Dies *By Rabbi Perry Netter. Afterword by Rabbi Laura Geller.*
6 x 9, 224 pp, Quality PB, ISBN 1-58023-172-1 **$16.95**

**A Heart of Wisdom:** Making the Jewish Journey from Midlife through the Elder Years
*Edited by Susan Berrin. Foreword by Harold Kushner.* 6 x 9, 384 pp, Quality PB, ISBN 1-58023-051-2 **$18.95**

**So That Your Values Live On:** Ethical Wills and How to Prepare Them
*Edited by Jack Riemer and Nathaniel Stampfer* 6 x 9, 272 pp, Quality PB, ISBN 1-879045-34-6 **$18.95**

# Meditation

**The Handbook of Jewish Meditation Practices**
A Guide for Enriching the Sabbath and Other Days of Your Life
*By Rabbi David A. Cooper*
Easy-to-learn meditation techniques for use on the Sabbath and every day, to help us return to the roots of traditional Jewish spirituality where Shabbat is a state of mind and soul. 6 x 9, 208 pp, Quality PB, ISBN 1-58023-102-0 **$16.95**

**Discovering Jewish Meditation:** Instruction & Guidance for Learning an Ancient Spiritual Practice *By Nan Fink Gefen, Ph.D.* 6 x 9, 208 pp, Quality PB, ISBN 1-58023-067-9 **$16.95**

**A Heart of Stillness:** A Complete Guide to Learning the Art of Meditation
*By Rabbi David A. Cooper* 5½ x 8½, 272 pp, Quality PB, ISBN 1-893361-03-9 **$16.95**
*(A SkyLight Paths book)*

**Meditation from the Heart of Judaism:** Today's Teachers Share Their Practices, Techniques, and Faith *Edited by Avram Davis*
6 x 9, 256 pp, Quality PB, ISBN 1-58023-049-0 **$16.95**

**Silence, Simplicity & Solitude:** A Complete Guide to Spiritual Retreat at Home
*By Rabbi David A. Cooper* 5½ x 8½, 336 pp, Quality PB, ISBN 1-893361-04-7 **$16.95**
*(A SkyLight Paths book)*

**Three Gates to Meditation Practice:** A Personal Journey into Sufism, Buddhism, and Judaism *By Rabbi David A. Cooper*
5½ x 8½, 240 pp, Quality PB, ISBN 1-893361-22-5 **$16.95** *(A SkyLight Paths book)*

**The Way of Flame:** A Guide to the Forgotten Mystical Tradition of Jewish Meditation
*By Avram Davis* 4½ x 8, 176 pp, Quality PB, ISBN 1-58023-060-1 **$15.95**

# Ritual/Sacred Practice/Journaling

**The Jewish Dream Book:** The Key to Opening the Inner Meaning of Your Dreams *By Vanessa L. Ochs with Elizabeth Ochs. Full-color illus. by Kristina Swarner.*
Instructions for how modern people can perform ancient Jewish dream practices and dream interpretations drawn from the Jewish wisdom tradition. For anyone who wants to understand their dreams—and themselves.
8 x 8, 120 pp, Full-color illus., Deluxe PB w/flaps, ISBN 1-58023-132-2 **$16.95**

**The Jewish Journaling Book:** How to Use Jewish Tradition to Write Your Life & Explore Your Soul *By Janet Ruth Falon*
Details the history of Jewish journaling throughout biblical and modern times, and teaches specific journaling techniques to help you create and maintain a vital journal, from a Jewish perspective. 8 x 8, 304 pp, Deluxe PB w/flaps, ISBN 1-58023-203-5 **$18.99**

**The Rituals & Practices of a Jewish Life:** A Handbook for Personal Spiritual Renewal *Edited by Rabbi Kerry M. Olitzky and Rabbi Daniel Judson*
6 x 9, 272 pp, illus., Quality PB, ISBN 1-58023-169-1 **$18.95**

**The Book of Jewish Sacred Practices:** CLAL's Guide to Everyday & Holiday Rituals & Blessings *Edited by Rabbi Irwin Kula and Vanessa L. Ochs, Ph.D.*
6 x 9, 368 pp, Quality PB, ISBN 1-58023-152-7 **$18.95**

# Science Fiction/ Mystery & Detective Fiction

**Mystery Midrash:** An Anthology of Jewish Mystery & Detective Fiction
*Edited by Lawrence W. Raphael. Preface by Joel Siegel.*
6 x 9, 304 pp, Quality PB, ISBN 1-58023-055-5 **$16.95**

**Criminal Kabbalah:** An Intriguing Anthology of Jewish Mystery & Detective Fiction
*Edited by Lawrence W. Raphael. Foreword by Laurie R. King.*
6 x 9, 256 pp, Quality PB, ISBN 1-58023-109-8 **$16.95**

**More Wandering Stars:** An Anthology of Outstanding Stories of Jewish Fantasy and Science Fiction *Edited by Jack Dann. Introduction by Isaac Asimov.*
6 x 9, 192 pp, Quality PB, ISBN 1-58023-063-6 **$16.95**

**Wandering Stars:** An Anthology of Jewish Fantasy & Science Fiction
*Edited by Jack Dann. Introduction by Isaac Asimov.*
6 x 9, 272 pp, Quality PB, ISBN 1-58023-005-9 **$16.95**

# *Spirituality*

**The Alphabet of Paradise:** An A–Z of Spirituality for Everyday Life
*By Rabbi Howard Cooper*
In twenty-six engaging chapters, Cooper spiritually illuminates the subjects of our daily lives—A to Z—examining these sources by using an ancient Jewish mystical method of interpretation that reveals both the literal and more allusive meanings of each. 5 x 7¼, 224 pp, Quality PB, ISBN 1-893361-80-2 **$16.95** *(A SkyLight Paths book)*

**Does the Soul Survive?:** A Jewish Journey to Belief in Afterlife, Past Lives & Living with Purpose  *By Rabbi Elie Kaplan Spitz. Foreword by Brian L. Weiss, M.D.*
Spitz relates his own experiences and those shared with him by people he has worked with as a rabbi, and shows us that belief in afterlife and past lives, so often approached with reluctance, is in fact true to Jewish tradition.
6 x 9, 288 pp, Quality PB, ISBN 1-58023-165-9 **$16.95**; Hardcover, ISBN 1-58023-094-6 **$21.95**

**First Steps to a New Jewish Spirit:** Reb Zalman's Guide to Recapturing the Intimacy & Ecstasy in Your Relationship with God
*By Rabbi Zalman M. Schachter-Shalomi with Donald Gropman*
An extraordinary spiritual handbook that restores psychic and physical vigor by introducing us to new models and alternative ways of practicing Judaism. Offers meditation and contemplation exercises for enriching the most important aspects of everyday life. 6 x 9, 144 pp, Quality PB, ISBN 1-58023-182-9 **$16.95**

**God in Our Relationships:** Spirituality between People from the Teachings of Martin Buber  *By Rabbi Dennis S. Ross*
On the eightieth anniversary of Buber's classic work, we can discover new answers to critical issues in our lives. Inspiring examples from Ross's own life—as congregational rabbi, father, hospital chaplain, social worker, and husband—illustrate Buber's difficult-to-understand ideas about how we encounter God and each other. 5½ x 8½, 160 pp, Quality PB, ISBN 1-58023-147-0 **$16.95**

**The Jewish Lights Spirituality Handbook:** A Guide to Understanding, Exploring & Living a Spiritual Life  *Edited by Stuart M. Matlins*
What exactly is "Jewish" about spirituality? How do I make it a part of my life? Fifty of today's foremost spiritual leaders share their ideas and experience with us.
6 x 9, 456 pp, Quality PB, ISBN 1-58023-093-8 **$19.95**; Hardcover, ISBN 1-58023-100-4 **$24.95**

**Bringing the Psalms to Life:** How to Understand and Use the Book of Psalms
*By Dr. Daniel F. Polish*
6 x 9, 208 pp, Quality PB, ISBN 1-58023-157-8 **$16.95**; Hardcover, ISBN 1-58023-077-6 **$21.95**

**God & the Big Bang:** Discovering Harmony between Science & Spirituality
*By Dr. Daniel C. Matt* 6 x 9, 216 pp, Quality PB, ISBN 1-879045-89-3 **$16.95**

**Godwrestling—Round 2:** Ancient Wisdom, Future Paths
*By Rabbi Arthur Waskow* 6 x 9, 352 pp, Quality PB, ISBN 1-879045-72-9 **$18.95**

**One God Clapping:** The Spiritual Path of a Zen Rabbi  *By Rabbi Alan Lew with Sherril Jaffe*
5½ x 8½, 336 pp, Quality PB, ISBN 1-58023-115-2 **$16.95**

**The Path of Blessing:** Experiencing the Energy and Abundance of the Divine
*By Rabbi Marcia Prager* 5½ x 8½, 240 pp., Quality PB, ISBN 1-58023-148-2 **$16.95**

**Six Jewish Spiritual Paths:** A Rationalist Looks at Spirituality  *By Rabbi Rifat Sonsino*
6 x 9, 208 pp, Quality PB, ISBN 1-58023-167-5 **$16.95**; Hardcover, ISBN 1-58023-095-4 **$21.95**

**Soul Judaism:** Dancing with God into a New Era
*By Rabbi Wayne Dosick* 5½ x 8½, 304 pp, Quality PB, ISBN 1-58023-053-9 **$16.95**

**Stepping Stones to Jewish Spiritual Living:** Walking the Path Morning, Noon, and Night  *By Rabbi James L. Mirel and Karen Bonnell Werth*
6 x 9, 240 pp, Quality PB, ISBN 1-58023-074-1 **$16.95**; Hardcover, ISBN 1-58023-003-2 **$21.95**

**There Is No Messiah... and You're It:** The Stunning Transformation of Judaism's Most Provocative Idea  *By Rabbi Robert N. Levine, D.D.*
6 x 9, 192 pp, Quality PB, ISBN 1-58023-255-8 **$16.99**; Hardcover, ISBN 1-58023-173-X **$21.95**

**These Are the Words:** A Vocabulary of Jewish Spiritual Life  *By Dr. Arthur Green*
6 x 9, 304 pp, Quality PB, ISBN 1-58023-107-1 **$18.95**

# Spirituality/Lawrence Kushner

**The Book of Letters:** A Mystical Hebrew Alphabet
Popular Hardcover Edition, 6 x 9, 80 pp, 2-color text, ISBN 1-879045-00-1 **$24.95**
Deluxe Gift Edition with slipcase, 9 x 12, 80 pp, 4-color text, Hardcover, ISBN 1-879045-01-X **$79.95**
Collector's Limited Edition, 9 x 12, 80 pp, gold foil embossed pages, w/limited edition silkscreened print, ISBN 1-879045-04-4 **$349.00**

**The Book of Miracles:** A Young Person's Guide to Jewish Spiritual Awareness
*All-new illustrations by the author*
6 x 9, 96 pp, 2-color illus., Hardcover, ISBN 1-879045-78-8 **$16.95** *For ages 9–13*

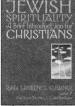

**The Book of Words:** Talking Spiritual Life, Living Spiritual Talk
6 x 9, 160 pp, Quality PB, ISBN 1-58023-020-2 **$16.95**

**Eyes Remade for Wonder:** A Lawrence Kushner Reader
*Introduction by Thomas Moore*
6 x 9, 240 pp, Quality PB, ISBN 1-58023-042-3 **$18.95;** Hardcover, ISBN 1-58023-014-8 **$23.95**

**God Was in This Place & I, i Did Not Know**
Finding Self, Spirituality and Ultimate Meaning
6 x 9, 192 pp, Quality PB, ISBN 1-879045-33-8 **$16.95**

**Honey from the Rock:** An Introduction to Jewish Mysticism
6 x 9, 176 pp, Quality PB, ISBN 1-58023-073-3 **$16.95**

**Invisible Lines of Connection:** Sacred Stories of the Ordinary
5½ x 8½, 160 pp, Quality PB, ISBN 1-879045-98-2 **$15.95**

**Jewish Spirituality—A Brief Introduction for Christians**
5½ x 8½, 112 pp, Quality PB Original, ISBN 1-58023-150-0 **$12.95**

**The River of Light:** Jewish Mystical Awareness
6 x 9, 192 pp, Quality PB, ISBN 1-58023-096-2 **$16.95**

**The Way Into Jewish Mystical Tradition**
6 x 9, 224 pp, Quality PB, ISBN 1-58023-200-0 **$18.99;** Hardcover, ISBN 1-58023-029-6 **$21.95**

# Spirituality/Prayer

**Pray Tell:** A Hadassah Guide to Jewish Prayer
*By Rabbi Jules Harlow, with contributions from Tamara Cohen, Rochelle Furstenberg, Rabbi Daniel Gordis, Leora Tanenbaum, and many others*
A guide to traditional Jewish prayer enriched with insight and wisdom from a broad variety of viewpoints—from Orthodox, Conservative, Reform, and Reconstructionist Judaism to New Age and feminist.
8½ x 11, 400 pp, Quality PB, ISBN 1-58023-163-2 **$29.95**

## My People's Prayer Book Series
Traditional Prayers, Modern Commentaries
*Edited by Rabbi Lawrence A. Hoffman*
Provides diverse and exciting commentary to the traditional liturgy, helping modern men and women find new wisdom in Jewish prayer, and bring liturgy into their lives.

Each book includes Hebrew text, modern translation, and commentaries from all perspectives of the Jewish world.
Vol. 1—The *Sh'ma* and Its Blessings
7 x 10, 168 pp, Hardcover, ISBN 1-879045-79-6 **$23.95**
Vol. 2—The *Amidah*
7 x 10, 240 pp, Hardcover, ISBN 1-879045-80-X **$24.95**
Vol. 3—*P'sukei D'zimrah* (Morning Psalms)
7 x 10, 240 pp, Hardcover, ISBN 1-879045-81-8 **$24.95**
Vol. 4—*Seder K'riat Hatorah* (The Torah Service)
7 x 10, 264 pp, Hardcover, ISBN 1-879045-82-6 **$23.95**
Vol. 5—*Birkhot Hashachar* (Morning Blessings)
7 x 10, 240 pp, Hardcover, ISBN 1-879045-83-4 **$24.95**
Vol. 6—*Tachanun* and Concluding Prayers
7 x 10, 240 pp, Hardcover, ISBN 1-879045-84-2 **$24.95**
Vol. 7—Shabbat at Home
7 x 10, 240 pp, Hardcover, ISBN 1-879045-85-0 **$24.95**
Vol. 8—*Kabbalat Shabbat* (Welcoming Shabbat in the Synagogue)
7 x 10, 240 pp, Hardcover, ISBN 1-58023-121-7 **$24.99**

# Spirituality/The Way Into... Series

*The Way Into...* Series offers an accessible and highly usable "guided tour" of the Jewish faith, people, history and beliefs—in total, an introduction to Judaism that will enable you to understand and interact with the sacred texts of the Jewish tradition. Each volume is written by a leading contemporary scholar and teacher, and explores one key aspect of Judaism. *The Way Into...* enables all readers to achieve a real sense of Jewish cultural literacy through guided study.

**The Way Into Encountering God in Judaism**   *By Neil Gillman*
6 x 9, 240 pp, Quality PB, ISBN 1-58023-199-3 **$18.99**; Hardcover, ISBN 1-58023-025-3 **$21.95**
Also Available: **The Jewish Approach to God: A Brief Introduction for Christians**
*By Neil Gillman* 5½ x 8½, 192 pp, Quality PB, ISBN 1-58023-190-X **$16.95**

**The Way Into Jewish Mystical Tradition**   *By Lawrence Kushner*
6 x 9, 224 pp, Quality PB, ISBN 1-58023-200-0 **$18.99**; Hardcover, ISBN 1-58023-029-6 **$21.95**

**The Way Into Jewish Prayer**   *By Lawrence A. Hoffman*
6 x 9, 224 pp, Quality PB, ISBN 1-58023-201-9 **$18.99**; Hardcover, ISBN 1-58023-027-X **$21.95**

**The Way Into Torah**   *By Norman J. Cohen*
6 x 9, 176 pp, Quality PB, ISBN 1-58023-198-5 **$16.99**; Hardcover, ISBN 1-58023-028-8 **$21.95**

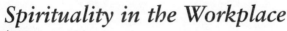

# Spirituality in the Workplace

**Being God's Partner**
How to Find the Hidden Link Between Spirituality and Your Work
*By Rabbi Jeffrey K. Salkin. Introduction by Norman Lear.*
6 x 9, 192 pp, Quality PB, ISBN 1-879045-65-6 **$17.95**

**The Business Bible:** 10 New Commandments for Bringing Spirituality & Ethical Values into the Workplace   *By Rabbi Wayne Dosick*
5½ x 8½, 208 pp, Quality PB, ISBN 1-58023-101-2 **$14.95**

# Spirituality and Wellness

**Aleph-Bet Yoga**
Embodying the Hebrew Letters for Physical and Spiritual Well-Being
*By Steven A. Rapp. Foreword by Tamar Frankiel, Ph.D., and Judy Greenfeld. Preface by Hart Lazer*
7 x 10, 128 pp, b/w photos, Quality PB, Layflat binding, ISBN 1-58023-162-4 **$16.95**

**Entering the Temple of Dreams**
Jewish Prayers, Movements, and Meditations for the End of the Day
*By Tamar Frankiel, Ph.D., and Judy Greenfeld*
7 x 10, 192 pp, illus., Quality PB, ISBN 1-58023-079-2 **$16.95**

**Jewish Paths toward Healing and Wholeness:** A Personal Guide to Dealing with Suffering   *By Rabbi Kerry M. Olitzky. Foreword by Debbie Friedman.*
6 x 9, 192 pp, Quality PB, ISBN 1-58023-068-7 **$15.95**

**Minding the Temple of the Soul**
Balancing Body, Mind, and Spirit through Traditional Jewish Prayer, Movement, and Meditation   *By Tamar Frankiel, Ph.D., and Judy Greenfeld*
7 x 10, 184 pp, illus., Quality PB, ISBN 1-879045-64-8 **$16.95**
Audiotape of the Blessings and Meditations: 60 min. **$9.95**
Videotape of the Movements and Meditations: 46 min. **$20.00**

# Spirituality/Women's Interest

**The Quotable Jewish Woman:** Wisdom, Inspiration & Humor from the Mind & Heart *Edited and compiled by Elaine Bernstein Partnow*
The definitive collection of ideas, reflections, humor, and wit of over 300 Jewish women.
6 x 9, 496 pp, Hardcover, ISBN 1-58023-193-4 **$29.99**

**Lifecycles, Vol. 1:** Jewish Women on Life Passages & Personal Milestones
*Edited and with introductions by Rabbi Debra Orenstein* 6 x 9, 480 pp, Quality PB, ISBN 1-58023-018-0 **$19.95**

**Lifecycles, Vol. 2:** Jewish Women on Biblical Themes in Contemporary Life
*Edited and with introductions by Rabbi Debra Orenstein and Rabbi Jane Rachel Litman*
6 x 9, 464 pp, Quality PB, ISBN 1-58023-019-9 **$19.95**

**Moonbeams:** A Hadassah Rosh Hodesh Guide *Edited by Carol Diament, Ph.D.*
8½ x 11, 240 pp, Quality PB, ISBN 1-58023-099-7 **$20.00**

**ReVisions:** Seeing Torah through a Feminist Lens *By Rabbi Elyse Goldstein*
5½ x 8½, 224 pp, Quality PB, ISBN 1-58023-117-9 **$16.95**

**White Fire:** A Portrait of Women Spiritual Leaders in America
*By Rabbi Malka Drucker. Photographs by Gay Block.*
7 x 10, 320 pp, 30+ b/w photos, Hardcover, ISBN 1-893361-64-0 **$24.95** *(A SkyLight Paths book)*

**Women of the Wall:** Claiming Sacred Ground at Judaism's Holy Site
*Edited by Phyllis Chesler and Rivka Haut* 6 x 9, 496 pp, b/w photos, Hardcover, ISBN 1-58023-161-6 **$34.95**

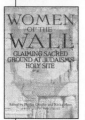

**The Women's Haftarah Commentary:** New Insights from Women Rabbis on the 54 Weekly Haftarah Portions, the 5 Megillot & Special Shabbatot
*Edited by Rabbi Elyse Goldstein* 6 x 9, 560 pp, Hardcover, ISBN 1-58023-133-0 **$39.99**

**The Women's Torah Commentary:** New Insights from Women Rabbis on the 54 Weekly Torah Portions *Edited by Rabbi Elyse Goldstein*
6 x 9, 496 pp, Hardcover, ISBN 1-58023-076-8 **$34.95**

**The Year Mom Got Religion:** One Woman's Midlife Journey into Judaism
*By Lee Meyerhoff Hendler* 6 x 9, 208 pp, Quality PB, ISBN 1-58023-070-9 **$15.95**

See Holidays for *The Women's Passover Companion: Women's Reflections on the Festival of Freedom* and *The Women's Seder Sourcebook: Rituals & Readings for Use at the Passover Seder.*

# Travel

**Israel—A Spiritual Travel Guide, 2nd Edition**
A Companion for the Modern Jewish Pilgrim
*By Rabbi Lawrence A. Hoffman* 4¾ x 10, 256 pp, Quality PB, illus., ISBN 1-58023-261-2 **$18.99**
Also Available: **The Israel Mission Leader's Guide** ISBN 1-58023-085-7 **$4.95**

# 12 Steps

**100 Blessings Every Day**
Daily Twelve Step Recovery Affirmations, Exercises for Personal Growth & Renewal Reflecting Seasons of the Jewish Year
*By Rabbi Kerry M. Olitzky. Foreword by Rabbi Neil Gillman.*
One-day-at-a-time monthly format. Reflects on the rhythm of the Jewish calendar to bring insight to recovery from addictions.
4½ x 6½, 432 pp, Quality PB, ISBN 1-879045-30-3 **$15.99**

**Recovery from Codependence:** A Jewish Twelve Steps Guide to Healing Your Soul
*By Rabbi Kerry M. Olitzky* 6 x 9, 160 pp, Quality PB, ISBN 1-879045-32-X **$13.95**

**Renewed Each Day:** Daily Twelve Step Recovery Meditations Based on the Bible
*By Rabbi Kerry M. Olitzky and Aaron Z.*
Vol. 1—Genesis & Exodus: 6 x 9, 224 pp, Quality PB, ISBN 1-879045-12-5 **$14.95**
Vol. 2—Leviticus, Numbers & Deuteronomy: 6 x 9, 280 pp, Quality PB, ISBN 1-879045-13-3 **$14.95**

**Twelve Jewish Steps to Recovery:** A Personal Guide to Turning from Alcoholism & Other Addictions—Drugs, Food, Gambling, Sex...
*By Rabbi Kerry M. Olitzky and Stuart A. Copans, M.D. Preface by Abraham J. Twerski, M.D.*
6 x 9, 144 pp, Quality PB, ISBN 1-879045-09-5 **$14.95**

# Theology/Philosophy

**Aspects of Rabbinic Theology**
*By Solomon Schechter. New Introduction by Dr. Neil Gillman.*
6 x 9, 448 pp, Quality PB, ISBN 1-879045-24-9 **$19.95**

**Broken Tablets:** Restoring the Ten Commandments and Ourselves
*Edited by Rachel S. Mikva. Introduction by Lawrence Kushner. Afterword by Arnold Jacob Wolf.*
6 x 9, 192 pp, Quality PB, ISBN 1-58023-158-6 **$16.95**; Hardcover, ISBN 1-58023-066-0 **$21.95**

**Creating an Ethical Jewish Life**
A Practical Introduction to Classic Teachings on How to Be a Jew
*By Dr. Byron L. Sherwin and Seymour J. Cohen*
6 x 9, 336 pp, Quality PB, ISBN 1-58023-114-4 **$19.95**

**The Death of Death:** Resurrection and Immortality in Jewish Thought
*By Dr. Neil Gillman* 6 x 9, 336 pp, Quality PB, ISBN 1-58023-081-4 **$18.95**

**Evolving Halakhah:** A Progressive Approach to Traditional Jewish Law
*By Rabbi Dr. Moshe Zemer*
6 x 9, 480 pp, Quality PB, ISBN 1-58023-127-6 **$29.95**; Hardcover, ISBN 1-58023-002-4 **$40.00**

**Hasidic Tales: Annotated & Explained**
*By Rabbi Rami Shapiro. Foreword by Andrew Harvey, SkyLight Illuminations series editor.*
5½ x 8½, 240 pp, Quality PB, ISBN 1-893361-86-1 **$16.95** *(A SkyLight Paths Book)*

**A Heart of Many Rooms:** Celebrating the Many Voices within Judaism
*By Dr. David Hartman* 6 x 9, 352 pp, Quality PB, ISBN 1-58023-156-X **$19.95**

**The Hebrew Prophets:** Selections Annotated & Explained
*Translation & Annotation by Rabbi Rami Shapiro. Foreword by Zalman M. Schachter-Shalomi*
5½ x 8½, 224 pp, Quality PB, ISBN 1-59473-037-7 **$16.99** *(A SkyLight Paths book)*

**Keeping Faith with the Psalms:** Deepen Your Relationship with God Using the
Book of Psalms *By Daniel F. Polish* 6 x 9, 272 pp, Hardcover, ISBN 1-58023-179-9 **$24.95**

**The Last Trial**
On the Legends and Lore of the Command to Abraham to Offer Isaac as a Sacrifice
*By Shalom Spiegel. New Introduction by Judah Goldin.*
6 x 9, 208 pp, Quality PB, ISBN 1-879045-29-X **$18.95**

**A Living Covenant:** The Innovative Spirit in Traditional Judaism
*By Dr. David Hartman* 6 x 9, 368 pp, Quality PB, ISBN 1-58023-011-3 **$18.95**

**Love and Terror in the God Encounter**
The Theological Legacy of Rabbi Joseph B. Soloveitchik
*By Dr. David Hartman*
6 x 9, 240 pp, Quality PB, ISBN 1-58023-176-4 **$19.95**; Hardcover, ISBN 1-58023-112-8 **$25.00**

**Seeking the Path to Life**
Theological Meditations on God and the Nature of People, Love, Life and Death
*By Rabbi Ira F. Stone* 6 x 9, 160 pp, Quality PB, ISBN 1-879045-47-8 **$14.95**

**The Spirit of Renewal:** Finding Faith after the Holocaust
*By Rabbi Edward Feld* 6 x 9, 224 pp, Quality PB, ISBN 1-879045-40-0 **$16.95**

**Tormented Master:** *The Life and Spiritual Quest of Rabbi Nahman of Bratslav*
*By Dr. Arthur Green* 6 x 9, 416 pp, Quality PB, ISBN 1-879045-11-7 **$19.99**

**Your Word Is Fire:** The Hasidic Masters on Contemplative Prayer
*Edited and translated by Dr. Arthur Green and Barry W. Holtz*
6 x 9, 160 pp, Quality PB, ISBN 1-879045-25-7 **$15.95**

---

## I Am Jewish
Personal Reflections Inspired by the Last Words of Daniel Pearl
Almost 150 Jews—both famous and not—from all walks of life, from all around
the world, write about Identity, Heritage, Covenant / Chosenness and Faith,
Humanity and Ethnicity, and *Tikkun Olam* and Justice.
*Edited by Judea and Ruth Pearl*
6 x 9, 304 pp, Deluxe PB w/flaps, ISBN 1-58023-259-0 **$18.99**; Hardcover, ISBN 1-58023-183-7 **$24.99**
**Download a free copy of the *I Am Jewish Teacher's Guide* at our website:**
**www.jewishlights.com**

## About Jewish Lights

People of all faiths and backgrounds yearn for books that attract, engage, educate, and spiritually inspire.

Our principal goal is to stimulate thought and help all people learn about who the Jewish People are, where they come from, and what the future can be made to hold. While people of our diverse Jewish heritage are the primary audience, our books speak to people in the Christian world as well and will broaden their understanding of Judaism and the roots of their own faith.

We bring to you authors who are at the forefront of spiritual thought and experience. While each has something different to say, they all say it in a voice that you can hear.

Our books are designed to welcome you and then to engage, stimulate, and inspire. We judge our success not only by whether or not our books are beautiful and commercially successful, but by whether or not they make a difference in your life.

For your information and convenience, at the back of this book we have provided a list of other Jewish Lights books you might find interesting and useful. They cover all the categories of your life:

| | |
|---|---|
| Bar/Bat Mitzvah | Life Cycle |
| Bible Study / Midrash | Meditation |
| Children's Books | Parenting |
| Congregation Resources | Prayer |
| Current Events / History | Ritual / Sacred Practice |
| Ecology | Spirituality |
| Fiction: Mystery, Science Fiction | Theology / Philosophy |
| Grief / Healing | Travel |
| Holidays / Holy Days | Twelve Steps |
| Inspiration | Women's Interest |
| Kabbalah / Mysticism / Enneagram | |

Stuart M. Matlins, Publisher

*Or phone, fax, mail or e-mail to:* **JEWISH LIGHTS Publishing**
Sunset Farm Offices, Route 4 • P.O. Box 237 • Woodstock, Vermont 05091
Tel: (802) 457-4000 • Fax: (802) 457-4004 • www.jewishlights.com
**Credit card orders:** (800) 962-4544 (8:30AM–5:30PM ET Monday–Friday)
*Generous discounts on quantity orders. SATISFACTION GUARANTEED. Prices subject to change.*

# For more information about each book, visit our website at www.jewishlights.com